IN BED WITH DOUGLAS Mawson

TRAVELS AROUND ANTARCTICA

CRAIG CORMICK

NEW
HOLLAND

The Antarctic present badly needs contact with the Antarctic past.

—Stephen Murray-Smith

This book was written almost entirely on a seven-week Antarctic re-supply voyage on board the RSV *Aurora Australis*, from 31 January to 20 March 2008. I am indebted to the Australian Antarctic Division's Antarctic Arts Fellowship Program, which allowed me to travel to Australia's three stations on the continent, and also to the helpful people from the Australian Antarctic Division who I was fortunate to have as travelling companions (you know who you are!). This book is dedicated to their enduring spirit of discovery, adventure, comradeship and love of both acronyms and the great white continent.

Thank you to Emma McEwin and the Mawson estate for allowing me to quote from Douglas Mawson's work, particularly his and Paquita's letters, and also thanks to Tom Griffiths for the excerpt from his speech at his well-deserved NSW Premier's Literary Award.

And a special big thanks to Bill, Nicki, Sally, Robyn and Gary, Mark and all the others who read the manuscript for errors and provided comments.

In Bed with Douglas Mawson

First published in 2011 by New Holland Publishers (Australia) Pty Ltd
Sydney • Auckland • London • Cape Town

www.newholland.com.au

1/66 Gibbes Street Chatswood NSW 2067 Australia • 218 Lake Road Northcote
Auckland New Zealand • 86 Edgware Road London W2 2EA United Kingdom •
80 McKenzie Street Cape Town 8001 South Africa

A record of this book is available at the National Library of Australia

ISBN 9781742570082

Publisher: Diane Jardine
Publishing manager: Lliane Clarke
Senior editor: Mary Trewby
Designer: Emma Gough
Production manager: Olga Dementiev
Printer: Ligare Printing, Australia

IMPERIAL-METRIC MEASUREMENTS
1 inch = 2.54 centimetres
1 foot = 30.48 centimetres
1 mile = 1.609 kilometres

Contents

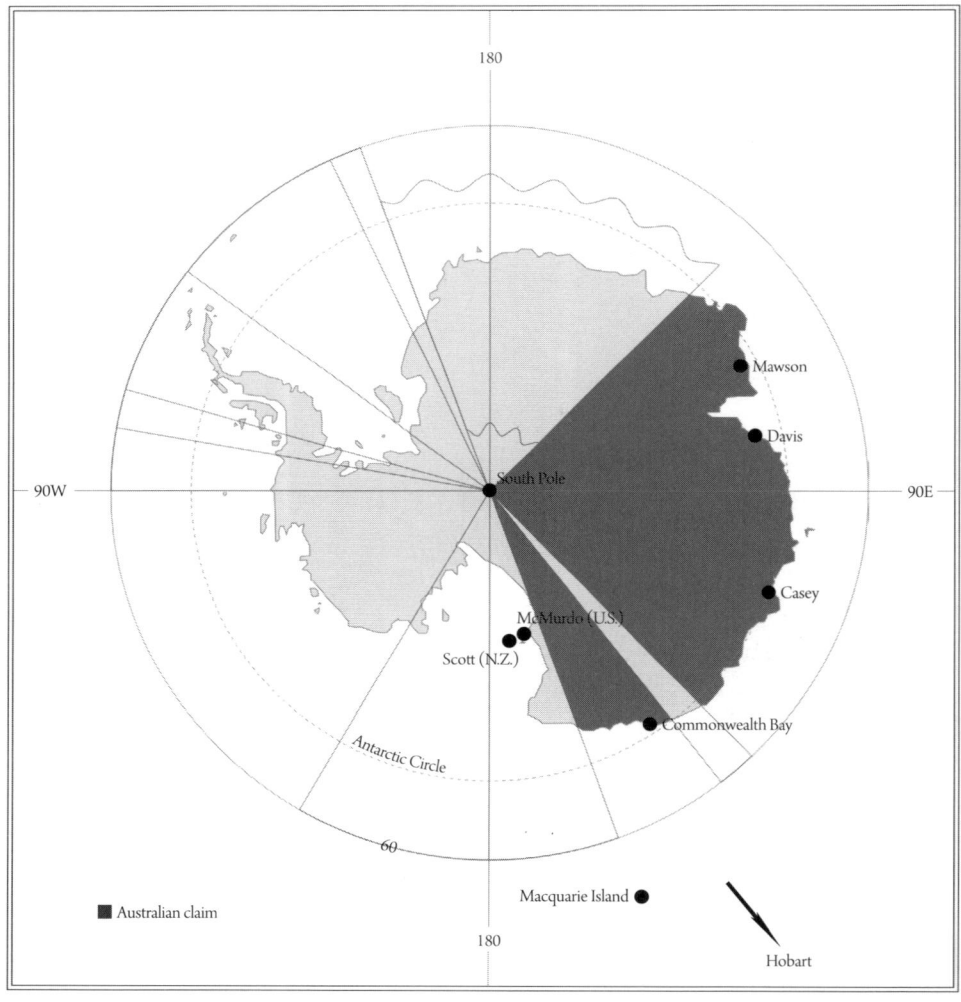

180

Mawson

Davis

90W

South Pole

90E

Casey

McMurdo (U.S.)

Scott (N.Z.)

Commonwealth Bay

Antarctic Circle

60

■ Australian claim

Macquarie Island ●

180

Hobart

Introduction

We will see the Antarctic ice soon. It is clearly marked on the ship's radar but the horizon is shrouded in fog. We are standing on the pitching bridge of the good ship *Aurora Australis*, Australia's re-supply vessel for the Australian Antarctic program, in early 2008, and we fill the time by talking about conservation. There are four of us in a small group on the port side of the bridge and another half-dozen or more over on the starboard side. The bridge is large enough for about 30 more people to fit in relative comfort.

My companions have all been south many times, to either the Antarctic continent or to subantarctic Macquarie Island, and all have many terrific stories to tell. But for now they are discussing conservation and preservation. They think it maddening that legislation does not allow for the salvaging of any artifact found in these territories. They say many historical things are washed up on the shores of Macquarie Island and many things are found around the Antarctic stations but it is forbidden to touch them. Even if it is aged rubbish it is forbidden. It is even forbidden to move things to a safer location where the oceans or the elements or time won't destroy them.

They think this is an example of the good intention of bureaucracy gone too far because they feel many interesting and priceless artifacts are in fact being lost due to the policy. 'But what can you do?' they say. 'What can you do?'

I don't yet know enough to make a comment. But I do know that on my voyage I've discovered that in Antarctica it is also possible to find stories washed up at your feet. Many are both interesting and priceless and it worries me that they might be lost to the elements or to time. So I have attempted, with due care, not to damage the stories or their tellers in any way, to collect them for preservation.

That's something I can do.

So my book is looking at the past, the present and the future of Australian involvement in Antarctica. The past, although well recorded, we know is sometimes open to interpretation. The present, although with us, is multifaceted and varies depending on your perspective of things. And the future is mostly conjecture so will always be a quite varied. Therefore, and importantly, whatever I have to say in this story reflects my experience and perspectives—not necessarily anybody else's.

Antarctic Dreaming

*I never saw or dreamt of anything so gloriously beautiful as some of the
stuff we have come through this morning. After lunch the country changed
entirely. In place of the confused jumble and crush we have had, we got
on to neve slopes; huge billows, half a mile to a mile from crest to crest,
meshed with crevasses …*

—Douglas Mawson, *The Home of the Blizzard*

I had dreamed of Antarctica a thousand times before ever I trod
upon its frozen shore. But none of my imagining prepared me for
that exhilarating feeling of walking up the gangway onto the *Aurora
Australis* at the wharf in Hobart. When I stepped onto the metal deck

of the large orange ship, I was grinning like an idiot. This was it. I was really going to Antarctica!

The voyage had actually begun in earnest many months before with my packing and medicals and re-packing and pre-reading and re-packing once again, yet it never felt like it was really, *really* going to happen until I stood there on the ship's deck early that January morning.

I had played this scene out in my mind so many times. In fact I had imagined the whole trip in detail many times, and each film I have seen or book I have read or expeditioner I have talked to added details to my imagining. But it always starts with Mawson. *The Home of the Blizzard,* the film of his 1911–14 voyage made by Frank Hurley, shows the expedition ship, the *Aurora,* leaving Hobart. There is a rapid-paced excitement to everything, like there always seems to be in old black-and-white films played at a slightly higher speed than they were recorded.

I can see the crates of supplies all over the ship and all the husky dogs in their deck kennels. The air is electric with adventure as the *Aurora* pulls away from the wharf, the crowd waving frantically. Then the ship is out there on the great Southern Ocean, rising and plunging through the swell, the icebergs just over the horizon and everyone busy readying their gear and selves for the ice.

And then the ship is ploughing through the whiteness. Hacking into the wide plains of ice that try and hold us back from the continent. But we endure. We reach the land and step off the ship onto the ice and walk ashore, planting our legs onto the snow-covered sparse land. We are here. In Antarctica. The last great wilderness on earth. The last great adventure.

I am finally filling that huge Antarctic-shaped hole within me with the many experiences I imagine over and over. Fighting against the elements to construct our shelter. Struggling with tents in the fierce flapping winds. Endeavouring to make headway against a blinding blizzard. Hauling heavy loads across the ice. Overcoming hardships and adversity to discover the inner strength of the human spirit. All enacted in grainy high-contrast black-and-white scenes.

And that's surely just how it will be.

Surely.

❄ ❄ ❄

'I thought it was bigger,' my wife Sharon had said to me the day previously in Hobart. She was looking down at the *Aurora Australis* from an office block window, staring out over the wharves, and there was a monster cruise ship that looked the size of a city suburb tied up there. I was looking at it for some time before I recognised the tiny orange shape beside it. It did look rather small by comparison.

The first time she had seen the ship we were staying at the hotel on Elizabeth Wharf and when we looked out the window in the morning this huge orange ship was docked there. I told Sharon, 'That's the *Aurora Australis,* and one day I'm going to go to Antarctica on it.'

Well, that's how I remember saying it. And I'd remembered the ship being bigger too. As big as my imagining of sailing to the icy continent. But the cruise ship had gone now, off to New Zealand or Melbourne or somewhere else that the thousand or so people on board could take photos of and buy souvenir T-shirts from. And the *Aurora Australis* did look bigger every step closer I took. As big as my imagining. I was really, *really* going to Antarctica.

❄ ❄ ❄

We had been promised that Sharon could come on board and attend our departure briefing with me, but as we stood in line at the security barrier, ready to board the ship, a small middle-aged woman in uniform held up a clipboard. She ticked off each of our names in turn, but Sharon's name wasn't on her list. She said Sharon therefore would not be allowed on the ship.

Sharon looked devastated. I appealed to the woman-in-uniform's better nature. I asked her to be reasonable. I said there must have been some mistake. But she wasn't having any of it. The list was the list. No name on it, no entry. 'Rules are rules,' she said, and turned to the next person. I was tempted, I must admit, to point to a name at random and say, 'Oh, that's her!' But I knew it would only get us both into trouble at some stage later when the name's real owner tried to come on board. And this woman before us had hands that seemed to me very skilled at body cavity searches of troublemakers.

(Note to self: Try and recall the unfortunate fact that, despite the romantic and adventurous notion of travelling to Antarctica with an official Australian expedition, it is as much an adventure in bureaucracy and regulation, and that almost everything in Antarctica is tightly governed by bureaucratic lists.)

So I hauled myself up the gangway on my own, following the line of expeditioners, and felt that tremendous flood of excitement as I stood upon the ship's deck. The RSV *Aurora Australis* is a purpose-built ice-breaker, constructed in Newcastle and commissioned in 1990, and it has been Australia's workhorse for the Australian Antarctic Division ever since. The ship can accommodate 116 passengers, is equipped with a trawl deck built for marine science and can house up to three helicopters, which are launched off the helideck at the rear of the ship. *Aurora Australis* , known affectionately as the 'Orange Roughy', is listed as being capable of penetrating 1.2 metre-thick ice, which I was hoping we would get a chance to witness.

About 40 of us assemble in the ship's conference room and old friends shake hands and colleagues who know of each other by scientific reputation size each other up and exchange cordial greetings. I am surprised at the amount of grey hair around me. I had expected this would be a young person's expedition, but ages stretch from early 20s up into the 60s. You can easily spot the first-timers though by their fidgety excitement. The old hands just look quietly pleased to be heading south once more.

Then Nicki, our voyage leader, calls us to attention. Nicki seems endlessly cheerful and ever in control, and I hope that she never ends up with a clipboard in middle age. She does a rollcall like we might be in school and then tells us that, although we have mostly roundtrippers on board, we will be leaving some people at each of the three stations we visit—Casey, Davis and Mawson—and we will be taking many people on board at each station, returning scientists or technicians who have finished either a summer or overwinter stay. We will have over 100 people on our return voyage, which will be near to full capacity.

She then tells us that we have a few international observers on board, a few Bureau of Meteorology people and also three arts fellows. Now it's a peculiar thing, at least to my way of viewing it, that while nobody turned a head at the mention of international observers there to monitor Australia's compliance with the international Antarctic Treaty, they all look around the room in curiosity at the mention of three arts fellows. And we have to hold our hands up so that everyone can eye-ball us like we are exotic creatures they have never seen before.

The Antarctic Division regularly takes arts fellows down to the frozen continent with the aim of expanding the ways that the Antarctic, and Australia's interactions with it, can be expressed. Some wonderful books and works of visual art have resulted from the program, but I have a personal belief that some truly weird stuff has resulted too. This was confirmed in my mind when I asked Jenny, who administers the program for the Australian Antarctic Division, to tell me what were the weirdest things that had been produced under the program. She dodged the answer as expertly as if she had a clipboard with a list of questions not to answer.

Catching my wandering attention, Nicki says we will be gone from Australia for about 49 days, give or take a day depending on the ice conditions, and we'll be back in Hobart just in time for Easter.

Most of the next two hours of briefings concentrate on death: how to die, or how to avoid dying, including a lifeboat drill and squeezing ourselves into emersion suits that can keep you alive in near-zero waters for anything from six to 30 hours, evidently depending on which programs you watch on the National Geographic Channel. The only downside is that I reckon it would take me anywhere from six to 30 hours to get into one and fasten it correctly while in a panic. It also gives us a chance to talk to some of our fellow expeditioners.

'So what do you do?' one of the very international observer-looking guys asks me.

'Oh, I'm one of the arts fellows,' I mumble.

'Yes,' he says. 'But what do you do? Paint?'

'No,' I say. 'I'm a science journalist.' This is my safe standard reply.

'Oh? What will you write about?'

I wonder if this is building to being some international observer question, so I decide to play it safe. 'Articles mostly.' But then I can't help myself and say, 'I'm also considering writing a book.'

'What about?'

Now I could have said, about Australia's hidden weapons of mass destruction in Antarctica. Or I could have said, about secret Nazi bases or UFOs, or any crap at all, and I think it would have sounded more credible than what I did say.

'About Mawson,' I tell him.

'Oh?' he asks.

'But it would be set in different times, like part contemporary and part in the past. You know?'

He nods his head slowly and I can see he knows that I'm making this up as I go along.

After the death talk we are each given a seasickness tablet to take. Lloyd, the voyage doctor, tells us it will make us drowsy, so we're not to drive, operate heavy machinery or pretend that we are clever, particularly if we get back off the ship for last farewells before departure time at 4 PM. And right up close to that time the last person climbs aboard, Kym the cook, to much hooting and cat-calling by the crew. But she calls back, 'You'd never leave without me.'

Only a few years previously families and friends could stand at the dockside and throw well-wishes and streamers to the ship, but that is a thing of the past now. Security demands that family are separated by a barbed wire-topped chain-link fence, so everybody on the ship taking pictures of their loved ones has shots of them pressed up against the wire fence, like their families are in a detention centre.

Then there are three blasts on the horn and the ship starts moving out from the wharf. It does a slow 180-degree turn, or the ship's equivalent of a hand-brake turn, and then we are away, at what seems like a brisk walking pace, heading out into the D'Entrecasteaux Channel.

All around the ship I see that people are squeezed into alcoves with their mobile phones pressed to their ears, saying more goodbyes to children or loved ones. As we head farther out to sea, it's an odd sight to see the way they continue this for an hour or so, peering at their phones every now and then to see how much reception they still have, to try and squeeze in those last words.

Dinner is served at 5.30 PM, with Tasmania still on the starboard side of the ship. The deputy voyage leader, Rob, sits at the table with me. He's fairly young, very cheerful and seems to only ever wear sandals, even when we reach the ice—so I just know he's a Tasmanian. He tells me he works as an executive assistant to the Antarctic Division's chief.

'So is this trip a reward or a punishment for you?' I ask.

'A reward!' he says, smiling broadly. Then he asks me, 'So what are you going to be working on?'

'I'm thinking of writing a book on Mawson,' I tell him.

'Oh?' he asks.

'But I'm sort of changing the timelines around and setting it in the past as well as the present and comparing his voyage with ours, if that's the way it all works out, of course.'

And I realise I've really got to come up with a better description of what I'm doing. Some of the guys say, 'I drive barges.' Or 'I study penguins.' Or one woman told me, 'I study mosses.' But me—I'm thinking of sort of writing a book about Mawson, which is really about this voyage, it's trying to compare the two, but it might just go in a different direction, or not at all, for you never know, you know?

I'll have to work on that answer, I think, or it's just going to get in the way of me ever writing anything at all.

When Mawson sailed out of Hobart, also at 4 PM, on 2 December 1911, aboard his ship, the *Aurora*, he wrote in his journal, *Left Hobart for Macquarie Island*. He expanded a little on this later in his book, *The Home of the Blizzard*, saying: *As we proceeded down the river … Hobart looked its best, with the glancing sails of pleasure craft skimming near the foreshores, and backed by the stately, sombre mass of Mount Wellington.*

The Governor of Tasmania Sir Harry Barron, the Premier Sir Elliot Lewis, and many of the citizens of the fair city had come to wave them off, and the Premier and a small party even followed them some way in a steamer to give them a final farewell. Mawson's farewell might have outclassed ours, but the reception he got from the Southern Ocean didn't. He wrote that during the night the wind and sea rose steadily, developing into a full gale, and added that although most of the men experienced a stage of seasickness, it soon passed except in the case of two or three.

What Mawson forgot to mention was that he was a poor seaman himself. On his earlier voyage with Shackleton he had been so seasick that he was described as both useless and objectionable, perpetually lying about in a sleeping bag at one end of the bridge and vomiting when he rolled to starboard.

Stories of seasickness and the harsh southern seas have given many of us first-timers aboard the good ship *Aurora Australis* cause for not a little concern. How seasick might we become? Should we take more seasickness tablets and walk around like complete zombies? Should I really have watched *The Poseidon Adventure* last week? But the sea remains kind to us as we move farther away from Hobart. But maybe it's also the ship that's helping. The *Aurora Australis* is quite an improvement upon the Steam Yacht *Aurora*. For a modern traveller used to creature comforts, it's not quite a luxury liner, nor is it the Starship *Enterprise,* but it's a lot more comfortable than the ships of yore that I've crawled over, such as the *Discovery* or the *Endeavour.*

Mawson's ship was a whaler, built in the Scottish port of Dundee in 1876 to work in the north seas. She was 165 feet long, or a little over 50 metres, and was 30 feet wide, or about 10 metres. The hull was made from thick oak, sheathed with greenheart timber and lined with fir (not fur). Thick beams reinforced the sides to resist the strain of pressing ice.

She used both sails and a 98-horsepower engine which was capable of 6 to 10 knots. When she set out from Hobart she was crammed, packed tight with all the expedition's gear, to the point that some of the expeditioners had to travel on the support ship *Toroa* and most of the cabins barely had room for those on board to sleep in them. Not that most got any sleep, by all accounts, for the sea was too rough for sleeping or cooking warm food.

The *Aurora Australis*, by comparison, is almost 100 metres long, has six decks we can visit, from the bridge up on A Deck to the gym down on F Deck. There are about 40 cabins on D Deck, most with four bunks set out as in a sleeper compartment on a train, but also with four lockable cupboards, a desk and light, power points and internet connection and a small shower-toilet cubicle. It's not too bad, I think. I've stayed in hotel rooms that were more uncomfortable. We also have the obligatory porthole, which is shaped like a rounded square rather than a circle, but have been told to avoid opening it. On previous expeditions unexpected waves have crashed in and flooded out rooms.

It's not until nearly 9 PM, just as the sun sets, that we finally see the last of the land falling away behind us. It feels like we're really entering the big, wide open seas. And it really does feel it. The roll of the ship becomes drastically more pronounced. Slow loping rolls forwards and backwards and side to side. But it's not uncomfortable. Yet.

The ship offers so many activities, from a well-equipped gym to a small library of books and another of DVDs, but most of us succumb to the influences of those little seasickness pills and, doing our best to avoid operating heavy machinery or driving, fall asleep in our cabins quite early. My cabin-mate is Nick, who is one of the other arts fellows. He's a visual artist and was born in England. He has a very droll and dry sense of humour and once we reach Antarctica I can say his humour is as dry as dry ice. He has an impressive short haircut that is as close to being shaven bald as it is possible to get and I wonder if he's planning to grow his hair long on this trip or find a way to keep it trimmed.

We wake at 7.30 in the morning, our first full day at sea. I am a little thick-tongued still and dry of mouth. The gentle motion of the ship is quite lulling and I'd be happy to lie there in bed all day, but breakfast is only served between 7.30 and 8.30. Come late and you have to forage for yourself on biscuits and coffee. We lurch like drunks down to the dining room, which the ship's company insists on calling the restaurant. It is somewhere vaguely below us, down a flight of stairs if we can find it and then through laboratories, or down a long corridor and then down a central stairwell. The ship is still a little bit of a maze and will take some time to become familiar with.

Our last-aboard cook Kym greets us bright and chirpy and I suspect she's a bit of a party girl when the ship reaches port. I tell her that her food is delicious. One of life's guiding truths is always suck up to the cook. Another one is don't piss off small middle-aged women with a clipboard. Anyway, cooks are very important to Antarctic explorers. It is often said that the cook is the most important job on any station. If he or she is good the Antarctic experience will probably be good; if the cook is not good it probably won't be. And the first person to sight Antarctica was a cook: Captain James Cook, in 1773–74, on board the *Resolution*. He and his shipmates crossed the Antarctic Circle in 1773, the first men to do so, and in early 1774 he proceeded several hundred nautical miles further to reach 71°10' South. He saw the Antarctic mountains reflected as mirages and wrote in his journal: *I can be bold enough to say, that no man will ever venture farther than I have done and that the lands which may lie to the South will never be explored.*

Cook also made it clear that if there were any mass of land to the south it must lie within the Antarctic Circle and be subjected to such stringent climactic conditions as to render it an unlikely habitation for humanity.

He was proven wrong in both of these assumptions, of course, as a long line of explorers followed after him, each getting farther and farther south, including Ross, Dumont d'Urville and Wilkes. The first landing on the continent itself, as opposed to the islands around the Antarctic Peninsula—that long tail that points towards, and comes close to touching, South America—varies, depending on whose account you choose to favour. It could have been Bellingshausen's Russian expedition of 1820, or perhaps Edward Bransfield's British expedition of 1820, or even Nathaniel Palmer, the American seal hunter, in 1820. You take your pick. (And each nation does.)

The next important Antarctic cook was Frederick Cook, who was on board the *Belgica*—the first ship to overwinter in Antarctica, in 1898. The leader of the Belgium expedition was Adrien de Gerlache, who, by all accounts, was not much chop as a leader and came close to having the men mutiny on him, particularly when he decided to winter in the pack-ice, seemingly as a spur-of-the-moment idea, with no proper equipment or provisions. The first mate on the voyage was none other than Roald Amundsen, and Frederick Cook was the ship's doctor and anthropologist. He wrote the sad story of how poorly the crew coped with the winter in his book, *Through the First Antarctic Night*, in which he said: *The darkness grows daily a little deeper, and the night soaks hourly a little more colour from our blood. Our gait is now careless, the step non-elastic, the foothold uncertain. Most of us in the cabin have grown decidedly grey within two months, though few are over thirty. … There is no one willing to openly confess the force of the night upon himself, but the novelty of life has been worn out and the cold, dark outside world is incapable of introducing anything new.*

Several of the crew went mad from the experience. When Mawson read Cook's book years later, he said that he was shocked by the account. The young Cook was widely praised for his role in keeping most of the crew alive and sane. Roald Amundsen wrote: *Frederick A. Cook, of Brooklyn, was surgeon to the expedition—beloved and respected by all. As a medical man, his calm and convincing presence had an excellent effect … It cannot be denied that the Belgian Antarctic expedition owes a great debt to Cook.*

Now here's the funny thing about this Cook: he was certainly a competent explorer and set some records for achievement in the Arctic, such as traversing the coast of Greenland, but two of his later great achievements appear to have been faked. The first was climbing to the peak of Mount McKinley in Alaska in 1906 and the other was being the first person to reach the North Pole in 1908.

At first both claims were widely supported until Robert Peary insisted he was the first man to reach the North Pole, in 1909, and that Cook had faked his claim. The two men's claims became the subject of a bitter press campaign between rival newspapers, each backing one or the other. After careful analysis of their expedition data, it has now been suggested they both missed it and Roald Amundsen was the first to the North Pole as well as to the South Pole.

Anyway, back to the dining room—sorry, restaurant—on board the *Aurora Australis*. The room is roughly divided into two large areas, sort of like a pair of lungs, with the kitchen—oops, galley—right across the top of them. The crew tends to sit on one side, all dressed in their orange coveralls, with the expeditioners sitting around in groups, either with those they already know or those they are getting to know. I wonder what it might be like being stuck in the ice for over 12 months with everyone here and who might be the first to go mad.

I suspect that no one I asked that question of would say it might be themselves.

❄ ❄ ❄

After breakfast I go back to my cabin. I can hear my bunk calling me. Just a half-hour's more sleep, it says, with that melodious allure of a siren tempting a ship onto the rocks. Why not? I reply, like thousands of sailors before me when they have heard the siren's song. Anyway, those little seasickness tablets still have me feeling dozy. I'd better sleep a little longer so that I'm more awake later.

Have you ever told yourself that? If I just sleep for half an hour now I'll feel much better. But then you wake up, in the middle of the afternoon or something, feeling dozier than ever? Anyway, I went back to bed. I woke up again maybe an hour and a half later and there was somebody sitting on the bunk opposite me. I rubbed the sleep out of my eyes, supposing it was Nick. But it was too tall to be Nick. Who was this in our cabin, just sitting there, staring at me? It took me a moment to recognise him. It was Douglas Mawson. Just sitting there, with those blue eyes watching me intently.

And before I could even think of what to say, he asked me, 'What's this about a book you're writing on me?'

Now would have been a good time to have the answer down pat, but I hadn't got it yet, so I said, 'Well, I'm sort of thinking of comparing your voyage of the past with this voyage now, looking at similarities and differences. You know?'

He is silent for some time and then he asks, 'How exactly does it start?'

'I'm planning on the first line being—"I had dreamed of Antarctica a thousand times before ever I trod upon its frozen shore",' I tell him.

He thinks upon that a moment, then says, 'Isn't it a little bit melodramatic?'

'Melodramatic?' I say. 'I thought it was great. It hooks the readers. Gets them into the story quickly. Let's them know what is coming.'

'Why?' he asks.

'So that they want to read the rest of the story. You've got to hook them with a great opening line.'

'Or what happens?'

'They might put the book down and not read it.'

He looks doubtful. But this is the man who began his own book, *The Home of the Blizzard*, about his 1911–14 voyage to Antarctica, with the riveting opening sentence: *Notwithstanding the fact that it has been repeatedly stated in the public press that the Australasian Antarctic Expedition had no intention of making the South Geographical Pole its objective, it is evident that our aims were not properly realized by a large section of the British public, considering that many references have appeared in print attributing that purpose to the undertaking.*

'How does this sound then?' I ask him. 'Notwithstanding that I had dreamed of Antarctica a thousand times before ever I trod upon its frozen shore, it was evident that my aims in realising the dream should appear in print, as the purpose of the undertaking.'

'It has a nice ring to it,' he says.

Now it is my turn to look doubtful. 'I prefer to stick to my original,' I say.

'It sounds too fanciful,' he says. 'You dreamed of it a thousand times?'

'It's a perfectly good line,' I say, quite defensively. 'And it's true.'

'Then tell me one of the dreams,' he says. 'Any one of the thousand.'

'All right,' I say. 'This is a dream I had just last week. I was with Anthony, who was a previous arts fellow, and he was my guide. I had just arrived at a hut near Ross Island, in the Ross Sea, where Scott and Shackleton had set up their bases, and he was going to take me to see both their huts, which are still there today. But as we walked over the ice towards them I noticed that one of the huge ice formations in front of us was actually concrete, and up close it was like an underground car park, with pillars holding the upper levels up.

'Anthony told me that a mall was being built in Antarctica and he would show me how to sneak in without paying the admission fee. He led me into a small ventilation shaft and we climbed up into the upper levels of the mall. It was huge and had all these shops selling Antarctic souvenirs, T-shirts and jackets with "Antarctica" written on them, but there weren't many people buying them because they were overpriced. Anthony showed me that we could look out from an upper balcony and see where there was a bridge under construction, to link the island to the mainland. He said it was so that more tourist buses could reach the mall and take photos of Mount Erebus, which was behind us.

'But when I tried to take a photo of the mountain it was obscured by cloud and mist and the other tourists. Then we hopped on a bus and rode it over the now-completed bridge and we could see where there were all these suburbs being built for medium-density housing. And even as we drove past in the bus we could see people moving into them. I tried to take a photo out of the back window of the bus, to prove this was really happening and wasn't just a bizarre fantasy from my imagination, but my camera froze and wouldn't take any pictures.'

Mawson is quiet for some time and then says, 'You should see the ship's doctor. You might be suffering some form of madness.'

'You asked for a dream. That was a dream that I had,' I tell him.

'And you have 999 more dreams like that?' he asks.

'Well, no. When I say I had dreamed of Antarctica a thousand times, I'm not saying there were a thousand different dreams that I can sit here and describe to you.'

'Then why say it?'

'Maybe I won't even use that introduction,' I say. 'Maybe I'll come up with a better one after I've been to the ice and back.'

This seems to satisfy him. 'Yes,' he says. 'Visiting the ice changes you.'

Sharon won't be happy to hear that. I have promised her that I won't come back an Antarctic bore. It has already driven her crazy that

I spent so much of the last week telling everybody I could, including people in shops and so on, that I was just off to Antarctica. That's one of the great things about my wife, she's a really good reality check. If she were here, she'd slap me and tell me to wake up and to stop imagining that I'm talking to Mawson and get on with the story. But there is so much that I want to ask him, for my book.

'Tell me how it changed you,' I say.

'By and by,' he says. And then he's gone. And I'm sitting in the cabin alone looking at my watch, seeing it is soon time for lunch. But first I should go up on the deck and look around at the ocean surrounding us on all sides and let the sea breeze blow all the cloying cobwebs of sleep out of my head.

❄ ❄ ❄

Okay—let's address the key question early. Why Mawson? I've been waiting for somebody to ask me that. If they don't get around to doing it until the voyage is nearly over, then it will be a problem putting it into the book in a place where it makes sense. Of course I could always ask Nick, my cabin-mate, to ask me, 'Why Mawson?' and then I could recount the story. But how could you trust that any writer who made up conversations was really telling you the truth about anything? Right?

So I'll have to ask myself. Why Mawson? Well, to my mind he's the most overlooked of the big four explorers of the heroic age: Scott, Amundsen, Shackleton and Mawson.

Scott and Amundsen used to get all the great press, with Amundsen being the dour but determined one of the two. The one who always used scientific analysis to get the best results. And Scott, who died in his tent a mere 18 kilometres from a food depot, was always seen as the most heroic of explorers—man-hauling over vast distances instead of relying on dogs, and even on his death bed singing praises of the noble efforts of his comrades.

That all changed a bit in 1979 when Roland Huntford published a book on Scott and Amundsen, which lionised Amundsen and accused Scott of amateurish bungling that led to his death. Since then, several writers, including polar explorer Sir Ranulph Fiennes, have worked hard to overturn these criticisms.

In the last decade or so people have rediscovered Ernest Shackleton—who, though he failed in his bid to cross the Antarctic continent in 1914 (he didn't even manage to set foot on the continent at all before his ship *Endurance* was crushed)—overcame tremendous odds and brought all his men home alive. He was flawed in many ways, but he overcame the odds nevertheless. He was a womaniser, he was always chasing a quick buck, but he became a hero. Sara Wheeler, who to my mind has written the travel book on Antarctica that all travel books should aspire to equal, *Terra Incognita*, said of Scott and Shackleton that we admire Scott because he was better than us all and we admire Shackleton because he was just like us all.

Mawson knew the two of them and it is his differences from them that define him. Both were eager to get the young geologist onto their own expeditions as he had already established a reputation for himself as part of a party that reached the South Magnetic Pole on Shackleton's 1907–09 *Nimrod* expedition, when Shackleton got within

160 kilometres of the South Pole. Scott and Shackleton both recognised Mawson's qualities, but he was put off by their intense rivalry and their obsession with racing to the Pole at the expense of scientific endeavour.

Shackleton had taken part in expeditions with both Scott and Mawson before the three men's more famous expeditions. He was a member of the 1902 *Discovery* expedition led by Scott, which trekked inland to a point 770 kilometres from the Pole, and perhaps the two men's greatest discovery was that they didn't get on at all. Mawson then went with Shackleton on his 1907–08 expedition. Amundsen, of course, had previously been south on the *Belgica* in 1897–99.

Shackleton's third expedition became so legendary that a telemovie staring Kenneth Branagh was made about it. And, as we all know, that's the mark of fame in the modern world—being made into a movie or a mini-series. It's a question I often ask people I meet: 'Who will play you in the movie?' And you'd be surprised how many don't have an immediate answer for you. What do they daydream about in their free time?

But to get back to the heroic Antarctic explorers. Scott has been portrayed twice, firstly by John Mills in the 1948 film *Scott of the Antarctic* and then later by Martin Shaw in the 1985 US mini-series *The Last Place on Earth*. Amundsen was played in that last one by the Norwegian actor Sverre Anker Ousdal, and he was also played by Sean Connery in the 1969 film *The Red Tent*.

But Mawson? He's still waiting for the Hollywood contract, which is ironic in a way since he was responsible for one of the first features ever filmed in Antarctica, *The Home of the Blizzard*. It was shot by the Australian photographer Frank Hurley, who later accompanied Shackleton on the *Endurance* expedition and made a film of that too.

'So why not make a mini-series rather than write a book?' I imagine Nick asking me in our cabin this evening, after I prompt him to ask it. And I can imagine myself saying, 'I'll answer that by and by, but there are a lot of other things to tell first.'

There is a rather famous quote of Raymond Priestley, who travelled with Scott. He said: *For scientific leadership, give me Scott; for swift and efficient travel, Amundsen; but when you are in a hopeless situation, when there seems to be no way out, get on your knees and pray for Shackleton.*

I would add to that, when you want to write a book about a polar explorer who hasn't been done to death by the publishing industry, even churning out management books in their name, give me Mawson.

And this is something that needs to be understood about Mawson: he chose to travel to Antarctica to conduct scientific research at a time when other explorers were obsessed with reaching the Pole, and he was more driven by exploration rather than adulation, as Amundsen, Scott and Shackleton clearly were. This was an era when very little was still known about the Antarctic continent. Its edges had been mapped and there had been some limited forays into its interior, yet there was a clear ideological difference between the need to know more about Antarctica, through mapping it and studying its wildlife and rock samples, and through engaging in a race to the Pole—even if rock samples and observations were collected sporadically along the way. It is this that sets Mawson apart from the others. He was primarily a scientist and that's a tradition that Australia's modern Antarctic expeditioners are quite proud of.

There's no doubt that the early explorers of the heroic age occupy a certain special place in the consciousness of those with a fascination about Antarctica. It's as if they are mythical people, which in a way they are. They have become the creation heroes of the land. Antarctica, unlike every other continent on our planet, has never had an indigenous people and therefore has never had the types of myths and legends that people develop to explain their relationship to the land. The closest we have are the stories of the age of heroes, as much as if they were Ulysses, or the Winjarning brothers, or Maui the Pacific Ocean fisher of islands. Heroic myths fit snuggly into a place in our heads where, if we do not have heroic myths, we have a tendency to create them. And if we don't have heroic myths in that place in our heads, I suspect that we too easily fill that place with short-term celebrities.

So that's why Mawson. Because he's a hero. Because he's Australian and because he fills that place in my head that makes me inured to the covers of check-out magazines in the supermarket.

All at Sea

The wind increased from bad to worse, and great seas continued to rise until their culmination on the morning of December 5, when one came aboard on the starboard quarter, smashed half the bridge and carried it away.

—Douglas Mawson, *The Home of the Blizzard*

D ay two, official situation report at 12 noon, Australian Eastern Standard Time: we are on a heading of 225, whatever that means, with a current speed of 11.7 knots and are 224 nautical miles from Hobart with 1658 still to go to Casey Station. The air temperature is 13 degrees, as is water temperature, and we are at a bearing of 45°33'4", 144°27'9".

Now it would be easy to say that after seven days at sea we reached the ice, but the fact is that for many people on re-supply voyages their Antarctic experience is made up more of being at sea than of being in Antarctica, and despite our impatience to reach the ice we have many days to fill in. We have spent most of the first two days getting to know the ship and each other. The atmosphere on board is a little bit like we are all mature-aged students settling into a college dormitory at sea. But without the alcohol-assisted social barrier breaking. The *Aurora Australis* is no longer the party ship it was reputed to have once been and the cozy bar down on the lower deck has been converted into the video library.

This evening, because we have a scientist on board who is going down to Mawson Station to study a poultry virus in emperor penguins, we decide to have a screening of *Happy Feet*. Gary, the aforementioned penguin expert, tells us that he was actually the penguin consultant for the film and had to dress up in an animation suit in the early stages to mimic the movement of a penguin for the artists. When his name comes up on the credits, after the film has ended and after about ten minutes of names, we burst out in applause.

For those who like to count these things, his name is the 1007th listed.

I check my email before going to bed and there is a message from Sharon. Emails from the ship are packaged and sent two or three times a day, depending on the conditions. It means delays in receiving replies sometimes but that can't be helped. Sharon says she is missing me but the friends she is staying with in Hobart are trying to keep her busy and not let her feel sad. It's nice to know she is in good hands. It also makes me think about Douglas Mawson and his fiancée Paquita Delprat. The pair became engaged to be married in 1910, shortly before Mawson left on a trip to Britain to raise money for his Antarctic expedition, and their letters show the difficulty of maintaining a relationship via correspondence over time and distance.

The last letter he wrote to her before leaving Australia, dated 1 December 1911, stated in part:

Sweetheart and more—far more,

I have a great longing to say something to you but I cannot in a letter communicate my feelings. You may be sure that I am going away this time far happier than last when there was no gem of priceless worth awaiting my return. You may be sure I will look after myself compatible with my dutiful endeavour to accomplish.

But I'm sure if he had a mobile phone he would have sailed out into the ocean with his ear pressed up against it too, whispering farewells in stilted formal English until he was out of reception range.

Mawson first met Francesca Delprat in 1909, when he was 27 and she was 17. They met again later that year in Broken Hill, where they were formally introduced to each other. They were both born in England and found they had many things in common despite their diverse upbringings. Mawson continued to 'woo' Paquita, as she was always known, back home in Adelaide, and she was quite happy to be wooed. Douglas finally asked her to marry him on a December evening in 1910 and she heartily agreed.

She saw little of him during 1911, however, as preparations for his upcoming Antarctic expedition took him to London and around Australia on many occasions. His departure on 2 December of that year must have happened far too fast for the pair of them. Mawson wrote her a final letter from Hobart, and then two letters were sent back from Macquarie Island, a few weeks later, but he had to wait until February 1913, over a year later, before he received his first letters from her.

It's not often told, but when Mawson left her Paquita believed she might become pregnant from his passionate kisses, although at some time during his absence the facts of life were obviously explained to her. In later letters she wrote, using what was obviously pretty hot language of the time: *When I look back at myself the time you left it seems a different person—so young & silly … I loved you then as a girl who knows nothing at all of life & now—as a woman!*

I look at the picture of Sharon that I carry with me, before I go to sleep, glad that she has loved me as a woman for some time!

❄ ❄ ❄

Day three and we awaken to feel the rocking of the ship has really increased quite a bit. Nevertheless, at breakfast there are a few faces we haven't seen before, only now just emerging from their cabins for a bite to eat. Some still look a little green around the edges but are slowly recovering. I ask one of the cooks if they need to cook less when the seas are rough and he says that, yes, when people are feeling a bit sick they definitely eat less, but they still need to cook for them as if they had a full appetite.

Walking around the ship is a lot harder now. It moves in unpredictable ways that catch you off balance. Still, the sea is nowhere near as terrible as Mawson described it was on his voyage. On day three in 1911, a huge wave struck the *Aurora* with such force that it smashed half of the bridge and damaged a life boat.

He wrote: *Toucher was the officer on watch, and no doubt thought himself lucky in being, at the time, on the other half of the bridge.*

The rough seas also got into one of their freshwater tanks, ruining it for drinking and forcing them to ration their water for the rest of the voyage. The men on board were thrown from their bunks into inches of cold inboard seawater and nobody washed or changed clothes until they reached safe port at Macquarie Harbour on 11 December.

It is a peculiar character of ice-breakers that they need to have a rather rounded bottom, which is good for being in the ice but makes them roll terribly on the open seas. Interestingly, with a few years to look back on his voyage, Mawson talked repeatedly about how lucky they were. In an article for the *Geographical Journal* of 1914, he wrote: *Our good fortune commenced almost immediately, for a violent gale was weathered off the Tasmanian coast without any more serious consequence than the loss of half the bridge and slight damage to the motor launch. Deeply laden as we were, the decks lumbered with cargo, we had every reason to congratulate ourselves on the Aurora's sterling sea-going qualities ...*

The main drama for us on day three of the *Aurora Australis* is a muster drill at 10 AM. I follow the procedure properly and put on my woollen socks and thermals, then drag myself into my bright orange freezer suit, then don my balaclava and snow goggles and put my Field Manual in my pocket—which we're all meant to have read—and then squeeze my life vest over my head and walk awkwardly down the corridor towards the stairwell, like an alien extra from *Dr Who*. Strangely enough, in each cabin I look into people stare back at me from their beds where they are lying and reading or dozing.

'Isn't there a muster drill on at ten?' I ask.

'10.30,' I'm told.

I go back to my cabin and sit there in my freezer suit until it is too hot and I have to take it all off again before putting it all back on once more.

It is quite windy on the outer deck and we all assemble slowly, not really sure where to stand or what to do. Some of us fumble with cameras, others press their backs to the rails or cargo, convinced that the freezer suits not only make their own bottoms look rounder than the ship's but make them look elephant seal-sized big. Then one of the crew comes around and ticks all our names off a list and gives us another cheery talk on the many ways that we can die in the open ocean.

The drill takes about 15 minutes, then everybody waddles back down to their cabins. Since I'm dressed for it, I stand by the railings for some time, watching the ship pitch into the deep, dark sea and the waves of spray this throws up. After that I go up onto the bridge, which spans the width of the ship. We're about 17 metres up, but the crewman on duty tells me it is not unknown to get waves that strike the bridge in rough seas.

'How high are the seas now and how rough are they?' I ask him.

'They're running at about 5 metres,' he says, 'and I'd describe them as average for here.'

Then I go up on top to the monkey island, which is what they call the open-air area on top of the bridge. From up there the view is gobsmacking: 360 degrees of dark moving ocean. The ship pitches and dives into the swell, sending large blooms of spray over the bow of the ship. If you stand with your legs apart, facing forward, you can imagine you are riding one of the largest surfboards in the world across the roughest ocean in the world. I lean into the pitch of the boat as if I'm the one tipping it forward and then lean back to bring the bow back up out of the water. It really makes me want to fling my arms out wide and shout into the wind, 'I'm on top of the world!'

Leonardo Di Caprio only had a fraction of this exultation in *Titanic*.

The Southern Ocean really is something to experience up close— feeling the wind on your face as the ship rolls and dips into each trough and the explosions of spray leap towards you in the air. The ocean's surface is like an endless moving carpet of turtle-back shapes, spread out over the dark grey-green sea. Notwithstanding the fact that it has been repeatedly stated, it's glorious!

(Note to self: try not to use up all the best adjectives too early, as you're bound to run out later when you really need them.)

❅ ❅ ❅

I go down to my cabin afterwards to have a nap and am woken to find Mawson sitting there opposite me on Nick's bunk.

'So,' I say.

But he cuts in. 'Tell me more about this book that you're writing about me. I don't think I really got the sense of it last time.'

'Well,' I say, 'It's just an idea at the moment really, but it will be like comparing your voyage to Antarctica in 1911 with this voyage.'

'Wouldn't it be better to re-enact it in 2011?' he asks.

'Maybe. But I'm doing it now.'

'So, you're going to sail down to Macquarie Island and then to Cape Denison?'

'Well, no. Not actually. We're going to neither of those places. We're going to visit Casey Station, then Davis Station, then Mawson Station.'

'But I never visited those places. How can you compare the voyages if I didn't go to those places?'

'Well, it's not a literal recreation—that's another part of the book I'm working on.'

'I don't understand. How is it another part?'

'Well,' I say, 'I've got this other idea, see, but I haven't really worked it out fully either but it goes something like this. We're in the future, in the year 2050 or something, and the world has changed enormously, like the governments aren't running the place any more, it's all run by major corporations, and for years and years the Antarctic has been tied up by them as a tourist destination. You know how people pay a fortune to sail down in some luxury cruise ship and take pictures of the Antarctic Peninsula. Well, imagine how it might be in the future. Imagine that the only unpolluted place on earth is Antarctica. Imagine that not even scientists are allowed to live there any more, only tourist operators. Like it's the reverse of how things are now. So, this is the scenario. Some tour company has this idea that they get people to pay money to re-enact heroic journeys. So in this instance there would be three people who have paid to be you and Ninnis and Mertz and they're going to re-enact that famous journey you three made across George V Land.'

'Why would they possibly want to do that?'

'Well, let's suppose that in the future there is no danger any more in life. No challenges or adventure, so people are willing to pay for it.'

'Hmmm,' he says, as if not quite convinced of the idea.

'Look,' I say, 'It's you they're following. They want to be heroic like you. Famous like you. I think it's a really easy thing to imagine.'

'And just the three of them do the journey?'

'No. There's a cameraman, or maybe two, who follow them, filming it all, so it's also like a reality TV show that people can watch. I mean, that's the thing about fame. You need to achieve something in front of an audience.'

I wait for him to say something, but all he says is, 'Go on.'

'Well, that's the idea so far and there's still a lot to work out, of course, but I'm going to spend this voyage getting all the details in my head as I visit Antarctica. I can't write it all too far ahead of myself.'

'So you're going to be getting ideas as the voyage continues?'

'Yes.'

'And are you going to re-enact my journey?'

'Well, no. It would be a bit too difficult.'

'Then how can you really know what to write about? Wouldn't you need to undertake the same journey to know it?'

'But it's not the actual same journey in my story. It's a re-creation.'

'So the people playing Mertz and Ninnis will have to die, like they did in real life?'

'Not necessarily. I mean there are lots of things that could happen instead. They could be airlifted away at the point where they would have died. Or they could play dead. Or lots of things.'

'Hmmmm,' he says again.

'But, as I said, I haven't really worked it out fully yet,' I say defensively.

'No,' he says, 'I can see that.'

And then he's gone. Damnit! I really am going to have to come up with a clearer definition of this book. Perhaps when the next voyager asks me what I'm working on, I'll say, 'It's a book about Scott.'

❄ ❄ ❄

The ship's passageways and stairwells are decorated with framed posters and maps of Antarctica, which I spend long periods examining. Everything aboard makes me think of Antarctica and highlights the absence of it around us. This ship is built to take us to the ice and all our expectations and longings are to be in the ice too. Everything else is just impatiently filling in time until we reach it.

Several of the expeditioners I talk to work for the Antarctic Division in policy or support roles, and this is their first trip to the continent after many years of working on Antarctic issues. The (then) head of the Division, Tony Press, was not able to travel to the continent for several years himself. Whether they view it as a reward for service, or an integral part of their jobs, they are all delighted to be finally going south.

The old hands on the ship are very helpful in dishing out useful and useless advice to us new hands. For instance, we're told some horror stories of past trips. Nicki, our voyage leader, tells me that during one trip she was on recently the sea was so bad that her time was taken up walking around collecting filled-up seasick bags. Lloyd, the ship's doctor, tells me that on one voyage the ship tossed so sharply that an expeditioner was flung out of his seat and suffered a neck injury. Another old hand, who shall remain nameless, told us how to make a pair of underpants last eight days without washing them by wearing them two days normally, then two days back to front and then turning them inside out and repeating that.

(Note to self: if you try this, don't admit to it.)

❄ ❄ ❄

We go to sleep at night feeling the swell rising higher than ever. The bunk curtains start sliding back and forth on their runners, then we start sliding up and down in our bunks. This is our in-cabin motion sensor that tells us when we are going to have a rough night.

There's a peculiar motion to a ship in a rough swell that needs some portraying, for the few lucky souls who may never get to experience it for themselves. It's different to the lurch and bump of a train, which has some regularity to it, and lacks the sudden drop of an airplane entering an air pocket. It's more akin to standing on a flat board, perched on top of a ball, and trying to maintain your balance. But imagine that the ball under the board is on top of a trampoline that is being held aloft by a dozen teenage boys with mischief in their hearts and they tilt it this way and that, changing the point of balance continually but with no pattern. Now imagine that you're the type of person who gets motion sick from reading in a car and you've just read a long magazine article with very small print. You know that woozy feeling that seems to be both in your head and in your stomach at the same time. Then add to that a light background smell of diesel fuel, like you're behind a slow-driving truck that is belching out clouds of fumes that are coming in your window. Got that feeling? Now add to that the smell of mushrooms and gravy and greasy sausages with vinegar that somebody had been eating previously and the aroma still lingers. Okay, we're starting to get close to it. Now add to that the feeling of being quite hung-over, with a tremble in your legs and arms, that terrible delicate stomach and a feeling like cotton wool pressing up against the backs of your eyeballs. We've very close now. But you also need to imagine that you're standing on that plank of wood, on the ball, on the trampoline, being tipped to and fro by the boys, with the aroma of diesel fumes and vinegar and onions and greasy sausages, that you are going to have to eat and, trembling legs and arms and stomach, and you need to stand there for five days continuously, and all you really want to do is curl up into a small ball in your bed and be left alone, but even if you do, the bed is also on the board on the ball, and so on.

Can you imagine that? Well, that's still not quite it, but is starting to get very close.

I wake late on Sunday, day four, to find the sea has calmed a little. Nick is up and about somewhere. He's spending a lot of time on the bridge sketching the waves. I have a shower and get changed. The shower cubicle is quite spacious, though the door needs a good shoulder charge to open it when you're inside with it pulled tight. The water has two main settings, too hot and too cold, which we've been advised of, and I'm pleased to be starting to master the art of both showering with one hand on the rail and peeing with one hand on the rail too (though not at the same time).

I wander down to the dining room—oops restaurant—and find it is deserted. The ship is like the *Mary Celeste* this morning. It gives me an idea for the story I'm planning. I eat and wander back to my cabin to work on my Sunday napping. We've been told that somewhere mid-voyage people start to get very bored and listless, after the excitement and newness of everything wears off and before we reach the ice front, which we'll reach on day six or seven. By comparison it took Mawson nine days just to reach Macquarie Island, which was only halfway between Hobart and Antarctica.

Mawson's stated intention for his expedition was to leave four parties at different locations. The first would be at Macquarie Island, where they would set up a radio antenna capable of receiving messages from the Antarctic continent and relaying them on to Hobart. They arrived at the island on 11 December, which Mawson described in his journal as: *Arrive in Macquarie Id. Monday. Toroa arrived 13th.*

The *Toroa* was the support ship they were using to bring additional coal and the remainder of Mawson's expeditioners to Macquarie Island, which was fortunate for when the *Aurora* came around the northeast side of the island they saw the remains of a shipwreck and two small huts on the beach. As Douglas Mawson describes it in *The Home of the Blizzard*: … *a human figure appeared in front of one of the huts. After* surveying us for a moment, he disappeared within to reappear shortly afterwards, followed by a stream of others rushing hither and thither; just as if he had disturbed a hornet's nest.

The men on the beach dragged out some planks and barrels and set up a flagstaff, which one of the them climbed atop of and by the use of flag signals informed the *Aurora* that they were survivors of the wrecked sealing ship *Clyde*. Mawson arranged for the men and their salvaged cargo of oil to return to Australia on the *Toroa*.

The expeditioners spent two weeks at Macquarie Island, ferrying ashore supplies, building huts and carting materials up the steep sides of a 110-metre hill, North Head, for erecting the wireless antenna. On Christmas Day, Mawson, in the style typical of his journal to date, wrote the only entry for that week: *Left Macquarie Id.*

Now it was full steam southwards to the ice. The plan was to find a suitable location to land a party of 12 men, to establish the main base, and then place two further parties of six and eight men at other points. If they could indeed find places to put them ashore, that was, as the area of Antarctica that they were heading towards was little known. His stated intention was to travel *along the meridian of 158°E longitude until reaching the ice pack.* For those armed with only a map of Antarctica, this meant he was sailing sort of due south from Hobart, and when he reached the ice, instead of turning left and entering the gulf of the Ross Sea where Scott and others had gone, he would turn right and explore along the coastline until he found a nice spot to set up camp. And not knowing what he was going to encounter was the point of the expedition, wasn't it? Mawson stated in his book that different explorers had encountered quite different conditions around this part of Antarctica. Wilkes had difficulties getting through the ice, but d'Urville had a much easier run of things. The German ship *Gauss* had been trapped in the ice farther to the west, but Scott had managed to sight land.

Being early in the season, they expected the ice to be thick and to present some problems for them. The farther south they went, the more they searched the horizon for signs of ice or the continent. *Already we are steaming through untravelled waters, and new discoveries might be expected at any moment,* he later wrote.

On 27 December they saw whales spouting all around them in the water, travelling from east to west, and albatrosses and petrels hovered about the ship. On several occasions they saw 'fantastic' cloud formations on the horizon, which gave them an expectation of land that was proven fruitless. They also encountered large masses of floating kelp, which was an indication of land ahead somewhere.

At the time there had been much speculation whether Mawson would encounter a continent, or a series of islands linked by ice. The earlier land sighting reported by Wilkes had already been found to be over-optimistic and large areas of what he claimed to be land were shown to be sea-ice when later ships sailed through those regions. Whatever they might find, Mawson knew it would, in all probability, be defended by sea ice, which would be their main barrier to reaching land, and it would be the thickness of the ice that would largely determine the success or not of the expedition.

I go up on the bridge in the early afternoon and, looking around the horizon, it does look like there might be land ahead. Hiding behind the clouds, there seem to be dark shapes low to the horizon that would easily form into a solid landmass for the expectant eyes of the hopeful.

❀ ❀ ❀

Mealtimes are becoming meetings of the Subversive Antarctic Historical Society. Almost everybody has stories that you never find recorded in official records about hijinks and disasters and personality problems on stations. Mick, who is coming down as a round-tripper to work in inflatable boats keeping the fuel lines cleaned, seems to know every underground story about Australia's stations that has been told. He's got larrikin blood flowing through his veins in pints and has been to all three mainland stations at different times. Today he's telling me about a former station leader who clashed with several of the staff, handing out so many official reprimands (which expeditioners refer to as being sat in the 'comfy chair') that one techie built up the Antarctic Division record of 30.

Most members of the Society have a clear and open dislike of the small-minded bureaucratese that sometimes governs operations, but conversely they are fulsome in their praise of the way the Division allows them to visit the stations to better do their jobs. It is a love-hate relationship, but there are parts of their jobs they just love so much, and other aspects they consider nothing but a burden for no reason. I used to believe you could either get a job you liked or nice people to work with, but not both. Over the years, though, I've learned that it is possible to have an interesting job with nice people, or a dull job with arseholes. I ask several of the long-term Antarctic Division employees what type of an arsehole filter they apply to stop sending down people who are just too difficult to work with. They all admit it is a problem, and even though psychology tests are applied, a few difficult people still slip through. It's worse when it's the station leader or a person who is critical to morale, such as the cook. They tell me stories of very unpopular cooks who heated up the same food throughout the day, whereas the best went that extra yard and even prepared meals, prepacked meals, for those going out on field trips.

Talking to the tradespeople and the scientists, it is apparent there is a strong culture of belonging that binds the Antarctic Division people together. Some are contractors who come and go every few years and some are permanent staff, but there is a commonality that unites them. I've read how in previous years there were strong divisions between the two groups, but this appears to be much less now, with more intermingling and social mixing. The worse days were at the height of the rebuilding program in the late 1980s to early 1990s, when the numbers of tradies far outweighed the number of scientists and, as Mick describes it, 'a few plank-heads ran things their way'.

I'm having dessert with Nicki, our voyage leader, who is telling me about her main job with the Division, which is handling shipping logistics. She says that the *Aurora Australis* is coming up on 20 years old. The ship is chartered from P&O by the Australian Government for five years currently, though it was initially ten. She says that in a perfect world Australia would have two ships, one to concentrate on marine science and one to serve as a passenger and cargo ship for re-supplying our stations, but currently the *Aurora Australis* does both.

In the next summer season there are plans for the ship to

be contracted to the Japanese for some Antarctic work and the Australians may then find another ship. I'm asking Nicki what type of ship Australia should have built for the future, when Andrew from the BOM squad (Bureau of Meteorology), comes in and tells us excitedly that there is a spectacular cirrocumulus effect on the starboard side of the ship and to grab our sunglasses and get up on deck quickly. So we muster a hell of a lot faster than we ever did for the muster drill and all spill out on deck with our coats and gloves and sunglasses and cameras and are looking all about us, saying, 'What are we looking at?' 'What is it?' Andrew tells us to bunch our hand into a fist to cover the sun and look up at it. Sure enough there is a faint sort of dirty orange ring in the clouds around the sun. The sort of thing you sometimes see wide around the full moon.

'Is that it?' we ask.

'Isn't it supposed to be like, lights and moving and things?' somebody asks.

'No. That's it,' we're told.

(Note to self: In the interest of shipboard harmony, don't mention that, standing out there on the deck of the Southern Ocean with the big wide world around us, a faint cloud ring around the sun doesn't seem so very spectacular.)

❄ ❄ ❄

I'm having a midday doze courtesy of seasickness tablets, trying to shake off one of the strange side effects, such as having old 1970s song lyrics go around and around in your head, which today is 'Did you boogie with you baby in the back row of the movie show?', and when I wake up I hear this voice beside me. 'How's the book coming along?' It's Mawson.

'It's coming along okay,' I say. 'I think I've got a good angle for it.'

'An angle?' he asks.

'Yeah,' I say sitting up. 'I've got this great idea. I'm going to make it a murder mystery.'

'Death of the author?' he asks.

It takes me a moment to get his irony. It's the slightly British accent, so beloved by South Australians of his era, that throws me. 'Everybody loves a murder story,' I say. 'It holds the reader, see. So we might start the story at Commonwealth Bay where they are going to begin the re-enactment and somebody has been murdered and nobody knows how it was done.'

'So how was it done?'

'Well, I can't give that away straightaway. That's the whole point of building up expectation and mystery.'

'I see,' he says. 'Well, build up expectation and mystery in me.'

'Okay. Let's say it's the day before the expedition has to set out and they wake up to find that one of the expeditioners is missing. And they search around for him and find his body in one of the old huts. There's this stab wound in his back but nobody can find the murder weapon.'

He stares at me with neither expectation nor mystery.

'Do you know why not?'

'No. Why?'

'Well, it turns out, I mean I won't reveal this straightaway, of course, but it turns out he was stabbed with an icicle and then left in a place where it would thaw out and melt so no murder weapon could be found. Clever, isn't it?'

'Why wasn't he just shot with ice bullets?' Mawson asks. 'They'd melt inside him too and be even more mysterious.'

I think about this for a moment. How would you cast ice bullets? And how would you fit them into casings? Then I see Mawson is taking the piss. 'You don't like the idea?' I ask him.

'Well,' he says. 'Murder in Antarctica is a delicate issue, of course and I've considered it many a time myself, particularly with Jeffryes, our radio operator, in 1913.'

'Seriously?' I ask him, leaning forwards.

'No,' he says.

'Oh,' I say a little downcast. 'I thought I had a scoop or something then.'

'An ice scoop?' he asks. 'Wouldn't that be an ice-cream?'

'You're not this sarcastic in your book,' I say.

'I had no need to be,' he says.

'Okay. They find this dead body and it's one of the three expeditioners and so it raises the question, should they go on or should they call it all off? And circumstances dictate that they have to go on with it.'

'Why?'

'Well, I'm not sure yet. Maybe they have contractual obligations, or maybe they just need to or they'll all go bankrupt, or maybe something else. I'll figure that out. But the point is that they have to go on regardless of their concerns and doubts. So they need to choose a replacement expeditioner at the last moment and they go through this process of selection.'

'What process of selection?'

'I don't know yet.'

'They could put an ad in the newspaper.'

I ignore him and keep talking. 'They have to work out who is next best to go and the one they take is, of course, the one who is most likely to be the murderer.'

'Why most likely?'

'Perhaps he has some well-known grudge with the guy who was killed, but he's the only other one who can ski properly, or is the only one who is in a good position, contractually, to undertake the trek. I'll figure that bit out later too, but the expedition starts off with the readers thinking that things are going to go bad for all the expeditioners and that possibly one of them is the murderer. That's expectation, see. And mystery. It keeps the reader turning the pages.'

'Uh-huh. But you need a surprise twist, surely.'

'What type of surprise twist?' I ask him.

'Like Agatha Christie. Did you read *Murder on the Orient Express*?'

'I saw the movie.'

'She set you up to think that it could have been anybody who committed the murder. And it was, wasn't it?'

'Umm, I saw the movie quite some time ago.'

'Well, you'd know what I'm talking about then.'

'It was very late at night.'

'Can you remember how it ended?'

'I think I fell asleep before it ended.'

Mawson says nothing for a while. Then he says, 'And it was the butler who did it.'

'That's right,' I say. 'It was the butler.'

'No,' says Mawson. 'It wasn't the butler. It was everybody. They all did it and the point is that the reader is trying to figure out which one of the many people with a motive did it, but they all took part in the murder.'

'But why would they all do it in my book?'

'They wouldn't,' says Mawson. 'It's a twist. Something the reader isn't expecting.'

'I'm normally a little sharper than this,' I tell him, 'but the seasickness pills make me a bit dopey.'

'I see,' he says, in a very unconvinced tone.

'Yes, I might use a twist,' I say.

'And what twist would you use?'

'Well, I'm not sure yet. You know what they say—no surprise for the writer, no surprise for the reader.'

'They say that, do they?'

'Yes. They do. They all say it. They say it all the time. They say it so bloody often that they can barely open their bloody mouths without saying it. And if you ask me who they are I'm going to ditch my idea for this book and write about Scott or Shackleton instead.'

That shuts him up. He turns his head a little bit and goes big eye. That look of staring out over a far, far distant horizon.

'Thomas Keneally knew what I'm talking about,' I mumble.

'Did he?' Mawson asks finally. 'In what way?'

'He wrote a book based on your expedition called *In the Footsteps of the Aurora*.'

'I think it was called *A Victim of the Aurora*.'

'Whatever, and he has this expedition from the heroic age arriving at the site of an Antarctic base where there had been an expedition gone wrong in previous years, and they find a man still alive, and he's been living there for all these years on his own. At first it is something they joke about, that they've seen a figure out there on the snow, because lots of Antarctic expeditioners have reported just the same thing—seeing or feeling another person there. When Shackleton crossed South Georgia Island on the final leg of his mammoth rescue mission, he said he sometimes felt they were four instead of just the three of them.'

'You're drifting off course,' he says.

'Well, the point of it all is that they eventually track down this survivor and he tells them that his name is Malcolm Chalmers but, in fact, it turns out, it's not. He's the other missing expeditioner, John Forbes. But he cannibalised Chalmers' body and the shock of it, or the isolation and madness, has somehow made him believe that he's Chalmers. Neat isn't it?'

'There will be no more talk of cannibalism!' says Mawson sternly.

I recall there had been whispers and questions and mumbled stories of confessions heard about Mawson having cannibalised the body of Mertz to survive. And I'm thinking of what that might have been like, Mawson struggling back into their base at Commonwealth Bay and proclaiming to everybody that he's really Mertz. That would be something, wouldn't it? I'd better not mention it to him though.

'No. You're right,' I say. 'There'll be no mention at all of cannibalism.'

But I'm wondering if I could build that into the book somewhere.

❄ ❄ ❄

We have a great lecture today. Bill was an expeditioner to Wilkes Station in 1961–62 and, in the conference room at the rear of the deck with all the cabins on it, he gives us a talk, accompanied with pictures, about his time there. Wilkes Station doesn't effectively exist any more. It was built by the Americans during one of the big cooperative events of the International Geophysical Year of 1957–58 and was handed over to the Australians to run in 1959.

Bill said it was built in about 16 days, out of prefabricated insulated plywood panels, but it had been poorly located and snow built up around it constantly. It was eventually abandoned when Casey Station was built nearby. All that can be seen of Wilkes today are the tops of the buildings sticking out of the snow.

Bill hasn't been back to Antarctica in the 47 years since he was stationed there, and is immensely looking forward to seeing the remains of Wilkes Station—even though, according to his stories, it's fortunate there is anything still to see. He said there was a constant problem with melt-water puddling under the station and mixing with spilled diesel oil. The huts were heated with hot air from diesel-fired furnaces, so they were a terrible fire trap. He said there was quite a bit of jury-rigged electric equipment that could have caused a fatal spark at any time.

His pictures have that slightly colour-faded look of old photographs, but it suits the mood well. Expeditioners with long, long beards, the damage to the station caused by a 200 kilometre-per-hour blizzard, the husky dogs and, of course, the spectacular scenery of ice and wildlife.

The older expeditioners nod their heads in memory of an era that is long gone.

Then Bill told us the story of the US Neptune aircraft that crashed at Wilkes. It was in November 1961 and the station had been advised that the plane would be stopping to refuel. It arrived, landing on skis fitted to its wheels and, as was the custom, the youngest had to do the refuelling work. Bill and a young American pumped the fuel into the plane and Bill said that he noticed that some was spilling out the back of the internal tank fitted into the plane's bomb-bay. The American told him that it was just normal spillage. So Bill let it be.

When the plane attempted its take-off, however, the Australians standing on the ice saw fire emerging from the rear of the fuselage.

'We thought, that's it, they've had it,' Bill said. And they saw the plane, now airborne, wheel to one side and strike the ice. It was soon engulfed in flames. They rushed over to it.

Bill said it was miraculous that four of the nine crew got out alive. One of the purposes of his trip down south, he said, was to promote the building of a memorial to the crew who died. He wanted to see the front ski-wheel of the plane dug out of the snow and mounted on a suitable rock with a plaque describing what had happened and listing the names of the dead.

When Bill had finished his talk he got a rousing round of applause. I couldn't help but wonder if he were going south not just to see about digging out that front wheel but to dig out some of his own memories. Bill, to us, is a living treasure from an earlier age. As heroic as the big four (though his own modest response to being called this is to claim that he was just a boy on a big adventure—but maybe that's why we all identify with him so much).

❄ ❄ ❄

The curtains in the cabin are sliding again today as the seas pick up once more, and things slide around on tables. Waves even reach up and splash against our portholes for the first time. The numbers at meals drop accordingly, like a barometer we can use to assess the size of the swell. 'Hmmm, it's a minus ten-person swell today, but tomorrow we expect it might be only minus five persons.'

Or we can be very precise and give it a Debbie rating. We have two Debbies on board, who both suffer seasickness pretty badly. On a calm day at mealtimes it might be a two-Debbie day, but if the weather picks up a bit it could drop to a one-Debbie day by lunch, and if the weather gets even worse it might be a zero-Debbie day by dinner.

Now, here's an interesting fact. As far as I can ascertain, there is no patron saint for seasickness—despite the apostles being mostly fishermen who would have surely suffered their share of it. There is a patron saint of travellers in general, Saint Christopher—who carried baby Jesus across a river on his shoulders—but that just doesn't evoke the same type of rocking and rolling motion of a ship on the high seas. (And an interesting fact on that interesting face: some clipboard-bearing official at the Vatican has actually had Saint Christopher removed from the roll of saints because there is not enough evidence he actually existed—like all those paintings and little statues sold by Catholic shops aren't evidence enough!)

But coincidently Christopher was the name of Scott's polar party's most nuisance pony. Oates was responsible for looking after it, and by all accounts the truculent beast could not be induced to stop for lunch or stand still, so Oates always had to delay his start each day so that he would end up with the others at the end of the day. The ponies were killed before the climb up the Beardmore Glacier to the Antarctic plateau, which they would be unable to negotiate, and were stockpiled for food for the return journey. On the return trip, when they dug up the remains of Christopher at the Southern Barrier Depot on 24 February 1912, Oates wrote: *Picked up the depot and dug up Christopher for food but it was rotten.* He proved a disappointment to them even in death. That comment was the last fragment of Oates' diary to survive (his mother had all his papers burned, but his sister Violet managed to transcribe some entries).

But, once again, I digress. If Sharon were here she would have slapped me a few paragraphs back and said get back to the story. So maybe there's another patron saint who can cover seasickness as a part of his or her duties. Saints Camillus and Michael the Archangel are patrons of the sick. And Barbara is patron saint of storms. Or what about Saint Martin de Porres, who is patron saint of the sick poor? Anyone who has felt seasick would agree to that, feeling both poorly and sick.

There are a couple of other possible candidates. Peter is the patron saint of shipbuilders. Michael the Archangel is also patron saint of peril at sea. Or if we go down the occupational level saints, Albertus Magnus is the patron saint of scientists.

But I'm thinking that if you're suffering seasickness so bad that you're praying for relief then it's going to have to be a coalition of the willing among all of these.

Or there's always Saint Jude, one of my favourites, the patron saint of impossible causes (not to be confused with the mythical Saint Jude Grammaticus, the patron saint of impossible clauses).

❄ ❄ ❄

Day five and we get an ominous email today, sent out to all the ship's expeditioners: *Let it be known— / That from the salty, salpy depths we stir. / Your ship makes speed, but time is ours. / And all that cross the veil of the south, / Must stand before the Ocean's Law.*

And of course the first question we all ask ourselves is what the hell is a 'salpy depth'? No one seems to know, but the email is followed with: *King Neptune has issued us a warning that he will be paying us a visit sometime in the next few days. He will come aboard with his merry team of helpers to ensure that all those who have not travelled south beyond 60 degrees south by ship pay homage to him and this passage south. We must all show due respect to his position as Ruler of the Southern Ocean, and welcome him aboard the good ship Aurora Australis.*

So we can't say we weren't warned.

The next afternoon there is a sudden beeping on the ship's intercom and the captain requests all on board to meet in the restaurant (his words) for an important meeting. Could it be another drill? Could it be an important update on the ice conditions? Maybe we are going to go after a Japanese whaler and they want volunteers to board her? Yeah, some chance.

So we are all sitting around at the tables when we hear a sudden crashing and bashing and shouting and then King Neptune's herald steps out, looking a bit like Kyle the cook with his body painted green. He tells everybody we must kneel and praise almighty King Neptune. So we do. And many take the opportunity to slip farther and farther up the back of the room. It does them no good, however. King Neptune, with his herald and three creatures in waiting, who also bear uncanny resemblances to the other galley staff, calls everyone forward in threes.

The first poor few who are made to kneel, including my cabin-mate Nick, have to drink from some foul green concoction, eat a part of the royal haemorrhoids and then kiss Neptune's fish—which is a real fish. Not even a particularly good-looking one. If Neptune doesn't think you've paid him enough homage, you are also likely to get smeared with green gunk. Those who successfully pass, however, get given a piece of royal Antarctic coral to bear them safely beyond the 60th parallel.

Now I'm thinking about a few points of order here. Firstly, shouldn't Neptune appear when we cross the Antarctic Circle, not the 60th parallel—which we aren't even at yet? Also, is he certain that the piece of coral he gives us is in accordance with the safety regulations on the ship? Personally, I'd think a freezer suit, life jacket and life raft might make for a safer passing of the line.

But of course I don't get an opportunity to even mention these as I'm next on my knees on the floor, sipping the green gunk, having some tipped down my shirt back and staring into the mouth of a fish with sharp teeth, looking for a quick kiss. Fortunately, or not, depending on your point of view, I don't get a chance to chew on the royal haemorrhoids. And then, after we've all taken part, the king and his party return to the depths and I'm left trying to rinse the taste of the gunk and the fish kiss out of my mouth, thinking to myself, well, I've had worse dates than that in my life.

Though it does make me recall a quote from Kim Stanley Robinson, who has written one of the most thought-provoking books about the continent, called *Antarctica*. He wrote: *Below the 40th latitude there is no law; below the 50th no god; below the 60th no common sense and below the 70th no intelligence whatsoever.*

It makes the ceremony seem a lot more purposeful, if nothing but to demonstrate the point.

The Ice

'Ice on the starboard bow!' At 4 p.m. on December 29 the cry was raised, and shortly after we passed alongside a small caverned berg whose bluish-green tints called forth general admiration. In the distance others could be seen. One larger than the average stood almost in our path. It was of the flat-topped, sheer-walled type, so characteristic of the Antarctic regions; three-quarters of a mile long and half a mile wide, rising eighty feet above the sea.

—Douglas Mawson, *The Home of the Blizzard*

And finally, on day nine—the Ice! The first sighting was of a lone and lost-looking distant iceberg about a kilometre or so from the ship on the starboard bow, and all the first-timers lined the railings with whatever zoom lenses they possessed, snapping pictures of it like a flock of paparazzi having sighted Paris Hilton and Britney Spears out shopping for therapists together. I turned around and took a picture of everyone taking pictures. It seemed more likely to turn out.

We have been running a sweep to guess the first iceberg sighting time and the winner is Peter the Vomit (Voyage Management in Training). I was wrong by a full day. However, I'm told that most of those in the know hadn't anticipated seeing ice this early either. We stand there on the upper deck, braced against the pitching motion of the ship, in the near-zero temperature, and watch the berg slowly pass away behind us. Then we all turn forward eagerly looking for the next one.

It is 24 hours before we sight another though. The radar on the ship's bridge shows several bright blips of icebergs, though often they are too far away to be seen through the fog and darkness. It is quite a magical feeling being on the bridge at night, staring out into the darkness with just the luminous glow of controls, the banks of dials and buttons, the radar screen and satellite screens and cool glass and metal across the panels, like I am actually on the Starship *Enterprise*.

With the early morning's light we see thin flurries of snow are falling. Light and joyous flakes that dance about the ship's windows. The icebergs on the radar start increasing and then we're among them. Big sombre blocks of ice, the waves beating against them, slowly wearing them down as the current carries them farther away from the ice shelves from which they have broken off.

There is something about the ice that I've been wrestling with for some time. How exactly should I describe it? How to get beyond the clichés of cold and white and icy? How not to use the word salpy?

I've looked over the passages of those men who saw the southern ice before anybody else to see what words they used.

Captain Cook, who called the icebergs Ice Islands and Ice Rocks, found that he had to defer to the words of others: *Dangerous as it is to sail among these floating rocks (if I may be allowed to call them so) in a thick fog; this, however, is preferable to being entangled with immense fields of ice under the same circumstances. … I had two men on board that had been in the Greenland trade; the one of them in a ship that lay nine weeks, and the other in one that lay six weeks, fast in this kind of ice, which they called packed ice. What they called field ice is thicker; and the whole field, be it ever so large, consists of one piece.*

Otto Nordenskjöld, who led the Swedish *Antarctica* expedition, was a little more prosaic than Cook. He wrote in 1902: *Ere we approached so near the land that any of its details could be distinguished, our attention was taken up by something else which we also saw for the first time—the Antarctic ice. Yonder, on the green water there comes floating towards us a glittering white, four-cornered, flat mass of ice, an iceberg: not one of the largest kind, it is true, but in our inexperienced eyes it appears overwhelmingly great. This sight, which, on any other occasion, might have led us to doing all manner of things, was not able, however, to enchain our eyesight very long at such a time as this. All our thoughts, all our attention, was directed towards the colossal shining mass which slowly rose out of the ocean before us, and soon filled the whole horizon. It was the most wonderful picture my eyes have ever beheld.*

In *The Home of the Blizzard*, Mawson explained that the types of icebergs that occur in the Antarctic are different in nature to those of the Arctic due to the difference in glacial conditions. In the Arctic, coastal areas are generally free from ice, except for valley-glaciers which bring ice down from the high interior of lands to sea level. And summer temperatures are moderately warm, helping the glaciers to decay quickly, forming many different types of ice shapes. In the south, the temperatures are colder and there is no appreciable thaw of glacial ice that is pushed into the water. The inland ice is therefore pushed out to sea in enormous chunks, where it remains long before it breaks away to form icebergs. These icebergs can be several years old, with snow settled on the top, forming a large cake shape, but the actions of the ocean underneath wears away the ice to the point the berg may completely turn over, thus revealing an unseen worn surface in a multitude of shapes.

Mawson described the different types of ice colours and formations they encountered as ranging from alabaster-white to pale lilac colorations and ochreous-yellow. Or labyrinths of ice and *majestic tabular bergs whose crevices exhaled a vaporous azure.* He waxed lyrical about lofty spires and splendid castles and fairy castles. *In the soft glamour of the mid-summer midnight sun, we were possessed by a rapturous wonder—the rare thrill of unreality,* he wrote.

In the face of this, how can one find new words?

You've probably heard it said somewhere, at some time, in reputable scientific journals like those you find on supermarket racks near the checkout, that the Eskimos have about a hundred words for snow, with each word depicting a different texture or type of snow. Pick up your hammer, because it's time to hit that myth on the head. The first thing we need to clear up is that there is no one Eskimo language— there are several, which are known as the Eskimo-Aleut languages.

And, yes, they do have many words for snow, often estimated to be about 40 different ones. Now that's still quite a lot of words, compared with the single English word—snow. But in fact, English has about 40 words for snow too, including frost, berg, hail, glacier, ice, slush, flurry, sleet, and so on.

The real confusion is caused by the fact that Eskimo-Aleut languages are polysynthetic, which means you can build up a word by adding suffixes to it that differentiate the particular meaning. German does the same. The captain of the steam-shipping on the Danube can be one long word (*Donaudampfschifffahrtskapitän*), as can the Eskimo-Aleut word for frosty snow that is sparkling.

This means that although the number of words for snow is actually limited, it is also near unlimited, as you can keep coming up with different single-word expressions. Is that now as clear as the driven snow that falls on the captain of the steam-shipping on the Danube River in Germany?

Yet, despite the possible combination of existing adjectives, it is still hard to find enough words to describe the ice when we see it. And it has been so long in coming that the actuality of it has been defined by our anticipation. Moving from wide open seas into the fog-shrouded rolling swells of the past days, the very air feels so much more chill and the spray off the waves freezes into small ice particles. It is as if every nautical mile farther south the conditions are more and more ice-ready.

And then *finally*, finally, the ice proper!

The lone floating, gnarled chunks of ice in the dark sea are becoming thicker and thicker, as snow starts falling, immediately filling us all with that first snow-chill lightness of heart. It flurries and dances about the ship, falling thicker, and we move into denser ice. Immeasurable floes, low to the water, soft icing-sugared snow on top, pavlovas of ice, meringues of ice.

There are so many textures of white: shaded white, bright featureless white, dark shadowed white, soft white, bluish-white, whiter-than-white white. Then a glimmer of swimming-pool turquoise beneath the surface. Shades of rusty brown on the older ice. The dark contrast of cracks as the ship forces the ice to part. So much ice. Ice chunks. Ice scraps. Ice pieces. Ice cakes. Ice figures. Ice clouds. Ice shapes. Ice ponds. Ice mosaics. Ice slabs. Ice playing fields. Ice jumbles. Ice mounds. Ice shards. Ice lumps. Ice dollops. Ice banks. Ice dunes.

Then the mountains of ice. The bergs that leave the lone, wandering, outcast bergs to the north to shame. They pass by the ship so slowly, a new feature on each side of them. Caves and cliff faces. Stark edges and soft curves. Then the excitement of a small group of Adélie penguins on a low floe of ice ahead of us. The ship is bearing right down on them, but veers to port and we pass by so close we can see their flapping indignation as they hurry to and fro before diving into the water.

Next a seal, lounging lugubriously on a floe. It turns and regards us with a huff of annoyance as it slides into the water.

The ice seems to slowly converge about us and is soon so closely pressed together that the colours and shades between the floes diminish into a single ice-whiteness. And the foggy sky appears to slide closer towards us, joining into one. (Is it an expanse of ice? A whiteness of ice? A oneness of ice?)

Standing on the outer deck, awestruck, it feels like every chill breath tastes of this new world about us.

In an essay on travelling to Antarctica, 'Regions of Thick-Ribbed Ice', Helen Garner complains of her need and those of her fellow passengers, to compare icebergs to other things. She says how she would rather see them in abstract terms, and that she doesn't want to keep going 'like, like, like', yet is unable to avoid it. But despite this, she does manage one of the most beautiful descriptions of an iceberg you are ever likely to read, saying it is *shaped like a chunk of frozen cloud that has been sliced off by a downwards stroke of a spatula.*

Talking of trying to find words for the ice, there is a verse from *The Rime of the Ancient Mariner* that is often quoted when talking about the ice: *The ice was here, the ice was there, / The ice was all around: / It cracked and growled, and roared and howled, / Like noises in a swound!*

But it has always left me thinking, what the hell is a 'swound'? Perhaps Samuel Taylor Coleridge, who wrote the poem, had the same thesaurus that King Neptune used and he could also tell me what a 'salpy depth' was. However, I have spent some time on the bridge with the crew and have been able to learn the finer distinctions between greasy-ice, bergy-bits and growlers. Greasy-ice is a patch of ice on the ocean that is more like a very thin excuse for a get-together that wouldn't even impede the progress of a penguin. Growlers are more substantial chucks of ice and are often half-hidden under the water and very hard to spot on radar. They can be anywhere from the size of a car to that of a bus. Bergy-bits are like icebergs with L-plates, although they are generally bits that have carved off larger icebergs and range from the size of a caravan up to a house. When they form together, they are pack-ice—just called 'the pack', like it might be circling and waiting to attack. Above that are the icebergs, those solid and silent majestic mountains of ice that demand to be photographed from all angles.

Stephen J Pyne, in *The Ice,* lists 80 different expressions for different types of ice, from brash ice, blue ice, vuggy ice and pancake ice through to ice flowers, ice fingers, ice walls, ice bastions and ice rumples. But standing there, watching the infinite variation of ice, I think that even 80 words are not enough.

Louis Bernacchi, an Australian member of the Borchgrevink expedition, the first party to overwinter on the continent in 1899, seemed to have a different attitude to the ice than most who have fallen under its allure. He wrote: *Approaching this sinister coast for the first time, on such a boisterous, cold and gloomy day, our decks covered with snow and frozen water, the rigging encased in ice, the heavens as black as death, was like approaching some unknown land of punishment, and struck into our hearts a feeling preciously akin to fear … It was a scene, terrible in its austerity, that can only be witnessed at that extremity of the globe; truly, a land of unsurpassed desolation.*

A cheerful chap, but he did pioneer a style of Antarctic writing in his book of the expedition, *To the South Polar Regions,* that was more than a list of daily weather observations and included the effects of the environment on individuals. Not everyone was happy with the result, however, particularly those he wrote about in a critical light, including Borchgrevink himself. Ah, the perils of writing about Antarctic expeditions, I think. And it brings to mind an old adage that I have long subscribed to: Before you criticise anybody, make sure you walk a mile in their shoes. Because, firstly, when they discover your criticism you'll be a mile away. And, secondly, you'll have their shoes!

✳ ✳ ✳

There is a lot of excitement among us first-timers, who are spending nearly every waking hour up on the bridge or hanging over the ship's railings, taking multiple pictures of every lump of ice we see or distant dark shadow that might be a penguin. There are going to be some very heavy-duty PowerPoint slide nights for family and friends when we get home.

Then we are asked to assemble in the conference room for our pre-Casey Station briefing because we may reach the continent tomorrow. After so many days of endless waiting, it is all moving so quickly suddenly. We are told, once again, about all the different ways to die, such as when transferring by barge or from sudden blizzard or while just wandering around. We are assigned sleeping quarters and toilet blocks on the station and are given a whole new list of acronyms to learn. PPE, JSA, OOS, RTA, TLA, WFT (Personal Protective Equipment, Job Safety Analysis, Occupational Overuse Syndrome, Return to Australia, Three Letter Acronyms and What the Fuck is That?).

✳ ✳ ✳

Mawson's journal is very thin on details, considering the troubles he had getting into land at Commonwealth Bay in 1912. He wrote on 29 December: *Arrived at the pack ice.* Then on 3 January: *Sighted Barrier ice.* Then on 6 January: *Sighted first rock.* And finally on 8 January: *Anchored under the Barrier near winter quarters site and landed.*

In fact, these were fraught days for Mawson, full of frustration and anxiety. His original intention was to land near to Cape Adare, that area of Antarctica that marked the corner entrance into the Ross Sea, where Scott had gone. Mawson had hoped to establish a main base there and then land two other teams somewhere suitable much farther to the west, but all along that coast his way was blocked by thick ice, forcing him farther and farther westwards. This was a problem, as the more distant he was from Macquarie Island, the more he was stretching the limits of their radio communications. Also, if he went too far west he would reach the land already sighted by d'Urville, which the French had a claim to.

For those geographically minded, Cape Adare lies at longitude 170°E, Commonwealth Bay lies at about 142°40'E (about a thousand kilometres distance) and the French claim begins very nearby, at 142°2'E going to 136°11'E.

Mawson fretted endlessly, wondering if he had set out too early in the season. Wondering if they would have to turn back in failure before finding a clear passage to the coast. Wondering if the whole venture, the years of toil, would come to anything.

The ship made its way forward with painstaking care, trying to find a passage southwards through the ice, but forever encountering barriers. Ice walls and huge bergs pressed close, forcing them to turn back, and steam ever farther westward. Although their small ship was ice-strengthened that was no immunity from a large iceberg, well-demonstrated in the northern Atlantic a few months later of that same year when the *Titanic* struck a large iceberg and sank.

The men aboard *Aurora* noted the change in wildlife about them. The albatrosses that had followed them south were now gone, replaced by petrels, and they encountered numerous seals and leopard seals—all a clear indication that land was nearby. Embedded in some of the icebergs they were also able to see rocks which had been carried down off the continent that was hiding somewhere nearby in the mists and ice.

They skirted around two large glacial tongues, having to turn away from the weather at times and shelter behind large bergs. The ice seemed endless and seemed to be working against them. But finally they found an open area of land and sailed along it until they found a small patch of rocks. They examined it carefully from the ship and decided it might be their best chance. They named the wide bay Commonwealth Bay, and the area they were to settle Cape Denison.

❄ ❄ ❄

It's an odd thing being in regular contact with home, but we're having a delay in our emails. Brett, our communications dude, sends and receives them as a group, three times a day if a satellite connection can be made—at 9 AM, 3 PM and 9 PM. And we are now two hours behind Australian Eastern Standard Time, so if Sharon sent me a message last night, asking me a question, I might not get it until mid-morning, and then my reply would not go out until 3 PM and I will only get her reply if she emails me back before 9 PM. Being used to near-instant email replies, the timelag is frustrating at times. But of course I only have to remind myself how good we have it compared with Douglas Mawson and Paquita, who sent their letters into a void of time and waited years to receive a reply.

I've heard some expeditioners talk about the problems of using satellite telephones from the ship or from Antarctica because all they tend to get is bad-vibes calls, which are long lists of complaints from their wives or husbands about what home appliances are broken and how the kids are behaving and what bills need to be paid, and so on. They say it demoralises them at a distance and sometimes makes them reticent to call home too often, and they prefer to use email. I suspect there might be a little more to it though. The myriad complaints might be more an indication of how lonely it is for the partner left in Australia, with no one to discuss the mundane day-to-day things in life that we all need to talk about. It sometimes amazes me how poor we can be as a species at communicating, or understanding others' needs, although we've worked at it for tens of thousands of years. Just watch the way parents and teenagers talk to each other. Bosses and subordinates. Husbands and wives. Authors and readers (well, let's hope not).

I log onto my laptop each morning hoping to find an email from Sharon telling me all the bits of news that I'm most wanting to hear, but sometimes I get all the bits of news that she most wants to tell me—such as how frustrating it is at work or that she can't find something at home and I might know where it is. I could tell her to stop sending me bad-vibes emails, but I don't. I send her emails telling her that I miss her and that I have her picture above my bunk so I can see her smiling face as I go to sleep at nights, watching over me. Or I tell her that I'm not even one week into the trip and am already starting to count the days until I'm back home with her and that I'm dividing the days up into sections. One tenth of the time gone. One week of the seven weeks gone, and so on.

I know it doesn't sound like the true Antarctic spirit of exploration. But Mawson and Scott and many of the other heroic explorers spent long hours missing their spouses and writing them long letters telling them so too.

Any trip to Antarctica is an awfully big adventure, but it also puts a strain on a relationship—simply because of the separation. I recall reading about the problems of overwintering and the toll it took on relationships. The question posed was whether overwintering in Antarctica was detrimental to relationships, and the answer was that it was separation that was detrimental to relationships. Many of the multiple expeditioners have stories about relationship break-ups and the hard choice between Antarctica and a relationship.

It's Sharon's birthday in a few days, and I'd dearly love to be able to share the wonders and the thrills of this trip with her. The best I could come up with before leaving though was to give her an envelope with instructions about where I've hidden her present. It's a toy phone that I've recorded my voice onto. She can push a button and hear me talking to her, telling her how much I miss her and that I'm sorry if she's sad I'm so far away. I guess, in retrospect, I should have got several different phones, colour-coded perhaps. One could be the 'I Miss You' phone and one could be the 'I'm Very Sorry I'm Not There' phone—which would probably get the most use—and one could be the 'Yes, You're Absolutely Right' phone—which she would probably hang onto for years and years in case I ever thought I had got the last word in an argument.

Mawson wrote two letters to Paquita that went back with the *Aurora*, both sharing his excitement about what he was experiencing and regret about not having her with him. On 3 January 1912 he wrote: *Here within a gunshot is the greatest glacier tongue yet known in the world—no human eyes have scanned it before ours. What an exultation is ours—the feeling is magical—young men whom you would scarce expect would be affected stand half clad without feeling the cold of the keen blizzard wind and literally dance from sheer exultation—can you not feel it too as I write—the quickening of the pulse, the awakenings of the mind, the tension of every fibre—and this is joy.*

He also wrote: *... I hope Paquita occasionally thinks of Dougelly—wrap me up in your arms sometimes dear and warm me. Perhaps it is your love warmth that already protects me from the cold, for I doubt if I feel it so much this time as last.*

Before going ashore for the winter in late January, and sending the *Aurora* back to Australia, he wrote a final letter to Paquita, telling her that she would not receive it until April or May, and might even hear news of him via wireless before that. He also expressed his first doubts whether she might still want him after one year apart.

He wrote: *Well don't let that be, for in this stern country of biting facts ones love gets frozen in deeper and there is plenty of time here to think over all the happiness that may be ours ... There is an ocean of love between us dear.*

❄ ❄ ❄

Later that afternoon I go downstairs for a few zzzzzs and sure enough Dougelly is soon sitting there beside me.

'It's beautiful outside, isn't it,' I say. 'Absolutely magical.'

'Do you think so?' he asks.

'Don't tell me you've become jaded as to the magnificence of first entering the ice?' I ask him.

'No. Never jaded,' he says. 'More like …' And I can see him unsuccessfully searching for the word. 'I don't know,' he says. 'But the beauty of it is deceptive, you know. It is also a harsh and cruel land.'

'Then why did you keep returning?' I ask him.

'In part due to its harshness, I suppose,' he says.

This is a rare reflective Dougelly, perhaps bought on by the emotions that come with sighting the first ice. 'Do you remember your first time, in the ice I mean?' I ask him.

'Of course,' he says. 'I was on the *Nimrod* with Shackleton. We had sailed into the Ross Sea in 1908. It was beyond my imagining. The ship slowed down to a crawl and the sea was so calm and the wind had dropped, though we could still hear the soft moan of it coming over the bergs. Most of us stood up on deck, bareheaded, mouths agape, trying to cement every new image in our memories.'

'Now we use cameras,' I say. 'We don't need to cement it. We just put a camera between it and us and it cements it for us.'

And Mawson shakes his head a little. 'That's a pity in a way. You forfeit control over your memory to your machines.'

'It's what we do,' I tell him. 'And we learned it from you. Our visual dreams of Antarctica were formed by Frank Hurley and Herbert Ponting and all the other photographers who came after them. It's their landscapes that press us to want to see the ice for ourselves.'

'Not our stories?' he asks.

'Perhaps,' I say. 'But who reads any more?'

'You do,' he says. 'And there are a few others around the ship who do.'

'Not too many,' I say. 'And go into each of the cabins in the quiet of the evenings. How many are reading and how many are watching DVDs on their laptops?'

We stare at each other a moment, then he asks, 'So why aren't you making a film of this trip instead of writing a book about it?'

I don't quite know a simple answer to that, so I ask, 'In what ways is the ice deceptive?'

And now he smiles. 'It looks so beautiful and looks so calm when you first see it. But it has a slow power that can crush your ship if it chooses to. It is many thousand years old and a piece of ice can shear off the shelf that is so large it has the force of moving continents behind it. It can sneak up on you and chill you to the bone. You can lose your fingertips or toes to frostbite. And you can feel completely insignificant in its presence. You'll feel that soon enough when you're out there on the continent. You'll get a feel for its power.'

'I've read that some expeditioners have been so overwhelmed that they immediately turned around and hopped back on the ship. Couldn't face the sudden reality and isolation of it.'

'Or the insignificance of themselves in the face of it.'

'Perhaps so,' I say. 'So why did you keep returning if it made you feel insignificant?'

'It does,' he says. 'But there is a point, a rare moment, when you almost feel a oneness with the ice. Feel a part of that grandeur. Feel something monumental. Feel way beyond your human being. Feel your place with the frozen continent. Sometimes beyond even your place with the whole planet.

'Wow,' I say. 'You never wrote that anywhere.'

'No,' he says. 'But that's how I remember it now.'

I want to ring Sharon before we reach land. The satellite telephone is by the stairwell in a storage cupboard which is full of soaps and cleaners. I find afterwards that I've developed an emotional soft spot for Sunlight soap. I call her at work and she is so surprised to hear my voice she squeals. I sing her 'Happy Birthday' and then hear her mumbling 'I miss you so much' and tears are choking her voice. The phone cuts in and out a bit as the ship pitches about, but it is great to be talking to her and I say that it's only about 40 more nights apart now. I've read somewhere that the constant references to 40 days and nights in the Bible actually means 'a very long time, longer than we can actually count to or figure out accurately, so we will call it 40'. I know what they mean. Forty days and nights seem an eternity sometimes.

I hang up after five or six minutes, not even thinking of the astronomical costs of the call, and smell the Sunlight soapy smell about me. Just walking past the cupboard later in the day I can open the door and inhale and it brings back the feeling of Sharon crying softly while talking to me. Ah, the heartening effects of Sunlight.

We move through the ice closer to the continent as the short night settles about us. An icebreaker doesn't actually crash its way through the ice. It has a very flat and low-angled prow and it rides up on top of the ice, which the weight of the ship crushes, breaking a path. We're actually close enough to move into the harbour outside Casey Station now, but the ship's captain has decided to keep us in the equivalent of a circling pattern over an airport, doing large circles, and then we will come into land in the morning. It's frustrating to know the continent is just there before us in the darkness somewhere, but we can't see it. It's also confusing the way the same large icebergs are on the left of the ship, then on the right. But my inner compass has long since succumbed to disorientation, so I go to bed, eager for what the new day will bring.

❄ ❄ ❄

I lie in bed thinking about the book that I plan to write and which direction it should go. It's got me wondering how much ice there might be around Antarctica in the near future. There are two schools of thought on this, depending on who I talk to. One has it that there will be less ice as temperatures will have increased and it will melt earlier. On the Antarctic Peninsula, in particular, there will be less ice. The other school of thought has it that there will be a lot more ice in the seas as the warmer temperatures will encourage ice to break off the ice shelves and fall into the ocean.

So maybe I have to come up with a scenario where there is more ice on the sea but less ice on the land. When Mawson landed at

Commonwealth Bay they found just one small section of rock where they were able to build their huts. How might that look in the future? I could start the book with coming ashore at that place, but try to avoid one of those lame-arse dialogues like, 'My goodness, look how much the ice has receded around the huts. It was much thicker when Mawson landed here in 1911. Must be the impact of climate change.'

(Note to self: try the idea out on Mawson when next you see him. He's bound to have an opinion on it, and will probably even want to be a character in the story, or a narrator or something. But what reader would fall for a clunky device like that?)

Casey Station

At 11 P.M. the Aurora entered a bay, ten miles wide, bounded on the east by the shelf-ice wall and on the west by a steep snow-covered promontory rising approximately two thousand feet in height, as yet seen dimly in hazy outline through the mist. No rock was visible, but the contour of the ridge was clearly that of ice-capped land.

—Douglas Mawson, *The Home of the Blizzard*

We wake up early the next morning feeling like children on Christmas Day. There is a very soft snow falling outside the porthole. And there is Casey Station. I rush up on deck and find a few other early birds are there too, looking around at the continent surrounding us on three sides. I feel like punching the air and shouting, 'Woo-hoo!' But I restrain myself. Down in the canteen/restaurant there is a sign on the noticeboard saying we will be going ashore about 10.30 and to dress appropriately, as if in our enthusiasm we might somehow step off the ship in our thongs and shorts.

We have had a special briefing from the ship's environmental officer, one of the Debbies, who is back on her feet again in calmer waters and gives us the corporate PowerPoint presentation on environmental awareness in Antarctica. Some of the older hands roll their eyes a little at it, but in very small circles, as if this is a Soviet-era ship and we are about to get a lecture from the political officer (smile and pretend you are enthusiastic or you might end up in Siberia). I'm reminded a little bit of that scene in *A Clockwork Orange* where they strap the leader of the gang into a chair and make him watch violent movies with his eyes forced open until he develops an aversion to violence. I've long ago developed the aversion to corporate PowerPoint presentations and my body either reacts by falling asleep or daydreaming of things long, long ago in galaxies far away.

Most of my shipmates seem to have adopted the first approach. I can see eyes around me drooping. The gist of the talk is that we have to be very, very careful about what we carry in with us. We need to remove any excess packaging and things that might shred. Fresh fruit and vegetables are banned. Polystyrene packaging of all kinds is super-banned. It's like we're going to be going through the mother of all tick-gates. But the screening is self-performed. We have to vacuum the pockets of all our clothes and turn our bags inside out so we don't bring any alien matter onto the continent (apart from ourselves). We each get a 20-minute turn with a vacuum with a stocking over its end to catch whatever noxious lint we have in our pockets and bags and on the soles of our boots and then it is bagged and sealed for analysis.

Somewhere some poor sod will be sitting down in a laboratory opening dozens and dozens of these envelopes and pulling out dozens and dozens of stockings and having to analyse them in great detail to confirm that none of the lint that has been found is noxious. Though Nicki tells me afterwards that they have found some very unwanted introduced pests in both Antarctica and Macquarie Island that proved difficult to eradicate. There are weeds growing at Macquarie Island and pesky little flies had been a problem in Casey Station's waste systems.

Nicki also tells me that previously they found about 20 seeds on the socks of an expeditioner who had been in North America. They were seeds of an extremely invasive plant and every one was viable—they were able to grow them to germination in the laboratory, showing what tough little buggers they were. We are told if we find something alien that looks like it doesn't belong, be it plant or insect, we are to notify somebody immediately so the offender can be destroyed. Fortunately, we have all seen both versions of the movie *The Thing* and have pretty clear expectations of both what an alien species looks like and the type of drastic means needed to destroy it. I ask if we will each be issued with a flamethrower to destroy any aliens, like in the movie, and am given that 'don't-be-a-smart-arse' smile so favoured by management everywhere.

All human waste has to be collected, which includes ALL human waste, and we're particularly told if we end up on a helicopter to make sure that any shit or piss we're carrying back is not just frozen in a single plastic bag, but the bag is placed inside the special waste containers. It's a particular sore point with pilots, we're told—there are too many horror stories of them ferrying waste, with or without the people who provided it, and the frozen turds thawing out inside the helicopter.

We are also given a run-down on how to treat wildlife and not to come within 5 metres of a seal or penguin at this time of year. If they are mating, the distance is much greater. Gary, the penguin expert who gives this bit of the briefing, also says that it is okay for the animals to approach us—but to be careful if that animal is a leopard seal. As anybody who has seen *Happy Feet* can attest, they are mean mothers and have been known to leap out of the water and grab people. In fact, Gary is able to fill in the details about a story I'd heard of an Australian scientist who was killed by a leopard seal. All I knew was that it happened at a British station. The popular version was that she was in the water under the ice, scuba diving, and had been working around leopard seals for years, but on this day one just up and bit her nearly in half and then carried her down into the depths. Actually, she was examining the impacts of icebergs on the ocean floor and was snorkelling along in the water when the leopard seal attacked her, biting her on the head and dragging her underwater. She had some very severe wounds around her neck and head, but died of drowning.

Gary gives his impressions of agro seals and sea lions and penguins, showing how they turn away, or give you the piss-off stare, turning their heads from side to side. He also says that on occasion you just might meet a psycho-penguin, who, for no particular reason, might run at you and start attacking you with its flippers. For the record, he tells us, that's definitely a case of the penguin approaching you.

❄ ❄ ❄

We are taken ashore from the *Aurora Australis* by barge on Saturday morning. There we all are, standing on the deck in our day-glo orange freezer suits and life jackets—oops sorry, PFDs (Personal Flotation Device)—and there in front of us is Antarctica. We stare fixedly at the snow and rocks and ice and clouds and the little coloured Lego blocks that are the station. It looks like a toy town at this distance. The run in takes about five minutes and we are all like children on a school excursion. 'When do we get there? When do we get there?' But we find that when we actually reach the dock we are like penguins standing at the edge of the ice, looking into the water, all waiting for somebody else to go first. Then one of the guys scrambles awkwardly up the metal ladder on the edge of the metal wharf and suddenly we are all pushing to get there.

My first steps on Antarctica are onto rock and mud and slush. But it is Antarctic rock and mud and slush. The first thing I do is go over to the snow, make a snowball and throw it at Bob, the incoming station leader. He looks at me in surprise and horror, and then throws one back.

Mawson wrote in *The Home of the Blizzard*: *The sun shone gloriously in a blue sky as we stepped ashore on a charming ice-quay—the first to set foot on the Antarctic continent between Cape Adare and Gaussberg a distance of one thousand eight hundred miles.*

Our landing is a little different, with trucks and barges and cranes all about us. We have been warned that walking on land that doesn't move to and fro like the ship might be a little bit difficult at first, but I have no troubles. Not until later than night, when I start wobbling and nearly fall over. At first I think I must have had some sort of dizzy-spell, but then I realise it's the readjustment thing. One of the other expeditioners tells me he got out of bed after his first night's sleep at Casey and fell straight over on his bum.

Mawson had written: *The overcrowded whale-boat disgorged its cargo at 10 P. M. on the ice-quay at Cape Denison. The only shelter was a cluster of four tents and the Benzine Hut, so the first consideration was the erection of a commodious living hut.*

The rocky area they had found was barely large enough for erecting their huts and, unfortunately, happened to be in one of the windiest places on earth. The landing party had their work cut out for them. First they had to blast the rock to set foundations for their huts, and then they had to work with wood that had been partly warped by seawater on the voyage. The men were plugging cracks that let the wind and snow into the hut for many months afterwards.

The strength to resist hurricanes, simplicity of construction, portability and resistance to external cold were the fundamental necessities of their hut, Mawson wrote. *My first idea was to have the huts in the form of pyramids on a square base, to ensure stability in heavy winds and with a large floor-area to reduce the amount of timber used … In this form the pyramid extended to within five feet of the ground on the three windward sides so as to include an outside veranda. That veranda … lent stability to the structure, assisted to keep the hut warm, served as a store-house, physical laboratory and a dog-shelter.*

The men worked hard against the tormenting weather to complete the hut's construction, adding a slightly smaller second hut to the first to give it its famous double-pyramid design. Mawson told them that they were all a long way distant from any trades hall and there would be no union nonsense, and that the men should expect to work very long hours to complete their accommodation, starting at 7 AM and finishing at 11 PM. He also regularly lectured the men on the value of work. I noted that, although our ship has union posters prominently displayed, when called upon the crew and those undertaking the unloading work equally long hours, until late in the night.

When his hut was completed, Mawson wrote: *Our hearth and home was the living Hut and its focus was the stove. Kitchen and stove were indissolubly linked, and beyond their pale was a wilderness of hanging clothes, boots, finnesko, mitts and what not, bounded by tiers of bunks and blankets, more hanging clothes and dim photographs between the frost-rimmed cracks of the wooden walls.*

At Casey Station everyone lives inside the Red Shed, which is a huge red metal building with a door like that of a freezer room. Inside is like coming into a large, busy ski lodge. Through the large foyer full of boots and jackets, immediately on the left there is a spacious cafeteria-style dining room and kitchen. Opposite is the public living area, nicely carpeted, with tall ceiling, mezzanine level, couches and pictures and plaques and an all-over feeling of coziness. Bedrooms, washrooms and so on are through fire doors on the far side. Outside, though, the general feeling of the station is that of a mining town in Lapland or Alaska. Lots of huge big trucks and huge big sheds and mud and dirt roads. The rest of the sheds are colour-coded, according to function (red is for living). Green is for the store and supplies, yellow is operations and science, and blue means you can't go in as there is electricity or fuel or something equally dangerous in there.

Each is a separate structure, not linked by tunnels or anything, so station staff have to walk around outside whatever the station weather. I reckon that when the bureaucrats completely take over Antarctica they'll erect the Beige Shed.

This Casey Station is the third base built in this location. The original, Wilkes Station, built nearby by the USA in 1957, was replaced in 1969 by Casey Station, named after the then Governor-General and former government minister, Lord Casey, who had been a staunch supporter of Australia's Antarctic program. The rebuilt station was opened in 1988.

We are given a grand tour of the base, conducted by Jeremy, the station leader, and we get to visit most of the coloured buildings, including the incinerator (called Warren) where waste including turds are roasted, and then the fire and emergency vehicle shed, the giant store shed, the workshop and the meteorological shed and the vehicle storage shed—but we don't go into the science shed because there are no scientists about at the moment. In fact, we are told, it has been a bit thin on the ground for scientists in the last several months. There are some interesting grumbles about this from different people, some suggesting that the huge amount of infrastructure here is surely to support science, but where is the science? Yet others say that the opening of the new Wilkins Airfield, about 70 kilometres inland up on the ice dome, the Law Dome, has enabled scientists to fly in and then fly out again and will increase the amount of science done here in the future. More on that later.

Then we are taken out into the field—not the airfield, the ice field. There are many looks of envy as us three arts fellows and Bill are handed survival gear and a pack each. Most people say that life down here really only gets interesting once you are off the station. And they are right. We hop into a small Hägglund vehicle with our guide Vonna, and are driven around the peninsula to the Wilkes Hilton, about 4 kilometres and half a world away. A little bit of background here. A Hägglund is a Swedish army vehicle designed for transporting troops in Lapland and the word is Swedish for 'shakes the shit out of your bones'. Vonna is employed as a guide by the Antarctic Division. Originally from the US of A, now resident in Tasmania, she is small and tough and with great senses of both humour and adventure—though she'd rather be tall and tough. And the Wilkes Hilton is a little shed, like one of the huts in the Kosciuszko high country, set nearby the old Wilkes Station.

We were very lucky to have Bill with us. He stayed a winter at Wilkes as a young lad and, although the station is almost entirely buried in ice now, he takes us on a tour over the roofs. He shows us where he worked and slept and the cell they had to build, the year before he arrived, when one expeditioner went mad and took to another with an axe and had to be air-lifted out by the Russians. Fascinating stuff. History coming to life. It is the snow-hidden equivalent of an archaeological excavation. We are able to get into the hut where Bill did most of his work, taking magnetic readings. He says the hut was constructed with copper nails so as to not distort the instruments. The wood of the buildings is highly weathered on the windward side, with the blizzard ice slowly chipping it away.

I have heard a story that a few years previously it was possible to get in through the roofs of some of the buildings, with a clearance of about 60 centimetres, and slide around on your stomach and look down through the ice and see things in the rooms, including an old piano. Unfortunately, the slow ice entombment of Wilkes Station is now almost complete and most buildings have only 15 centimetres or so of space between the rising ice and the ceiling, and many are then covered in heavy snow drifts.

The curved wooden support ribs of the store buildings appear like the ribs of whale skeletons sticking out of the snow. And scattered all around are junk and detritus. Old rusted drums. Machinery. Wooden crates of soaps and foods. I'm told that when the snow melts down the extent of the discarded junk is really apparent, and bits of husky carcasses can even be seen. It's an unfortunate relic of the past that needs to be cleaned up for the future. In fact, the amount of junk that is carted away from the stations each year is impressive, but it is going to take many years to clean up a place like Wilkes.

Bill says it is all very different to his memories—it was always a living station to him and now it isn't. It is the near-obscured remnants of a base. It is the rusted iron stakes of a base. It is the broken weather packing cases of a base. It is the stranded whale carcass of a base.

Later we accompany Bill up the hill overlooking the bay, across from Casey Station, where two expeditioners are buried. One, Reg Sullivan, died of asphyxiation in 1968 and the other, Hartley Robinson, was run over by his own tractor in 1959. It is a beautiful location, looking over the station and the bay and the ice. But it is still a grave site. Bill is silent for a long time and then he thanks everyone for this opportunity. The wooden crosses are very weathered on one side. Vonna tells us the bodies are still under the rocks there. Bill had asked for permission to bring back a small stone off the grave of Reg Sullivan, for his family, and said the decision went all the way up to the Minister, but it was refused. That's sad. So is the final line of the inscription on Hartley Robinson's grave. 'We miss you Dad.' The wind and the cold and the moment combine to bring tears to our eyes.

We leave the many ghosts of Wilkes Station after a reflective hour or two and ski across towards the penguin rookery in the distance. When we stop on a ridge to sit and watch the distant penguins, some Adélies come up to check us out. They are the crazy Latino penguins in *Happy Feet*. How can anybody watch an Adélie penguin and not be joyed by it? You have to love the way your first Adélie penguins come to check you out. Three of them waddle up to see who the hell is that and what the hell you are doing there, and they keep stopping and having these little subcommittee meetings before deciding to come closer. They approach to within about 5 metres and give you a careful looking over, probably surprised to see you are much taller up close than you looked from a distance. And then one of the penguins might decide it is unhappy with the general state of the world, or some subclause in the Antarctic Environment Protection Act that allows people to smile like idiots and photograph them, and will go 'Aaargh aargh aaargh' a little at you, which we believe is probably penguin speak for, 'Who the hell are you and what the hell are you doing here?' Then they might all lose interest at once and plop down onto their stomachs and toboggan away, their feet propelling them along. You gotta love them penguins.

In the late evening we were graced with the most amazing sunset of reds and oranges and pinks across the water, behind the icebergs drifting into shore and the sea so calm and the sky so perfectly still. Suddenly, everything seems to slow and the size of the place is so overwhelming and I feel the age and the vastness of the place and a calmness all about, and I think I understand what those new-agers at the Salamanca Markets in Hobart are talking about, and I start to drift a little out of kilter into another consciousness. If Sharon were here, she could slap me and say, stop that hippie shit and get on with the story!

I had asked to sleep out in a tent to get the feel of the heroic age a little, wanting to experience that thin feeling of protection afforded by a tent in the snow—the illusion of safety offered by a sheet of canvas and the light and the shape of the pyramid over my head. But Vonna laughed and said I'd be sleeping in a bivy bag. A what? Well, basically, it's a large sleeping bag cover, but you crawl into it. So I laid a mat on the rocky ground behind the hut, put in my sleeping bag and crawled in and—surprise, surprise—I really slept well outside on the ground, except for being pecked at twice during the night. (Gary, the penguin expert, told me it's not unknown for a penguin to come and give you a small peck if you're sleeping anywhere near the penguin highway—their curiosity gets the better of them. I can just imagine the subcommittee going, 'What the hell is that and what is it doing here? It sure as shit wasn't here yesterday. One of us better go and give it a peck and find out if we can eat it.') But a penguin peck isn't so bad when I was more worried that an amorous elephant seal might think that I was a female elephant seal inside my bivy bag!

Inside the nearby Wilkes Hilton hut the others were lounging by the warm stove wearing genuine Hilton Hotel slippers, wondering if it were possible to get Paris Hilton to come and officially open the hut one day. Then they placed bets on how long it would take me to come in from the cold before they crawled into their sleeping bags and went to sleep themselves.

It took a little while for me to fall asleep outside. I found it odd that the rocks weren't rocking like I'd got used to on the ship, and they certainly weren't as soft as the bunk mattress I'd been sleeping on. But when I did drift off it was into a deep, deep sleep—though I was also visited by a long series of bizarre dreams. Later, I realised that I'd hardly been dreaming on the ship, which might have been one of the side effects of the seasickness tablets. If so, my night on the rocks made up for it.

Sitting inside the hut the next day, cooking dinner, it brings to my mind what it must have felt like inside Mawson's Hut. The old wooden floors and fibro walls and things hanging from hooks and the wooden shelves laden with food. At the modern Casey Station there is an old shelf unit from Wilkes with tins of food and drink from the 1950s and 1960s and I'm thinking that one day this hut is going to be as much a museum piece as Wilkes or Mawson's Hut is. Tourists might come here and poke their heads in and a guide will tell them that this is the hut known as the Wilkes Hilton, the old radio transmitter hut for Wilkes Station, which has now been removed entirely because of environmental guidelines for cleaning up Antarctica.

And that is going to be a big job. Some serious decisions will need to be made about what is classified as Antarctic heritage items which cannot be touched or moved and what is junk that needs to be returned to Australia. This varies, according to the heritage purists and the heritage heretics. The heritage heretics can tell junk from heritage items and say, 'That's crap. Let's pick it up.' The purists say, 'Put that back just where you found it or I'll report you.' I sympathise with the purists, but I've got to tell you, sometimes rubbish is just rubbish.

In the hut, when I'm reaching up to get something off a bunk, I get a large splinter under my thumb. 'That's a heritage splinter,' the others say. 'You can't touch it or move it.' We even tell Bill that he's now a heritage item and we won't be able to take him back with us and will have to leave him here.

Lynette, our historian arts fellow, has decided to brave the outside toilet, which is basically a plastic bag in a bucket in a little wooden dunny shack atop a rickety mount in the snow. Lynette is a history lecturer at the University of the Sunshine Coast and is writing a biography of an Australian Antarctic surveyor, Syd Kirkby. She is in her late 40s, but looks a lot younger when she smiles. Every time somebody goes outside we say, 'I'm just going outside to the toilet. I may be some time.' But Lynette comes back and says, 'Well, that was a heritage-listed experience.'

The hut has a row of double bunks around the walls, a long table running down the middle and a squat iron stove right in the centre. There is also a gas stove and an electric light, for those who want things a little easier. And we, in the hut, are explorers, of sorts. Exploring the past and the present and the links between the two.

While we're preparing dinner Vonna drops the cheese onto the floor. Twice. She laughs and looks up at me, as I'm sitting on a couch writing. 'You're going to write this stuff down, aren't you,' she says.

'Am I?' I ask, writing it down because she put the thought in my mind.

Bill has some absolutely fascinating stories to tell about Mawson's Hut, and he stares back into the past and tells me how he was almost the first person to stand at Cape Denison since Mawson left after his 1929–31 BANZARE (British, Australian and New Zealand Antarctic Research Expedition) voyages. He tells me that on his return trip to Australia from Wilkes Station, in 1962 at the age of 23, he went ashore with the legendary Phillip Law, the first head of Australia's Antarctic Division, and was about to hop out of the boat to make it secure when Phil shouldered him aside, not wanting to miss the historical step for himself.

The two of them were ashore first on that day and they looked over Mawson's Hut, which was already showing significant signs of weather damage and was filled with ice. Bill said that it really stuck with him and it drove his lifelong interest in the hut. He had it listed on the National Register—nobody else had thought to do so. When he was in Britain several years later, he was fortunate enough to meet Sir Vivian Fuchs—in 1958 he became the first man to traverse Antarctica, and that's pronounced Fooks or Fox or Foosh or anything but the obvious—and later met Sir Ernest Shackleton's son (Lord 'call me Eddie' Shackleton) in Sydney and had enlisted them both as supporters.

Bill's vision was that the hut should be bought back to Australia and erected somewhere, under a dome for instance, where visitors could walk up a wind tunnel, suitably dressed in parkas, and feel the wind and the chill, and then come into the hut. The problem with leaving it down in Antarctica, he said, is that so very few people would ever get to see it. Over the years it has become a fairly well-known icon, being promoted through Project Blizzard and other organisations, or appearing on breakfast cereal boxes and in school project publications—the twin-roofed hut looking something like a Mayan pyramid of stained wood planking. However, the elements have been taking a serious toll on the hut and in places the timbers have been worn down to one-third of their original thickness.

This has led to a long debate on whether to leave Mawson's Hut where it is and conserve it there, or whether to bring it back to Australia. Some have claimed that the arguments have sometimes led to inaction. The current thinking is to conserve it on site. Bill calls this the argument of the purists, but he also says they are making things hard for themselves because it is impossible to conserve the hut without changing its appearance in any way.

While in Hobart at the Antarctic Division, getting kitted out for the trip, I met a man with a Mawson's Hut conservation T-shirt on and asked him about it. He said he had just returned from working on the hut. The main objective at the moment was to make the building weather-tight, he said, so that they could get the ice out. He said they had applied a sealing layer over the roof and then fitted a replica of the baltic pine wood roof over that. And that they had been able to remove several tonnes of ice, but that there were a hell of a lot more still there.

There was a story in that fine journal *The Hobart Mercury* that I cut out with a picture of the eight-person team. It said they had spent five weeks at the hut undertaking conservation work funded largely by the Mawson's Hut Foundation. The expedition leader said that the cladding put down to keep further snow from trickling in was doing a good job.

The first major conservation work undertaken by the Mawson's Hut Foundation, in 1997–98, may have saved the main hut from collapse in that they replaced one of the main wooden beams supporting the apex of the building. Earlier work was undertaken by Project Blizzard in the 1980s, but because the hut was heritage listed they were restricted in what they could do.

In 1991 Australia's own adventuring entrepreneur, the electronic Dick, Dick Smith, had gone down to Mawson's Hut and found that it was largely filled with ice and impossible to enter, and noted some serious deterioration of the exterior timbers. Alf Howard was on the same voyage. He had been a scientist on Mawson's 1929–31 expedition, and said that back then they had climbed into the hut through the roof and found lots of things left behind from the 1911–14 expedition.

The year 2011 marks a hundred years since Mawson's landing and erection of the hut. I will watch with interest to see what decisions are made on how best to preserve it.

Bill says he'd much rather that many Australians could see the hut and go inside and look at the bunk where the two planks of wood were taken to make the cross for Mertz and Ninnis. He says it should be possible to make a replica on site if need be, but that the main hut should be moved to where the most people can share in that special feeling he got from seeing it all those years ago.

Bill, who has continued to be one of the champions of Mawson's Hut, tells me that it has led to other interesting things, such as when students of the former Canberra College of Advanced Education built a one-to-twenty scale model, based on the original plans. It was taken to Sydney and set up in the international airport terminal. Bill says that Eric Webb, who was the chief magnetician on Mawson's expedition, visited the exhibit and was able to point out in great detail where they worked and who had slept where and relate how he had fallen down on the ice just outside the hut one day and was nearly blown right out to sea. Bill said there were all these photographers taking photos but nobody had a tape recorder to record Eric Webb talking, which was a great pity.

The day before we had sailed, I went to the Tasmanian Museum and Art Gallery where there was an exhibition on Antarctica. It included a model of Mawson's Hut, which had the roof raised clear of the structure so it was possible to see the great detail of the bunks and the shelves and where the men stood and sat and worked. And the storage areas around the sides of the huts were moved away so it was possible to see how they also provided insulation. I could clearly see where the dogs lived down one side in their own kennel area. I could imagine standing behind Bill in the airport terminal, listening to Eric Webb, and peopling the hut in my imagination.

Another of Bill's stories is about obtaining a first edition of *The Home of the Blizzard.* He tells me that only 400 copies were printed before the press burned down and so 'they are as rare as rocking-horse shit'. A friend in Britain, who was looking out for a copy, was on a train coming back from a book-buying tour one day and got to talking with the woman in the carriage with him. She asked what he did and, when he told her that he was an antiquarian book dealer, she asked if he had a list of the types of books he was looking for. She ran her eyes down it and said, 'I think I've got that one.'

Bill says he's taken it to the National Library to get advice on how best to store it and that he intends, ultimately, that it form some part of a Mawson heritage exhibition. He says he'd never wish to sell it.

Bill tells me that it's been a frustrating experience, trying to get support for bringing Mawson's Hut back though, as many of the big Antarctic names who were supporting him have now died and it had been in the too-hard basket of bureaucracy for too long.

It's a common theme in the books and articles written by the modern explorers and adventurers, that the heroic age of Antarctica has been replaced by the heroic bureaucracy age that excessively limits the individual. When the trio of Gareth Wood, Roger Mear and Robert Swan trekked across Antarctica in 1985–86 on a private expedition, for instance, they were officially denied any support or assistance from New Zealand's Scott Base and the US McMurdo Station, although individuals at those bases went to lengths to help them. The expedition had fallen victim to a joint policy drafted by the USA and New Zealand governments, which ruled out any assistance to private expeditions and was aimed at preventing limited resources being diverted from science missions. The policy has proved rubbery, depending on political influence—there are cases of politicians insisting that aviator friends receive refuelling assistance at McMurdo. One such pilot was Brooke Knapp, whose husband was close with Ronald Reagan. She was able to receive support from McMurdo Station after flying from New Zealand on her way over the South Pole to South America.

As often happens, the blanket rule of bureaucracy, often implemented with good intentions, can come up looking as if it has no regard or compassion for the human spirit. It's unfortunate, but I've spent a lot of my life working with the developers of government policies, and have learned to be very cautious of ideologues, as if they were snoozing leopard seals. Usually quite harmless, but don't let their inaction fool you. For their intentions, those of bureaucrats not leopard seals, may be well-meaning—but they are often too far divorced from on-the-ground situations or unable to be flexible to individual cases.

For a final word on Mawson's Hut and its importance to the nation, I'd like to defer to the author, academic and free-thinker Stephen Murray-Smith, who wrote in his fine book *Sitting on Penguins* that when he sighted Mawson's Hut on his 1995–96 voyage: *I don't know if it was a great moment for the others, but it was for me. I felt a rather embarrassing rush of patriotism. This is where we Australians put our roots down in the south—or, rather, blew holes in the rock to hold the stumps of our first building.*

And I can well imagine a very grumpy Mawson appearing on the end of the beds of many bureaucrats and architects over the years and demanding to know why so much work has been done to preserve Shackleton's Hut and Scott's Hut and even Borchgrevink's Hut, while people bicker about what and how and whether to work on his hut, leaving it to deteriorate to the point that the weather-stained wood looked like rotted teeth.

The numbers of people who visit Mawson's Hut each year has been slowly climbing, reaching 400 in 2008–09, and access to the hut is limited to three people at a time for ten minutes each. What the future will bring is uncertain. The visitors might be able to visit Cape Denison and go inside the fully restored hut, and really get a feeling of what it was like to live there, with all the old tins and photographs and bunks, just as Mawson had left it. Or it might be possible to visit Cape Denison and find nothing there, the ruins of the hut blown out into the bay. Or it might be possible to sail in and spend one week trying to get through the ice, unsuccessfully, and see nothing. Or it might be possible to walk through a reconstruction of the hut in one of Australia's capital cities, as Paquita believed Mawson would have preferred. They are all possible futures. All imaginable. All the ghost of times that may or may not come about.

✻ ✻ ✻

There is a lot of talk at Casey Station about the recently introduced airlink. To some it represents the future, to some it represents an end of the past, which aren't necessarily the same thing. The project has been several years in the making—locating possible sites for a runway, obtaining all the regulatory approvals, scoping the type of airplane to use, organising logistics on the ground, including preparing the ice surface for a plane to land on. The first official flight of the Airbus A319 from Hobart to Antarctica was made in January 2008, not very long before our arrival at Casey Station. Those aboard for the nine-hour return flight included the then Environment Minister and former Midnight Oil frontman Peter Garrett, and the then head of the Australian Antarctic Division, Dr Tony Press, both of whom were visiting Australia's Antarctic Territory for the first time. The trip received oodles of great media coverage, including the $47 million cost of the project. Those who had to do the on-the-ground, or on-the-ice, support, however, found the flights quite exhausting.

The blue ice runway, known as the Wilkins Runway after the extraordinary South Australian Antarctic explorer Sir Hubert Wilkins, has been constructed on 500 metre-thick ice and is 4 kilometres long, allowing planes to land smoothly on their wheels. But landing on the continent is really only half the journey. The runway is about 70 kilometres from Casey Station, which can be a rough four-hour trip by Hägglund, about the same time as it takes to fly one-way from Hobart.

Although that does make me recall that in *The Guinness Book of World Records* I saw that the record for the fastest journey to the South Pole was in a custom-adapted six-wheel drive vehicle that drove from the Patriot Hills to the Pole in less than three days! For comparison, Edmund Hillary did it on a New Zealand tractor in 80 days, in 1958, and Amundsen got to the Pole in 53 days with dogs. And there was that *Top Gear* program in which the guys drove to the North Magnetic Pole in four-wheel drives, sometimes making crap progress and having to dig their way through hillocks and ice, but sometimes just ripping along in, well, in top gear.

But back to the airlink. Most of the flights during the 2007–08 summer season were successful but two had to turn back due to inclement weather. In the future it is hoped that 10 to 12 flights per season might carry in a dozen or more passengers each trip, mostly scientists and Antarctic Division staff. Almost everybody I talked to has a strong opinion on the airlink, or an interesting anecdote, though many would only tell me in a lowered whisper. One expeditioner counted 360 working hours in preparation for a single flight in, not counting the clean-up afterwards. Some think it a huge waste of money, which is being spent to hook politicians and VIPs to come down to the ice, whereas others think it an enormous asset for getting more high-quality scientists down to the continent. It should be added that using the airlink for tourism has been ruled out. So far.

It is a conundrum of Antarctica that the measure of a nation's successful involvement tends to be on the basis of the science undertaken, yet the more major rebuilding programs and projects such as the blue ice runway, which require huge resources to complete, the less science is undertaken. There were many comments by Casey Station staff that scientists have been a bit thin on the ground the summer I was there, and that of the 19 overwinterers who would stay to maintain Casey Station throughout the 2009 winter, none was a scientist. Coincidentally, this was the same number of men at the main base on Mawson's first expedition, from 1912–13, who did all the work—and this included the scientists.

And 19 is also the number of scientists who were flown in on the airlink in its first year of operation, which only amounted to 10 per cent of the total passengers.

Despite the airlink's PR successes, the real measure of its success, over the years ahead, will be whether it is a feasible way of landing targeted people on the Antarctic continent quickly and efficiently. It will be telling to see who is climbing off the plane onto the ice five years from now. Will it be invading hoards of VIP-wannabes, or junket-addicted journalists and bureaucrats, or will it be top-class scientists and political leaders who can make a difference? I'm sure those cushy seats will be filled, but by whom?

It all makes me recall the last lines of the 1951 movie, *The Thing,* in which the reporter, broadcasting the battle they have fought in the snow and ice with the alien, issues a warning, 'Watch the skies. Watch the skies!'

❄ ❄ ❄

I spend my next day at Casey doing slushie duty. A slushie is Antarctic-speak for slave. The idea is that you help the cook in the kitchen, but it can mean doing any manner of things. I start off by cleaning up the mess from the night before's drinking at the bar. Then I vacuum the common area of the Red Shed. It is very much like the living room of any large communal house situated near the Antarctic Circle. Then I clean out the toilets. But I do get the privilege of choosing the music to play throughout the shed. The first song I put on is 'Summertime' and I sing along, 'Slushie-time, and the feeling is easy …'

Then I do a bit of helping in the industrial-sized kitchen, talking to Richard and Frank, the cooks, who are top guys and the first people I've met who are a little awed that I'm a writer (what's wrong with the rest of these guys?). Frank is leaving with us on the ship and Richard will be station cook over the winter. Richard asks me to help him unpack some things in the green food shed. This is Antarctic-speak for come and help unload the whole year's supply of food from huge shipping containers and put it on pallets and put the pallets up on shelves, some over 6 metres off the ground. But it's a really fun day.

So many people talk about the importance of food in Antarctica but few get such a close-up view of it arriving and being stored. There is a warm room, which is in fact a giant refrigerator, for foods that need to be kept cool but not frozen (the shed goes well below freezing in winter).

There are drums and drums and drums of cooking oil, and drums and drums and drums of flour, and several huge bags of porridge and there is half a pallet of rice and one whole pallet of different types of chocolates. It's a bit like going through the shopping trolleys of a hundred or so people at the supermarket and piling all their things into one large eclectic mix. One shipping container, when unpacked, is spread across 14 pallets, which are over a metre square each. Some of the foodstuffs I hold up in amazement, like Parisian Essence, or crab paste, and Richard shows me where to stick them, down a back corner of the shed, where several years' worth of Parisian Essence are hidden.

There is self-raising flour, rye flour, gluten, raw sugar, white sugar, cooking chocolate, ground black pepper, salt, oregano and sage, rice noodles, cordial, jam, condensed milk, Wheat-bix, tinned peas and corn and tinned peaches and chamomile tea and home-brew ingredients and biscuits and dried coffee and soy sauce. And on and on it goes.

Richard tells me that it is difficult to get the food order just right because they don't really know if the winterers are going to be huge Vegemite eaters and they will run out, or if they are going to love taco shells instead. The food order was prepared at the Antarctic Division headquarters in Tasmania, he said, not by him, and when it all arrived they just looked at some of the things and shook their heads, wondering who thought it would be needed. I ask who supposed they needed as many artichoke hearts as they have packed here. He shakes his head and says the most valued things are fresh fruit and vegetables and that the many boxes of potatoes and onions will keep fairly well until after the winter, but apples and oranges don't last as long.

'Is there anything that expeditioners really miss?' I ask.

'Sex,' he says without missing a beat. Then the unpacking deteriorates into a bad punning competition.

'Here's beetroot,' I say. 'And you can't beat a root.'

'Let's spice up your life,' he says holding up some spices.

'We need a cordial place for the cordial,' I say.

'Who wants crushed nuts?' he asks, holding up a bag of same.

'I hear you can make a lot of dough as a cook down here,' I say pointing to the flour.

Richard holds up a packet of German red cabbage. The label says '*rotkohl*'. 'Do you know what this means?' he asks.

'It's German for "road kill",' I tell him.

I stop to write down some of the foods around me.

'Are you writing all this down?' he asks.

'I'm going to do a chapter on the most lame-arsed puns in Antarctica,' I tell him.

'You should write about the history of food in Antarctica,' he says. 'That'd be more interesting than the official histories.'

It's not a bad idea, I think. From Pemmican to Parisian Essence.

I ask Leighton, the Welsh store-manager who has worked with the Antarctic Division for well over 20 years, if he can tell me any of the stories he has accumulated over the time. But he politely declines. You've always got to respect that. So I ask Richard if he has an Antarctic moment that he'd rather didn't follow him back to Australia. He says that there was one instant that involved him losing a bet and having to substitute a piece of vital clothing with a strategically placed piece of uncooked chicken and run through the common area—and as a result nobody wanted to eat chicken for a few days.

I tell him that's obviously why there are such restrictions on bringing poultry into Antarctica—it's not to do with preventing bird diseases from being passed on, it's to do with preventing him from performing unnatural acts with them.

He says, 'You're not going to put this in your book are you?'

I say, 'If I do, I'll leave out the sordid details.'

❄ ❄ ❄

'I've got this great idea,' I tell Mawson. I've been wondering when he's going to show up. I'm in the converted shipping container that is the sleeping quarters for four of us.

'Oh?' he asks, as if he doubts that I do.

'Yes,' I say. 'Aliens!'

'Aliens?' he asks.

'Yes, aliens!'

He gives me a look of pain. Like somebody has shot him. With an ice bullet.

'Let me guess,' he says. 'There are aliens in Antarctica. And you discover them where nobody else has ever seen them?'

'Don't be like that,' I say. 'Aliens have been a part of Antarctic stories for a long time. Spaceships crashed into the ice and were accidentally thawed out by scientists, you know, and the alien goes rampaging around trying to kill the scientists—it becomes this battle in the polar darkness. Who is going to get the other first? Will the alien destroy everyone or will the humans find a way to destroy the alien? It's great. It's got tension and drama and everything.'

'So you're going to write a book about my expedition that includes aliens in it.'

'Well, it won't be your expedition as such, it will be a re-creation of it. But we need to find something to account for the deaths.'

'Just falling into a crevasse isn't good enough any more?'

'Well, sure, but finding some alien species would make it much more exciting. I mean, maybe it's a life form that only lives in the super cold and finds that humans are destroying the cold through global warming and so decides it needs to kill the humans to protect itself.'

'By digging a crevasse and letting them fall into it.'

'Well, no, obviously it would have to be a bit more thrilling than that. We'd have to start out with something more mysterious. Something unexplained. And then we could build this tension that something was out there tracking them, hunting them, and they had to escape it to survive.'

'We could make it one of those body-snatching aliens that has taken over Ninnis's body and he emerges from that terrible crevasse and starts attacking people.'

'Yes,' I say. 'That's not bad.' Then I figure it out. 'You don't like the idea, do you?'

'Whatever makes you say that?'

'I can tell by your tone. You're going to denigrate it before I can even work it up into the story, aren't you?'

'Am I?'

'Of course you are! Any idea I come up with that is any deviation from the facts of your precious expedition you consider trivial or unworthy. It's like the only way to tell the story is to glorify it and make it this wonderful heroic journey that is too sacred to be considered in any other way. But what if the whole idea I'm developing is to ask a reader to think about all the other possibilities—not to detract from what you did, but to imagine what types of things, in a modern context, would be just as great?'

'Like defeating aliens?'

'Yes. Like defeating aliens. What if the reader gets to the end of the story, to the point where the lone survivor finally defeats this alien that has been trying to kill her as they trek across the snow, and says to herself, wow, now I really understand what Mawson went through.'

'You really think anyone would think that?'

'Maybe.'

'And when you came up with the idea of putting aliens into the story, that's what was driving your thinking?'

'Maybe.'

'Maybe?'

'All right, I just thought of that now. But that doesn't alter the fact that it could put a whole new perspective on how people relate to your trek across George V Land. I mean, aliens are something that more people will understand than just trekking over the ice. We've all seen

alien movies and have wondered how we might act in the same circumstances. So, if you think of it like that, then, yes, aliens are real because
we've all seen them in movies and have thought about how things
might have been if we were the ones the aliens were hunting down.'

'You use the words "we" and "us" very liberally,' he says.

'I mean "us" in the broader sense, not just you and me. Obviously.'

'And what about communists?'

'What have communists got to do with it?'

'Well, the boom in alien films was a direct parallel to the cold war
anti-communist hysteria. These aliens that stole people's minds. Aliens
that tried to take over communities. They were thin metaphors for the
danger of communism. Most of the films were made in the 1950s and
if you replace alien for communist you have a propaganda medium
that aligns with the official paranoia of the day.'

I stare at him for some time.

I want to say, 'That doesn't hold up. That doesn't apply to the
modern films on aliens. That doesn't take into account the way we
view aliens in movies these days.' But I suspect he's just going to tell
me that in modern films the notion of an alien can be replaced with
an Islamic extremist. That it's all political propaganda. And I have a
terrible inkling that he's right and I'm not going to win this argument.

So all I can say, quite feebly really, is, 'If you'd seen *Alien Versus
Predator*, in which two aliens battle it out in the Antarctic, you'd think
differently about it.'

'I'm sure,' he says dryly.

'And there's nothing 1950s about these aliens,' I tell him. 'The
predator is an alien being from some race that exist as hunters, see, and

they have all these high-tech killing weapons and body armour that can make them near-invisible and they travel the universe looking for planets to land on and hunt things. But their one drawback is that they don't see things on the same wavelength that we do, they see things like in infrared or something, and it is possible to mask yourself by hiding your body heat.'

'I'm all ears,' he says, even more dry than dryly.

'And the alien, who is just called the alien, although the predator is an alien as well, is much more primitive, and sort of exists as a wild killing beast, and is really cunning and strong. But the thing about this alien which is its trademark is that it lays its eggs inside people and an alien pops out of them, ripping out of their chests.'

'Hmmm,' he says, so dry that he can't even mutter a single word. Just a short sound.

'So it's been conjectured for a long time, see, if the predator and the alien met up to fight it out, not just aliens versus humans, but alien versus alien, then which would win? That throws a spanner into the works of your theory, doesn't it, because it's like saying, what if the communists fought the Islamic extremists and how is that political propaganda in any way?'

'Hmm,' he says again. Even shorter.

I can see he's not buying it.

'Maybe I won't do the alien thing,' I say. 'It was just an idea.'

'Hm.'

'But I've been doing some interesting research to get the feeling of what it must have been like in your hut and camping out on the snow,' I tell him.

'In what way?'

'Well, I spent a night at the Wilkes Hilton and slept outside, you know, to really get the feel for it. How it must have been.'

He stares at me for a long, long time and then says, softly, 'You spent a day hanging out in a warm hut with a gas cooker. You had electricity. You had calm weather. You had fresh food. How could you know what it was like for us cooped up in our hut through the months of darkness, unable to go outside for days because of the winds?'

'Well, I mean, I got some feel for what it was like to sleep in the Antarctic wilderness.'

'Within 10 metres of a warm hut and warm food? You were inside two sleeping bags inside your jacket. And you had a full belly with warm food.'

'I was pretending it was dog food.'

And Mawson says, 'Dog food. Luxury.' Sounding like a poor imitation of that Monty Python sketch.

'I was pretending it was dog,' I lie.

'Luxury,' says Mawson again.

'I was thinking of tipping Vonna down a crevasse or feeding on her.'

That tips him over. 'There will be no talk of cannibalism!' he says sternly.

'And I was pecked by a vicious penguin,' I say.

❄ ❄ ❄

So I'm sitting in the library, upstairs in the Red Shed at Casey, surrounded by books, the Antarctic continent just outside the window, working on my own book and thinking, this is it. This is really, *really* it. This is something I've dreamed of for years and now here I am. Creating a book among books in the Antarctic. It's almost a surreal feeling. And I can recall the feeling I've had from being tucked up in libraries working on some project in different cities all around the world—in Helsinki, in Adelaide, in Penang, in Brisbane—walking among the stacks of books and feeling hugely content with the world. They're my special library moments. It's the same feeling here but it's exacerbated by being one of the most remote libraries in the world. The room is roughly the size of a small classroom, with three walls lined with bookshelves, and down the centre of the room is a double-sided shelf. One wall has largely Antarctic books only. One has old journals and logs and an encyclopaedia, and the other has fiction and non-fiction. The largest number of shelves are devoted to fiction, followed by science fiction, followed by history, religion, sea and sailing, mountains and exploration, sport, photography and cinema, then things like poetry, plays, economics and health. There are even language books if you wanted to learn Latin, Japanese, Russian, the Hawaiian language or Esperanto.

I look through the station log books to see what happened the day I was born. The entry is from Wilkes Station and only the carbon copy pages remain in the book. They are as faded as the past itself. The entry begins with the date 29 February, which is then crossed out and replaced with 1 March. A lot of it is very hard to make out, but I can see the entry starts off that it is a calm day and that the wind is starting to blow gently from the west with the prospect of choking up the bay with ice again. There is a page and a half that details maintenance and weather conditions, and so on.

It also mentions that Bill *by way of initiation into the 'snocats' had been debagged and anointed suitably with a jar of home brew. Taken in good spirits apparently and no share of hard feelings.* It then goes into more maintenance and repair details and ends with: ... *end to a day which almost threatened to become perfect.*

I'll have to ask Bill about the initiation from his point of view later.

I snoop in the library returns basket and see the books there: Lonely Planet's guide to Antarctica, Tim Bowden's Antarctic book *The Silence Calling*, Harlan Coben's *One False Move*, Arthur C Clarke's *Space Trilogy*, Alice Sebold's *The Lovely Bones* and Charles Darwin's *The Origin of the Species*. Hmmmm. So these are the books being read. I browse around the shelves and find a very eclectic collection, particularly when there are multiple titles from one author. There is a whole pile of old Alistair Macleans from the 1960s, another pile of Hammond Innes from the 1970s, some Len Deightons from the 1980s, Tom Clancys from the 1990s and Matthew Reillys from the 2000s. It's like a history of popular reading. Scattered on the shelves I also find some Peter Carey and Tim Winton. They also have *The Da Vinci Code*, of course, but I can't find anything by Mawson's favourite author Robert Service. He'd be disappointed. Maybe at the Mawson Station library though? Service was a Scotsman who moved to America and became a bank clerk. He made his name with poems about tough men toughing it out in tough places, like the Yukon, and refusing to lie down and die when things got really difficult and slogging on through any adversity. You can see why Mawson loved him, it was almost as if the poems were about him.

I'm told that most of the books are left behind by expeditioners so the library is also a catalogue of their readings tastes. It looks to my mind a lot like the type of collection you might find in suburban secondhand bookshops, with the recent and popular mixed in with the old and hard-to-move-off-the-shelf reads. But it's a collection that I wouldn't be unhappy to spend a long winter working through.

Tom Griffiths, who wrote the wonderful Antarctic history, *Slicing the Silence*, said in a speech at the NSW Premier's Literary Awards in 2007: *The history of Antarctica testifies to the potency of written words and the seductiveness of books. On the ice, books got blubbery with beloved use. Imagine what book you would choose to take on a sledging journey … you had to make a judgment about its weight, both physical and spiritual. Is it light enough to carry but heavy enough to sustain you? Will it offer you 'compressed nourishment' like pemmican? Polar expeditions took vast libraries, not only as a source of vital information, but also as a kind of insulation against the elements. On Ernest Shackleton's expedition of 1908–09, Professor Edgeworth David would read aloud for hours after supper in the winter hut. Sometimes these midnight readings were only stopped by a firm reminder from Shackleton, called out from his cabin in the corner, 'that it was after one o'clock and time all "good" explorers were in bed'.*

Now here's a great Mawson story I heard from Robyn, who is Gary's partner and who has done tours into Mawson's Hut. She told me about a man they took down with them a few years back who had been obsessed with visiting the hut since he was a small child. He had opened a bank account and started putting a little bit of money into it whenever he could. And even when he got married and his wife asked him what that account was, he told her it was his Mawson's Hut account and could not be touched. Throughout his life he kept adding to it, umpiring cricket on weekends and adding the small amounts of money he got from doing that to the account too. And then, at 55, when he retired, he cashed it in and sailed south. Robyn said that the days they visited Commonwealth Bay the weather was perfect and they got onto the shore and also got to go inside the hut and she said that this man just cried to have his childhood dream realised like that.

❄ ❄ ❄

I tell Bill at dinner about the journal entry that I found about him and he's able to give me more information about it. The 'snocats', he tells me, was the name of their band, Tar Brush Hickey and the Snow Cats. He said that most of the instruments were homemade, but he had one of the few real ones, which was a kettledrum that he had brought down with him. The other instruments included a type of tea-chest string bass and a lagerphone.

He also tells me that the anointing with homebrew wasn't quite what an historian analysing the text might think it to be. They did brew their own liquor, but it wasn't like the homebrew that they so proudly produce on Casey Station today. It was a very strong spirit that was over-proof alcohol and they all pretended that they were knocking them back happily and then gave Bill a whole glass to drink. He said that he was so sick the next day that he couldn't take his geomagnetic readings and the station boss wasn't too happy about it.

And Lynette tells me that she was going through the station logs and found a bit more about the expeditioner who went mad with the fire axe. She said that the Russians didn't airlift him out, they only came to provide some expert medical advice (what does that say about the Russians?) and he was largely rehabilitated. He was taken out by ship at the end of the season—though his superiors were given instructions to make sure he was fastened into a straightjacket (what does that say about his superiors?).

It's interesting how oral and written histories differ and each are subject to errors of interpretation.

I go for a wander around the station with a group of other camera-totting expeditioners in the afternoon (what is the collective noun—a clique of photographers, a paparazzi of photographers?) and we are cutting through this rock field where much of the moss around the station grows. Now we've been told that Casey Station is the Daintree of Antarctica as the mosses here represent a veritable rainforest of growth compared with those on the rest of the continent and, as they grow infinitesimally slow, to be very careful walking near them. Well, we're walking right through them, stepping carefully from rock to rock, and as I step on one large rock and ask if anyone knows if it is really granite or perhaps something else, as rocks hate to be taken for granite, it slips and I watch it slide slowly down the larger rock it is lying on and go boof into this big bed of moss. I look around and see everybody is staring at me in horror like I've just chopped down a dozen hectares of rainforest.

'Oops,' I say. Nobody says anything. 'They'll deport me for sure for that,' I say. 'They'll stick me on the first ship home and send me out of here.'

Everybody turns around and keeps walking down towards the harbour where we are hoping to get some spectacular shots of the ice out on the horizon as the sun sets. I photograph the crushed moss bed. Notwithstanding the fact that it has been repeatedly stated that we should be careful not to harm the moss, it's all I can think of to do.

❄ ❄ ❄

On our last full day at Casey Station we are going to put a proposition to the test: is it possible to take too many pictures of penguins? I think not. Vonna tells us that she has about ten thousand already and is going to shoot some more today because we're being taken over to Shirley Island, the closest accessible penguin colony to Casey Station. As with everything in Antarctica, the preparation sometimes takes longer than the actual event and we have to check that we all have the right clothes—Gore-Tex or our bright orange freezer suits—so that we look like an Antarctic Hare Krishna gathering. Then we need food and hot drinks and survival packs with a change of clothes and tent and bivy bag. When we are all loaded up we go down to the equipment store and get survival suits. Strangely, there is no acronym for these. They are also orange, but a reddish-orange, and can float, and they fit over our freezer suits so that we are all walking like the Michelin man and have to waddle down to the boat ramp. It's good practice for seeing the penguins, as we are all now walking like them.

Two zodiacs are launched into the dark chill water—everything is done in twos for safety in Antarctica, even helicopters have to fly in twos. We climb in and are off, zooming across the chill, calm water, occasionally feeling the taste of salt on the spray. The harbour has some more floating ice in it today and we weave and dodge about it, getting up close to the strange formations and feeling the exhilaration as we accelerate away.

Then we are at the island and clamber awkwardly ashore. First prize is given to the first of our party of seven to fall over on the slippery rocks and ice, which is not me today, and then we strip off our awkward survival suits and head off to get UCP (Up Close and Personal) with the penguins.

The colony is spread out all over the island and the first thing we notice is the pink penguin shit everywhere on the snow and the smell of pink penguin shit. Vonna says it's not too bad today, and is worse when the weather is warm, but even that is nothing like elephant seal shit. That's something to look forward to at Davis Station in a few days.

Now here's an interesting statistic. It has been estimated that the amount of Adélie penguin poo, deposited by the approximately ten million of them in Antarctica, is 3750 tonnes a day, or over 1.3 million tonnes a year. You'd be well advised to store those numbers in your memory for when they are asked at a quiz night some time.

Up close and personal, the penguins don't look like they look in photos. They are scruffy and pink-stained and very, very noisy. Vonna tells us this is because the young penguins are molting, losing their soft chick feathers and growing out their adult feathers in preparation for heading out to sea in a few weeks. We're told it's the penguin equivalent of adolescence—awkward growth and grumpiness. Most of the young penguins stand around flapping, trying to get the feathers off, and others cry noisily for food. The adult penguins are still feeding the chicks with regurgitated food from their stomachs, even though the chicks are nearly as tall as they are. (Is it a fluff of chicks? A molt of chicks? Or is it a squawk of chicks?)

Over and over throughout the day we see a pair of twin chicks chasing a mother penguin for food, running around the rocks, like one of those Benny Hill chase scenes. It makes us laugh every time. But all the while large predatory skuas, like gangster seagulls on steroids, glide stealthily in circles over the colony, looking for lone chicks to grab. There is ample evidence on the ground where they have been successful. Small piles of bones and flippers where they have ripped out a penguin's inside and left only the indigestible remains. The sad mummified remnants of the dead and weatherworn penguins are trodden into the ground. We watch one skua descend slowly into the midst of the penguins, like a Harrier jet landing, to feed on something we can't see. Those penguins nearest turn their backs as if not seeing will make them safe.

The noise is a mix of so many cries, something like the baaing of sheep, or the braying of donkeys, or the cry of parrots, or that laugh of dolphins, but not quite any of those.

Many writers before me have attempted to capture that special joy of watching penguins, some succeeding better than others to my mind, but several are worth quoting. Apsley Cherry-Garrard, who travelled with Scott, wrote: *They are extraordinarily like children, these little people of the Antarctic world, either like children, or like old men, full of their own importance and late for dinner, in their black tail-coats and white shirt-fronts—and rather portly withal.*

Helen Garner described them as ridiculous and helpless-looking creatures that were always in a flap. They looked like a person trying to walk in an inverted sack, she wrote. And Tim Bowden thought them: *Liquored-up freemasons in their dinner jackets, stumbling home in the early hours of the morning after a late night session at their lodge.* My favourite penguin quote, though, is from Joe Moore, although I've no idea who he is. He said that it's practically impossible to look at a penguin and feel angry. Joe, I can only agree with that.

It's got very cold now, at least minus six degrees, but of course colder in the wind, and our camera batteries are dying, one by one, as we take happy snap after happy snap. We cross the island and then come back very slowly through the centre of the colony. We have to keep at least 5 metres from the penguins and watch for any signs that we are distressing them. It is a far cry from the early days of expeditions and explorations like Mawson's, when penguins were a staple food, or even of the early days at Australian stations when films show penguins that have been dressed up in top hats and carry bags waddling undignifiedly around, or being picked up by men and flung into the water as a jest for the camera.

We find a spot out of the wind and settle down just to watch these crazy birds for some time. It's like watching a huge family gathering in a park. We see one penguin stealthily stealing stones from the nest of another penguin, to impress the lady birds with the size of his rock pile, while some other penguin is stealing stones from his. A chick is chasing its parent for some tasty regurgitated pink slime. To our left two penguins are squawking at each other, heads back in the air, as if involved in a heated argument. One fluffy chick is huddled down, shoulders up about its head, looking depressed. One penguin, higher up on the rocks, is standing alone, head thrown back, flapping its wings as if saying, 'Look at me—aren't I a damn good-looking bird!' One young chick is standing on its toes, flapping crazily, squawking a long 'not-happy-Jan' cry in penguin-speak. Two fluffy chicks are lying down on their stomachs beside each other, looking for all the world like a pair of fluffy slippers, just waiting for somebody to stick their cold feet into. Some birds are walking in that funny way that Adélies do, head forward and flappers back, peering down in front of them as if they've just dropped their car keys. Another bird, with a beautifully sparkling clean white stomach, fresh from a swim, is turning its head back and forward so that everybody can see just how clean it looks. It's another busy day at the penguin colony.

While we're sitting there and I'm taking notes, Vonna asks me if I'm going to put her in my book and, if so, how will I describe her.

'How would you like to be described?' I ask her.

'Nice. Beautiful. And …'

I wait for her defining adjective.

'Six feet tall.'

So I tell her that's just what I'll say.

It is soon getting late and the cold is biting at us, despite our heavy clothing. And here's another discovery about penguins—when the Adélies no longer look so funny and you can't feel if your face is smiling or not, then it's time to go back to civilisation and leave the birds contentedly alone, standing there in what to them is pleasant balmy weather, where penguins can just be penguins, with no one to anthropomorphise them into little comic people.

❄ ❄ ❄

The night we're due to leave Casey Station I sit up in the library taking advantage of the hotmail access to send Sharon some penguin pictures and write up some notes. Downstairs they are cranking up the music for the changeover party. I'll go down and join them soon. It's great talking to the locals, finding out where they have come from, what they do and what they came down to the ice for. Everyone has an interesting story about something to tell, and I listen to them all, and many of them I write down and take away. I think that I've become an Adélie penguin in this, getting stories from other people and putting them into my pile. But perhaps I'm too easily reverse-anthropomorphising, and that's not the best analogy. Perhaps I'm one of the heritage heretics picking up the stories that are scattered across the Antarctic continent, determined to save them from fading away.

The music goes up a few decibels, calling me downstairs, but for now I just sit looking out the window at the snow and rocks that stretch up to the horizon where the ice takes over and heads towards the Pole for hundreds and hundreds of miles. I look out onto this scene, which I've come to regard as familiar but know that I will probably never see again. I stare at it as the setting sun sets the snow alight and I stare so hard I hope to burn the image onto my optical nerves so that I can conjure it up easily at any time in the future. I'm trying to think of a way to describe how it feels, but can't quite get the words, and as I sit there a single tiny snow flake drifts down across the dark sky and disappears into the snow.

Yeah, it feels a bit like that, I think.

Downstairs it's like any workplace happy hour with people standing around the darts board and pool table and the bar, talking and drinking. After an hour we assemble around the central lounge area, the wallow, and witness the official handing-over ceremony, as Jeremy hands over the ceremonial station key to Bob. He also gives him the official ceremonial stamp for central office correspondence, which is a rubber stamp that says, 'I don't have time to read all this crap.'

There are about 60 at the farewell party and half of us will go back to the ship tonight. The departing summerers and winterers will come out to the ship tomorrow. That will leave 19 people for the winter. They will be glad to have the station to themselves, I'm sure, but it's going to feel very empty here tomorrow night, I suspect.

On the Sea Again

*The ice closed in, and shock after shock made the ship vibrate as she struck
the smaller pieces full and fair, followed by a crunching and grinding as
they scraped past the sides.*

—Douglas Mawson, *The Home of the Blizzard*

Just after noon we up anchor and are away. The 20 extra Casey
people stand on the helideck and look wistfully back to the land.
In ten minutes the station is just a tiny speck among the vastness of
ice and snow. I ask a few of them what they will miss the most. Jeremy,
the former station leader, says the people. Michelle, one of the BOM
squad, says the continent. I suppose different people will have different

answers, which is why so many of them choose to stand on their own and feel the loss of leaving individually.

It is Saint Valentine's Day today. The Antarctic Division has been pretty good about this, offering to organise flower orders for people on the ship to send home and even has a flower catalogue in the cupboard near the phone for selecting flowers. I ring Sharon as soon as I drag my puffy-eyed body out of bed in the morning and wish her a happy Valentine's Day. I've already organised a huge bouquet of flowers to be delivered to her, but she hasn't got them yet. She tells me some news and then gets quite teary, saying she's missing me so much. I tell her I miss her too and we exchange our special lovers' words. We talk for about ten minutes and then I go and look over the railing at the ice. Being in contact is so good, but it also accentuates the loneliness of being away from her for so long.

I go down to my cabin and, by the magnified light of the ice coming in through the porthole, I read over Mawson and Paquita's letters. She wrote him several letters from the European trip her family had taken her on while Douglas was on the ice, and she tells him how much she misses him and how often she thinks of him, interlaced with updates of her travels. Some passages in particular I circle because I feel the meaning in them more deeply today.

From the ship she wrote: … *one man I have particularly chummed up with. He is married but rather young & we get on very well. He misses his wife & I my Dougelly, so we get consolation! But whenever we are talking I have always the feeling I could easily help him overboard if it would bring me you just for a few minutes.*

That makes me smile. I wonder who on board I might consider

pushing overboard to conjure up Sharon in their place. A few tetchy candidates do spring to mind. I also smile at this: *I am sitting comfortably in bed. East west, home is best! I shall like to go away later on to come back to you again & be home. Will you also tuck me up warmly like my mammy does & kiss me goodnight? Then you can get into your nest and I'll get out to tuck you up and so on until we both fall asleep on the floor!*

But the following section makes me sad again: *I'm thinking of you hard every night & wondering whether you are hungry or cold or lonely. If you were only here now. How your Paquita would warm you. I don't feel cold here at all. Must be my warm heart … My love, my love, how I miss you. I close my eyes and lift up my lips but feel nothing. How very far you are …*

And from a later letter: *First of all I love you even more than when you left & there has not been a day—an hour almost—that you have not been in my thoughts. You will have a warm welcome on your return—my arms are open for you already as I think of it … But I had no idea I should miss you like this. Dearie, don't go away again. I'm longing to hear you say you've wanted me often.*

And this, in closing that letter, such a similar sentiment to that expressed between Sharon and me, even if a little less amorous: *Seventeen months without one caress! One embrace. We shall have something to make up for …*

Few people on the ship talk openly about how much they miss their loved ones, but it is pretty apparent on the looks of the faces of anyone coming out of the closet—the telephone closet that is.

In addition to our extra passengers we have loaded aboard an impressive array of rubbish, and it is heartening to know that it is no longer dragged out onto the ice to wait for the summer thaw to sink into the ocean. Almost all stations around Antarctica are engaged in some level of cleaning up the junk of the past, and recognition has to go to Greenpeace for its role in changing attitudes to pollution and dumping. From 1986 onwards Greenpeace regularly travelled down to Antarctica, visiting 40 stations and documenting environmental abuses which it publicised widely. This led nations to change their policies towards environmental impacts. But problems still occur. A recent Swedish study surveyed 71 stations and found that half of them lack any kind of sewage treatment. And a dive team who visited Antarctica in 2006 listed an enormous array of junk they found at several locations, including batteries, pipes, metal sheets, cutlery, lamps and old boots. Cleaning up junk in the Antarctic waters is not going to be easy, but clearly being out of sight is not going to make it out of mind.

As we head out to sea we encounter thick sea ice. It is magnificent. The bridge and the upper decks are filled with the paparazzi brigade, digging out their zoom lenses. The ship bumps and crashes its way through the ice, steering a path between the larger bergs. There is a very special feeling that has to be felt to understand, of lying in your bunk and looking out the porthole window and suddenly seeing a large iceberg passing by.

There's a game that Nick and I play in our bunks in the evening, trying to estimate how much of a carbon footprint our voyage is leaving. We think it an odd thing to have scientists studying climate change while contributing to it. Nick has all the figures. He says that the ship carries one and half million litres of fuel, which is well over a million dollars' worth, just to take us on this journey. He's convinced there should be a more internationally cooperative way to do the science without so many nations sending so many people down to the Antarctic. But he also admits he's very happy and privileged to be on the ship. Lots of the scientists are very passionate about using alternative energy sources, but they are onboard the ship as well. There's never an easy answer.

Andrew, who works for the BOM squad, is going to Mawson Station to do meteorological work over the winter. He's in his early 50s with a balding head, a beard, and wiry muscles, so he looks a lot like Popeye. 'It'll just be standard observations for climate change,' he says.

He says that people just haven't been paying enough attention to global warming. You don't see much ice loss on the main Antarctic continent, he says, but you see it a lot on the Antarctic Peninsula. Retreating glaciers in the Andes will probably give us our first climate change refugees, from not enough water, long before the Pacific Islanders have to up and move in large numbers because of rising sea-water levels, he says. He's been climbing in Peru and mixes mountaineering anecdotes with opinions on the science of climate change.

One consequence of global warming is going to be more snow falling on Antarctica, but the build-up of snow into ice will be offset by the movement of ice off the continent. And if the breaking of ice shelves continues to increase we're all going to be up shit creek, he says (or is that up shit glacier?). The two largest ice sheets, the Ronnie and the Ross, contain so much ice that if they both broke off they would raise sea levels by about 7 metres world wide, he reckons.

An even bigger immediate problem, to his mind, is the methane in the permafrost in the northern hemisphere. As the permafrost thaws, the methane is released into the air and it is about 25 times more effective than carbon dioxide as a greenhouse gas. But, he says, it's all firmly in the too-hard basket.

'In fact, it's beyond the too-hard basket. People just don't want to know about it.'

He's also convinced that biofuels and electric cars are just dicking around with technologies that pass the problem from one source to another, and that we really need to take renewable energies, such as solar, wind and tide-power, seriously.

The government, corporate and public commitment he'd like to see is a little hard to imagine. I saw some statistics relating to the 2008 flight to Antarctica by Environment Minister Peter Garrett:

- *112 billion tonnes was the net loss of Antarctic ice in 1996*
- *196 billion tonnes is the net loss of Antarctic ice in 2006*
- *6 tonnes is the amount of carbon offset needed to compensate for the flight that took Peter Garrett to Antarctica.*

However, I am told that Peter Garrett does partake very seriously in carbon offsetting. It is a similar issue for people like Al Gore, Bono and other climate crusaders. Flying around the world to spread their message is important, but in doing so are they contributing to the problem and setting poor examples, even with carbon offsetting?

It's an old adage of science journalists that we don't have all the answers—we just have the best questions.

Our new shipmates take a while to mix in with the rest of us, but we have anticipated this and all make an effort to sit with new faces when eating. At the latest meeting of the Subversive Antarctic Historical Society, at one of these mealtimes, the attendees are talking about booze in Antarctica. Almost everybody has a story of how dangerous it can be, or of piss-pots who didn't have the common sense about when not to get too drunk.

In the early days of the good ship *Aurora Australis*, I'm told, beer and wine were allowed, but not spirits. Predictably, people would regularly smuggle spirits aboard and have cabin parties, or just take it down to the bar after hours. Because the bins in the corridor outside the cabins often contained empty whiskey bottles, contrary to regulations, one of the voyage leaders had to go so far as to formally request that those drinking spirits should not be so dumb as to leave empty bottles lying around. All it led to was an increase in empty bottles being thrown out of portholes. I suppose none of them had messages rolled up in them. Anyway, a complaint was made about it to senior management and so the *Aurora Australis*, which we might better call the AA now, is a dry ship except for four special events—parties on reaching the ice and leaving each of the three stations, at which we are allowed three cans of beer or three glasses of wine each.

There is another story of a Frenchwoman who got very drunk and went down to one of the ship's doors, swung it open and then climbed up on the open door, hanging out over the ice and ocean for others to photograph her. Management were apoplectic when they found out. There is also a story that a few years back, while people were down in the bar getting drunk, an announcement came over the intercom that they had come upon a Japanese whaling fleet. Lots of the expeditioners ran up the bridge and went out onto the decks and dropped their pants, showing the whalers what a pod of white whales might look like. The Japanese responded as the Japanese do at any unusual sight, and photographed it, which ended up causing a bit of an incident. Again, management was not very happy (but neither were they invited to any of these parties).

There was also a legendary story about two heavy-drinking plumbers at Mawson Station, who took down enough booze to keep a small country town supplied for a few years, and they set to drinking it through the winter. One of the men, the story goes, took 40 bottles of whiskey alone, and had so much beer that it had to be carried in by helicopter and at the end of the winter he still had 24 slabs undrunk. When they were leaving the station, by helicopter, the pilot noticed that the two plumbers and their mate were cradling a bottle of whiskey between them and told them that they would not be allowed to take it onto the ship. So during the five- or six-minute flight the three men drank the bottle empty.

There was even a story of two scientists who almost missed having their scientific equipment delivered ashore on the last ship for the season, because the delivery of beer took precedence.

According to reports, alcoholism has been a problem on some stations at some times, and there has been difficulty knowing quite how to handle it. On the one hand, having a beer is such an Australian cultural tradition that it is hard to enforce total prohibition but, on the other, if not monitored and policed properly, the drinking can be very dangerous in the extreme conditions.

I spent two years in Scandinavia, where heavy drinking was quite a chronic problem, and it was not uncommon to read reports of a drunk who had fallen over somewhere stumbling home on a winter's night and had frozen to death. The scientists I talked to said that their main fears were not to do with heavy drinkers doing something stupid to themselves, but to them causing a fire or something catastrophic to the station. One, who had been down in the Antarctica at the turn of the millennium, said he went to stay in one of the huts out on the ice one night because he seriously feared the stationers would get so wasted they would burn the place down. His fears were a bit like the Y2K virus though—more concern than was warranted.

Another tale I've heard from the Subversive Antarctic Historical Society, about which I'm trying to track down more details, is of two hippies who stowed away on one of the Antarctic re-supply ships a few years ago. All I know is that he was a flute player who, with his girlfriend, snuck onto one of the ships because he'd decided he wanted to go south. I have so many questions, of course. Where did they hide on the ship? How were they found? Were they put in the brig or confined to quarters? Were they asked to pay their fare?

One of the most famous Antarctic stowaways was Perce Blackborow, a young English lad who snuck aboard Shackleton's *Endurance* in South America. Shackleton was evidently enraged when he discovered him and gave him a very strong public dressing down, but then Perce was appointed assistant cook and accounted very well for himself, becoming something of a ship's favourite. There is a famous picture of Perce Blackborow standing on the deck with his sleeves rolled up and the ship's cat Mrs Chippy on his shoulder. Mrs Chippy, who was actually a him, was also a bit of a favourite on the ship, to the point that he once fell overboard and the ship was turned around to rescue him.

I've been talking to Robyn about my book on Mawson. She is going to overwinter at Mawson Station as a field assistant, studying a poultry virus in emperor penguins. She has also written a book on Mawson. I sigh. Just what every author wants to know. I ask her why Mawson? She tells me that she read his story as a young girl and became enthralled with him, but over the years of her research she discovered he was a flawed man in many ways. I can only agree with her, and hope that I don't end up having a fight with Mawson about having done so.

It leaves me pondering what it is about Antarctic explorers that grabs our imaginations, despite any flaws we may discover in their characters? Why is it important to know about them? I've been pondering that every time I read a book about the heroic era, or a book about polar travel, and I've been asking it of people around the ship and also of myself. Is it the sheer audacity and endurance of the human spirit? Is it a human being pitted against the most inhospitable places imaginable? Is it that it reminds us of the desire to strive for success against all odds? Or is it just the simple drive within us to explore the last unexplored landmass of our planet?

Or perhaps it is something that isn't so easy to put into words. Something we feel but can't as easily articulate. Something that requires the length of a book to state?

Now, if Sharon were here with me she'd slap me at this point and tell me that I was in serious danger of disappearing up my own philosophical butthole and that I should just get on with the story.

Okay, but first a quick digression. Sharon, personally, doesn't think that risking your life to climb the highest mountain, or go to the coldest place, or eat the biggest hotdog, is a clever thing to do. One of her life philosophies is that there's no cure for stupidity, and life has shown her that just about anybody is capable of doing what she thinks are stupid things—like going down to Antarctica. And yet I have heard her on the phone talking to her mother or friends, telling them that, yes, she will miss me terribly while I am away, and would rather that I didn't go, but that since it's such a dream of mine she wouldn't want me to not experience it.

That's why I love her.

Dougelly would know what I mean.

❄ ❄ ❄

I've got more information on the stowaway. He wasn't two hippies, but one. He was a Hobart activist who had his own yacht in town and played the panpipes. He stowed away on board the French vessel *L'Astrolabe* as some protest and presented himself to the crew soon after departure to make his petition or whatever. They decided to make him stay on board for the trip down to Dumont d'Urville Station and back. He entertained them with his panpipes for the voyage, I was told.

The complex evolution of good stories and good history is interesting to untangle.

A few lucky people up on the bridge have seen whales in the ocean, which has brought a host of jokes about expecting to see Japanese whalers soon and that in turn has brought a host of comments on this season's variation of the stowaway story, the two Sea Shepherd activists who boarded the Japanese whale factory ship—sorry, research vessel—the *Nisshin Maru* to deliver a petition to the captain, and were detained on the ship for several days as it sailed away with them. Opinions about Sea Shepherd are divided—depending who I talk to on our ship: they are either a bunch of ratbag troublemakers or are inspired activists.

For those who came in late, as they say in the comics, the Sea Shepherd Conservation Society was founded by Canadian environmental activist Paul Watson, who was one of the three founders of Greenpeace. They made their name by attracting big-name celebrity support, cutting driftnets, ramming whaling vessels and sinking some in port. In 2007, two of the ships operated by Sea Shepherd, *Farley Mowat* and *Robert Hunter*, were struck off the British shipping register for their activities, but were able to register under the flag of the Kahnawake Mohawk nation—not usually thought of as one of the world's major shipping nations.

In January 2008 two activists, the Australian Benjamin Potts and Briton Giles Lane, boarded the Japanese whaler *Nisshin Maru* from their ship, the *Steve Irwin* (the ship formerly known as *the Robert Hunter*, as the pop star Prince would say), to deliver a petition in protest against the Japanese intention to catch 935 minke whales and 50 endangered fin whales, for what the Japanese claim is scientific research. The two men were, according to your point of view, taken hostage or detained on board the vessel.

Some on our ship reckon they should have been arrested as pirates, others think they did the right thing and more should follow their lead. Interestingly, Greenpeace and Sea Shepherd had a falling out some years back and members snipe at each other whenever they can. Sea Shepherd accuses Greenpeace of grandstanding for the cameras rather than really taking action to prevent whaling, calling them the 'Avon ladies of the environment movement'. They have also claimed that Sea Shepherd has a budget of only two million dollars compared with Greenpeace's well over one billion dollars, and thus the older organisation could afford to do a lot more.

Greenpeace, in turn, accuses Sea Shepherd of excessive tactics, such as scuttling nine ships in port. And having your ship sunk in port is a sore point for Greenpeace, after the sinking of the *Rainbow Warrior* by the French security service in Auckland in 1985.

Potts and Lane became the centre of a media and diplomatic storm for several days, with Sea Shepherd trying to lay kidnapping charges against the Japanese, saying that their men were assaulted and tied to the railings of the whaler. The Japanese countered by accusing the men of having thrown acid onto their ship and endangering the lives of crew members. Eventually the Australian Customs Service vessel, the *Oceanic Viking*, took charge of the pair and handed them back to the *Steve Irwin*. When they got back to Hobart, the two men were greeted as heroes, according to press reports.

Within a few weeks they were back at sea and Sea Shepherd and the Japanese whalers were again at war, both in the ocean and in the media. Paul Watson, Sea Shepherd's activist supremo, claimed that the Japanese shot at him, and that the bullet pierced his Kevlar vest and was only stopped from killing him by an anti-poaching campaign badge on his shirt underneath. The Japanese, in reply, accused him of engineering the stunt, but admitting that they had thrown several percussion grenades, known as thunder flashes, after the protesters had thrown bottles of butyric acid at them.

The latest clashes between Sea Shepherd and the Japanese got international coverage in January 2010 when the whaler *Shonan Maru No 2* collided with Sea Shepherd's *Ady Gil*, sinking it. A bit of background: the *Shonan Maru No 2* has been accused of being a spy ship, whose object is to tail the Sea Shepherd ships and report their movements to the whaling fleet. And the *Ady Gil*, formerly known as *Earthrace*, is an advanced trimaran craft that looks more like a space ship. It runs on biodiesel and holds the world's record for the fastest circumnavigation of the earth—just over 60 days. But the owners of the vessel were forced to sell it in 2009, due to mounting debts, and the Californian businessman and animal rights activist, Ady Gil, paid over a million dollars towards its purchase by Sea Shepherd. Amid the accusations and counteraccusations—whether the *Ady Gil* rammed the *Shonan Maru No 2*, or the *Shonan Maru No 2* rammed the *Ady Gil*—Sea Shepherd clearly came out on top in the PR war, despite the loss of their ship.

Kyle, the trendiest and youngest of our cooks, tells me that when he's not working on the good ship *Aurora Australis*, he often works on the *Oceanic Viking*, the Norwegian boat that Australian Customs uses to tail Japanese whaling vessels. I'm also told that it's not unknown for the *Aurora Australis* to be diverted to check up on possible illegal fishing in Antarctic waters. I'm guessing this is for the Patagonian toothfish, which has to be seen to be believed. The fish are about a metre long and are so ugly that their mothers must have a hard time kissing them good night, so I'm very glad the crew didn't manage to dig one up for our crossing-the-line ceremony. Kissing a cod piece, if that's what it was, was traumatic enough.

On the topic of dubious fishing, I walked down the passageway on the ship one evening and did a sudden stop as I glanced into one of the cabins. Leslie, our larrikin barge operator, who had put a sign on his door offering extended tourist trips for a princely sum, had a fishing rod sticking out his porthole window. I wondered whether fishing in these waters was as much a no-no as opening your porthole was. I decided not to worry about it. If he caught anything big enough to get really, *really* excited about, he probably wouldn't be able to fit it in through the porthole.

But he tells me later that he does have a permit and he had caught a fish already. He showed me a picture of it, a rather strange-looking piece of cod that I'm glad we didn't have to kiss at the crossing-the-line ceremony either. He tells me that every time we are stopped for some reason he heads out to the trawl deck at the back of the ship for some CFT (Critical Fishing Time). You can always tell a keen fisherman. But you just can't tell them very much!

❄ ❄ ❄

Avoiding any lame segue about Mawson not being able to do much fishing during his first winter in Antarctica due to the inclement weather, he was plagued by the repeated blizzards that confined them to their hut. They regularly recorded winds of around 145 kilometres per hour, strong enough to bowl a man over if he should try and walk around outside, evidenced in the footage that Frank Hurley shot of men stumbling on the ice and the wind sending them slithering across the ground.

As early as 30 March 1912, the day Scott probably died, Mawson wrote: *Blizzard. Digging out boxes in front of house and taking round to the aeroplane hut. Bage and Hodgeman go with frame. Chimney of stove in small hut is now put through roof. Draws badly. Caruso [sledge dog] shot.*

His diary entries from then on through the winter consist of variations of the same thing:

18 May Saturday. Heavy blizzard continues.

20 May Monday. Blizzarding—terrific puffs hit the Hut at lunch time.

22 May Wednesday. Violent Blizzard.

2 June. Strong blizzard.

3 June. Blizzard.

8 June. Blizzard.

9 June. Blizzard.

10 June. Blizzard.

11 June. Blizzard very hard.

And so on it goes. Trying to capture the feeling of it years later in *The Home of the Blizzard,* he wrote: *We had found an accursed country. On the fringe of an unspanned continent along whose gelid coast our comrades had made their home—we knew not where—we dwelt where the chill breath of a vast, Polar wilderness, quickening to the rushing might of eternal blizzards, surged to the northern seas. Already, and for long months we were beneath 'frost-fettered Winter's frown'.*

It was difficult for the men to achieve much. The winds blew down their wireless masts and blew their small boat out to sea and blew small amounts of snow incessantly into the hut. Outside, the men had to dig tunnels to get around and came to regard the wind as the enemy that had to be avoided, even learning strange ways of walking to prevent being tipped over and going the way of the wireless mast or the boat. Yet Mawson would not tolerate idleness. He kept the men busy preparing their equipment for the expeditions planned for the warmer months, training the dogs and taking scientific readings and even building a snow cave depot, which the men named Aladdin's Cave, at the top of the Antarctic plateau above the hut.

On midwinter's day, 21 June, the men celebrated with a breakfast of bacon and eggs, honey and marmalade on bread, and for lunch they added cherry cake and cheese. Mawson wrote in his journal: *After lunch the howling, only stronger than ever, heard, and waves come from the SW. The ice slopes to S are now absolutely free of snow. Our uniform temperatures indicate an insular climate ... Today the temperature has dropped and we appear to be in for a colder time in the future.*

The Hut has kept at only just above freezing point for some days now despite our efforts to keep it up to 40°F. The wood of the ceiling has shrunk and a fall of snow takes place in several spots in the Hut, partly direct, partly the chill of the Hut moist air. There are now 5 inches of ice on the windows, several inches of ice on the wall below my bunk, on the roof and ceiling, and on the upper wall. My bed is frozen to the wall on that side. The ice itself is no discomfort, but we all look forward to the showerbath we shall have when the temperature rises.

When the first signs of spring appeared he was, naturally, chomping at the bit to get out and about. He had a continent of snow and ice to explore and a reputation to establish.

❄ ❄ ❄

There is quite a variety of opinion among people I talk to as to whether living through a winter in Antarctica causes extreme psychological stress or not. Almost everyone agrees that it certainly adds psychological pressure, but as to whether that is manifest in any way, most say it is not.

There have been several studies done on the effect of greatly reduced daylight and isolation on people, leading to a syndrome known as SADS (Seasonally Affected Disorder Syndrome). I have read reports stating that the period leading up to midwinter is usually fine, but the period afterwards is worse, when people must face the fact that there is still the other half of the winter to get through and the initial excitement of being in Antarctica has worn off. Most of the cases of severe depression or psychological conflict are anecdotal though.

On Australian Antarctic stations, midwinter's day, 21 June, is traditionally a holiday—the only real holiday of the year. A celebration is made of the day and for some there is even a midwinter swim through a hole cut in the ice. It is also a tradition to put on a pantomime, something that dates back to Mawson's days, with a bawdy Cinderella being the most popular. But then it is a long, long wait until the longer days of spring and the return of wildlife.

Psychologists label Antarctic research stations as isolated, confined environments (ICE), and say that psychological stresses are often exacerbated by the condition of being so remote from family and friends, not being able to leave the small environment and having to interact with the same people day after day. US researchers have studied the behaviour and psychology of people living in Antarctica to figure out how astronauts can prepare for the mental and emotional hardships they may endure in space. They have catalogued the effects of midwinter, its darkness and confining weather as leading to increased depression, insomnia, fatigue, irritability, slowed cognitive and physical responses, inability to concentrate, social withdrawal, lack of attention to personal hygiene and hostility. Also, they believe there is an increase in cases of rebellion against authority, assault and sexual harassment during this time.

The study also found that after the last plane or ship left for the season, the typical reaction of the overwinterers is of celebration and rebelliousness, whereby the station staff bond by doing things that were previously prohibited. A major problem may develop, however, for any individuals who feel that they do not fit in, and they may develop some strange coping mechanisms, such as fantasising about murdering a colleague who is bothering them, often going into minute detail as to how it will be done and how the body will be disposed of. There was one story I found of a US researcher who admitted to imagining how he would kill a colleague by spraying him with a supersoaker water-gun filled with an acetate mixture, which would burn right through his clothing and skin; then, after killing the man, he would leave his body under a snowdrift to be eaten away so there was no trace of the victim or the crime.

The only real possible murder that has occurred in Antarctica is that of Rodney Marks. Perhaps. He was an Australian astrophysicist who died at the US Amundsen-Scott South Pole Station in May 2000. The facts are fairly straightforward, but the conspiracy theories are all over the place. But the facts first.

Dr Rodney Marks was spending his second winter at the South Pole Station, where his fiancée, Sonja Wolter, was also staying. One day he went to the base's medical centre because he was vomiting blood and was having difficulty breathing. Dr Robert Thompson, the duty doctor, reported that he was 'nervous, anxious and upset', and noted two needle marks on Marks's arm but did not ask about them. After observation the astrophysicist was sent back to his room, but returned to the doctor twice that day, complaining of hurting all over. Then, later in the day, his heart stopped and he was unable to be resuscitated. His body was kept on ice, literally, for six months, until it could be removed.

The US National Science Foundation issued a statement saying that Rodney Marks had 'apparently died of natural causes, but the specific cause of death has yet to be determined'. The Scott-Amundsen Station is run by the US National Science Foundation, though much of the actual work is subcontracted to Raytheon's Polar Services— and more about Raytheon in a moment. A postmortem was finally carried out on Dr Marks's body in New Zealand and a large amount of methanol was found in his system; the finding was that he died of methanol poisoning.

Now we can start getting into the conspiracy theories. If you trawl the internet you'll find some great components for a whodunnit. Dr Marks is said to have drunk heavily to mask a case of Tourette syndrome. The New Zealand investigators reported that the US agencies involved, particularly Raytheon, were less than cooperative. The likely scenarios are that either he might have drunk the methanol intentionally, he might have drunk it accidentally, or somebody might have given it to him to drink as a prank or indeed to murder him.

Some of the internet comments on the case include:

He was working on the Remote Observatory Project ... Maybe he saw something? Maybe he wanted to talk?

This is total fucking bullshit. The guy was offed, for some reason.

I remember there was a lot about the south pole observatory being discussed here about 3 years ago. Then I tried to google it a year later and found nothing. Why are things melting so fast?

A reconvened coroner's inquest in Christchurch yesterday heard that police had faced a largely fruitless four-year struggle to get information from the NSF and contractor Raytheon Polar Services ... ahem, Raytheon, cough, cough

So who exactly are Raytheon? Well, for all you conspiracy hounds out there, in the company's own words, they are: *A global leader in technology-driven solutions that provide integrated mission systems for the critical defense and non-defense needs of our customers. Raytheon's integrated businesses assure mission success with a broad range of products and services in government electronics, space, information technology, technical services, business, aviation and special mission aircraft.*

In other words, they are one of the major military contractors in the USA specialising in missile systems. Can you see the connection? Missile systems. Astrophysicist. Get it? Don't worry if you don't, because there are lots and lots of people out there who apparently do.

The subsequent death of an American employee of Raytheon Polar Services, Joshua Spillane, in April 2007, triggered its own amount of internet conspiracy traffic. Spillane was determined missing from the US National Science Foundation's research vessel *Laurence M. Gould,* on a routine cruise between the US Palmer Station on the Antarctic Peninsula and Punta Arenas in Chile. He had worked on over 30 such cruises over the past ten years. Comments posted (with typos) included:

Joshua disappeared off of a US research vessel on April 17th 2006, he is still missing. Nobody knows what happened to him. We still have no answers as to whether he is alive or gone. Neither the company he worked for or our government will help. They have lied to us and hidden things from us. Not

*everything written about his disappearance is accurate or honest and we
have spent the last couple of years trying to find out why.*

*… for the most part what Raytheon did say or do was misinformation
or untrue. We would find out later that they had misinformed us on many
things.*

*Why do they have so much power that even the governmental agencies
in the US cover from them?*

Sounds like someone stumbled upon something they shouldn't have.

Posts also state that Rodney Marks's former fiancée, Sonja Wolter,
was also on the ship that Joshua Spillane disappeared from, adding
further to the conspiracy theories.

I asked around to see if anyone on the ship had particularly
imaginative plans to kill people, but only found one that involved
pushing a colleague who was generally disliked through a hole in the
ice. At first I thought the killing fantasy a bit odd, but later on the voyage
I was to find how easy it is to succumb to. I was booked to do a reading
in the conference room at 2 PM and had spent half the day preparing for
it, but when I went to the room to set up there was some dick screening
a documentary on Mount Everest for his mates. (A handful of dicks?
A pocket of dicks?) I asked him how long it would run for, as I had
the room booked, and he said only about half an hour more. So I sat
and patiently waited, watching several people I had invited stick their
heads in and then walk out again. After 40 minutes the documentary
seemed a long way from finishing and I sat behind this dick and found,
quite uncharacteristically, that running through my head were all these
different ways I could kill him. I could stick my pen right up his nostril
or into his ear. I could smack him over the head with my laptop. I could

strangle him with my laptop power cord. Or I could even ask around if there was a supersoaker and any acetate mixture on board, not to mention the possibility of the ice bullet idea.

Murder fantasies aside, those who had spent several winters in Antarctica told me that it was just as important to teach somebody how to learn to overwinter as it was to teach them how to do their job, and people skills were often considered the most important skills a person could have. Jeremy, who was the summer station leader at Casey and had had the role for several winter seasons, said he had never personally experienced any severe psychological problems with station staff that was just caused by the winter or the darkness—any problems were more often caused simply by separation from home and the fact they were all living in a very close environment.

'It's important to plan something for the springtime to look forward to,' he said. 'Such as a trip away from the station. By the end of the winter people have been down there a very long time and may still have to wait some time until the first ship comes.'

I discovered fairly quickly on our voyage that there is a well-established social hierarchy in Antarctica, with the highest on the ice ladder being those who have overwintered multiple times. This is followed by the single overwinterers. After them come the multiple summerers and then the single summerers. The lowest of the low are the round-trippers! And of course, being Antarctica, there is an acronym for everything; we round-trippers were mostly JAFAs and JAFOs (Just Another Fucking Academic or Just Another Fucking Observer). The Division is working hard, however, to get rid of these no-longer politically correct terms but I decided to defend their heritage by instigating another: JAFAF (Just Another Fucking Arts Fellow).

I think it is fair to say that those who have overwintered aren't just at the top of the Antarctic social hierarchy, but develop a different outlook on life. When asked what they would miss most, many of those I talked to had a lot of trouble articulating it easily but summed it up generally as 'the place', meaning the people and the environment and the experience and everything. Those who had overwintered several times seemed to have a slightly different concept of what constituted strange behaviour during the winter period, probably as a result of those behaviours becoming norms to them. One station leader who has done several stints in Antarctica is known to put on a wedding dress quite frequently. I had the good fortune to see him dressed in it on a station on our voyage, and was more interested in the reactions of others. Those who had overwintered or spent time with him didn't bat an eyelid, the summerers smiled and laughed, but several of the round-trippers clearly didn't know quite how to react to it.

The blog that comes out of the US station at McMurdo under the colourful title Fucked-Up Winterover, states authoritatively: *For the record, it won't take some guys three months to get weird, because they show up here weird, as do some of the ladies.*

But of course it's not just winter that brings out the weirdness in people, demonstrated by the story of Christmas 2005 in which a fight at the South Pole resulted in an emergency flight to airlift one man to hospital in New Zealand, and another being sacked and sent home to the USA. Unconfirmed reports said the fight was over a woman and both men were put on a US Air Force Hercules for the eight-hour flight to Christchurch. One with a broken jaw and one with a broken employment record.

Both men worked for Raytheon. Press reports stated that polar medivac flights are rare occurrences, one of the most dramatic being a rare midwinter flight in 1999 for a doctor who developed breast cancer and needed urgent treatment. Not only did she make world headlines and write a book about her experience, but a telemovie, *Ice Bound*, was made with Susan Sarandon playing her.

❄ ❄ ❄

'So how's that book coming?' Mawson asks me. I look up and see him there sitting on my bed.

'Well, I'm not sure if I should start it on the ship or at Mawson's Hut, you know.'

'Does it matter?'

'Of course it matters. It's called the point of engagement. Starting your book at just the right point is as important as taking a cake out of the oven at just the right point.'

'The expression half-baked comes to my mind for some reason,' he says.

'It's not just hooking the reader,' I say, ignoring the comment. 'It's about the starting point of the story being in the right place for the structure of the book.'

'Don't you just start at the very beginning?' he asks.

'Yeah, yeah. Let's start at the very beginning, a very good place to start. But it's not as easy as Julie Andrews made it sound. Think about

Moby Dick starting just where it does with Ishmael declaring who he is and what has brought him awhaling. Think of Harry Joy telling you that he's died three times and you're going to witness his first death in Peter Carey's *Bliss*. Think of the mad voice of the Indian Chief introducing us to the asylum in *One Flew Over the Cuckoo's Nest*.'

'I'd always considered a point of engagement the place where you asked your wife to marry you. For Paquita and me it was by the beach at Brighton near Adelaide.'

'You're such a literalist!'

'To my advantage, I've always thought it.'

'Except when you start a book with *Notwithstanding the fact that it has been repeatedly stated in the public press …* '.

'What's wrong with it?'

'Your point of engagement actually doesn't kick in for several pages until you write *An unknown coast-line lay before the door of Australia*. Now that's a good line. A good point of engagement.'

Mawson sulks a bit. Then he asks, 'Well, tell me where you're going with your book after your point of engagement.'

'By and by,' I say.

'Does that mean you don't know.'

'No. It means I don't yet know. It's like science. You need to do the work sometimes to see where it has taken you. You need to experiment and see what you get. You need to discard some things and recognise the unrecognisable in others.'

'So you don't know.'

I ignore him. 'I am wondering in my mind though what the huts might look like in the future. I mean, will they still be there?'

Mawson now leans forward in his chair, looking a little distressed. 'Of course they will still be there. There are teams of hardworking men and women working to preserve them. It was a near thing though, you know, the main hut was severely worn by the force of the blizzards.'

'Well, I'm wondering if I might have the hut relocated to a Gold Coast theme park and a plastic replica put there in its place.'

He's looking even more distressed now.

'Or maybe an ice-sculpture hut.'

He looks at me carefully.

'Or even a hologram of the hut.'

Now he knows I'm taking the piss. He scowls at me a bit and then says, 'You should consider having the people who are doing the re-enactment all reading my book, and they could be duplicating what I said or did on each day of the venture. I mean, particularly the character who plays me. He should have a firm grasp of my point of view and philosophy, don't you think?'

'So you're going to write this book now?' I ask him.

'Just providing constructive ideas,' he says with a slight huff.

I close my eyes and mumble, 'Notwithstanding the fact that Mawson's spirit is starting to piss me off, I'm going to write a good book by and by.'

❄ ❄ ❄

The latest meeting of the Subversive Antarctic Historical Society is dealing more with current events than historical ones—in particular, the level of bureaucracy that governs all activity in Antarctica. I found this a rather interesting topic because there were several people taking part who could loosely be described as bureaucrats, representing the Australian Antarctic Division, and they mostly agreed as well that there was far too much bureaucracy governing things these days.

Many of the activities that were once taken for granted now need reams of paperwork before they can be undertaken, including risk assessments and occupational health and safety assessments, to the point that it was clearly frustrating the work of many. It's not a new phenomenon, of course, and I even heard it said that the reason that the venerable Phil Law resigned as the first director of the Australian Antarctic Division back in 1966 was that he worn down by the bureaucracy of things.

Talking to the expeditioners, it appears that the more rules and restrictions that are brought in, the more it encourages an attitude of subversion, which leads people to either avoid activities that require excessive paperwork or to find ways around them. Not that the Antarctic community is any different in this respect to most other areas of modern life, where the rule of law is the rule of paperwork and regulations. But the concern that many who work on the ships and the stations have is that there is a strong divide between Central Office, in the suburb of Kingston in Hobart, and those in the field. And those in Central Office rarely have any experience in the field (although that isn't true in all cases), yet make decisions that affect those who are.

And it is the small things that most people complain about. The decision to make the *Aurora Australis* a dry ship. The decision to limit fatty foods at smoko on the stations where bacon had been a long-running favourite for the men working in the cold.

Despite the close communications links, there is a strong sense on the stations that they are a long, long way from Australia—more distant than the physical kilometres. Yet despite the ever-present fog of bureaucratic regulations, there seems a commonsense approach to making relevant decisions to suit conditions on the continent. One of the station staff tells me that the reason he really likes coming down to Antarctica is that it is thousands of miles away from Hobart and many hours apart, which means that often on-the-ground decisions are made that might not be in accord with best policy practice, but are very commonsense on location.

'The decision is already made and it's all been taken care of before they're even out of bed in Kingston,' he says.

It amazes me that there is such a large general divide between those who work in Central Office and those who go down to Antarctica. Several of the Antarctic Division employees on the ship have been working at Central Office for seven or eight years and this is their first trip to the ice. They all tell me how much it has changed their perspective of things. If the Division ever asked me what I felt might be changed to improve the effectiveness of the organisation, I would include a few weeks working in the Central Office for all station leaders, both before and after their terms, so they really get involved in things, and I would find a way to ensure that senior management spent some time working on stations. The lack of opportunities for cross-fertilisation and job exchange is to the Division's detriment at the moment. It entrenches the separate cultures and the beliefs that the policy pushers have no idea what goes on in the field nor any real idea about the impact of their policies and that those in the field have no strong understanding of policy contexts and what drives decisions.

It's too much like small colonial nations resenting the interference of the mother- or fatherland. If the stations had their own wealth-generation capacity I can almost imagine them pushing for independence. Almost. The Republic of Casey, the Democratic Nation of Davis and the Mawson Federation.

Sounds crazy? Well, if we're projecting into the future, anything is possible if you can chart a logical course to get there. In this instance, if the stations were generating their own income, through tourism or minerals or leasing scientific access, you can envisage a point where they would grow to become large places like the US McMurdo Station, which houses over a thousand people. Outsourcing would lead to them becoming company settlements like some of the mining towns in remote locations. After that they would be bidding on the open market for staff and supplies and would soon see the benefits of becoming independent because the policymakers would be less and less relevant to the directions the companies and the settlers wanted to go.

Perhaps the airlink will be used to break down this separation though.

I do like the idea of an Antarctic settlement, however. If you browse the internet you might find the story of the Antarctic colony of Nadira. The story goes that in the mid-19th century, a North American utopianist, Samuel Brundt, was inspired by a vision to lead an expedition to Antarctica to establish a utopian colony there. Fortunately, the colony discovered a chemical substance they called

Heaven's Fire, which was a chemical compound that provided both heat and light and could also be used for excavating in the ice.

The records of Nadira show that the colony went through the similar formative years of most utopian societies, struggling with logistics and fundraising, but between the years 1845 and 1850 three survey expeditions spent time in Antarctica scouting possible locations for the colony. They built a staging base in the jungle of Venezuela as a half-way camp between North America and Antarctica in 1852, and by 1855 were far enough advanced to send an expedition of engineers to start building tunnels in the ice for the colony. The history also states that the American Civil War prompted many of the colonists to flee south and by 1866 there were 147 souls living on the continent.

As the colonists dug deeper into the ice, they claimed to have discovered the remains of an ancient civilisation and used many of the markings and icons they found as designs on the money the colony printed—later to be known as dream dollars. The currency had denominations of 1, 4, 7, 13, 28, 52, 91 and 365 dollars, with different designs for spring, winter, autumn and summer. They are intricate pink and red banknotes with strange symbols that make the pyramid and the eye on the US currency look tame, and are supposedly more full of hidden meanings and symbols than a Where's Wally puzzle.

In 1887 major divisions within the colony appeared after the sudden disappearance of Samuel Brundt. The next major crisis was the global recession of the 1890s, which delayed re-supply ships to the colony for several years, and in particular led to a shortage of Heaven's Fire. The last known records of the colony were dated August 1899 and when a rescue mission finally arrived in 1901 they could find no trace of the colonists, not even graves or bodies. Throughout the 20th century the dream dollars became highly prized collectors' items, often being reprinted, and they were particularly popular with the Beat generation of the 1950s in New York—who performed dream readings among poetry and music performances—because the dollars were said to be able to provoke and control dreams.

During the 1960s dream dollars were said to be very prized by hippies, who used them to assist in LSD sessions of altered states of consciousness. In 1999, the hundredth anniversary of the disappearance of the colony, dream dollars made a comeback, as did awareness of the colony.

The truth, however, is slightly less fantastic, but just as dream-filled. Nadira and the dream dollars were dreamed up by the New York artist Stephen Barnwell, who has created currencies for many fictitious countries, such as the State of War. I download a copy of the currency from the internet and show it to several people on the ship. Most are amazed at how gullible people are, though they never admit to me if they'd believed the story or not as I told it to them.

❄ ❄ ❄

We wake up the next day and the sea is covered in ice again. I go up on the bridge and look out over a seascape that resembles a paved garden of ice slabs—but each paving piece is the size of a backyard, joined by thin, dark ice and slush. It is a giant mosaic of ice slabs disappearing into the white fog on the horizon on all sides.

The ship slows down to a crawl, then stops. The ice is too thick to proceed. We back up slowly and move forward again. Eventually the ship finds a break and we are moving forward again. But very slowly. I ask the captain why we have headed into the ice rather than open water. And he confides to me one of the problems of Antarctic navigation, even with satellite images and radar: 'It wasn't meant to be here,' he says grimly.

The ship is turned towards a northerly direction and presses on as the light drops, trying to break clear of the ice. Nicki tells me that the ship has been stuck in the ice on several occasions, with the longest period being five weeks back in the mid-1990s. Brownie, the cook who runs the galley like he's taking part in street theatre and he's the Pirate King, says it was his first voyage and they were all getting a bit stir-crazy before they were freed. He says they always have an extra 30 per cent of food on board for emergencies like this, but as the time dragged by everyone was getting, in his own eloquent words, 'bored shitless'.

At a meeting of the Subversive Antarctic Historical Society the topic for discussion is early voyages of the good ship *Aurora Australis*. I'm told that the first three voyages were all bits of disasters in their own ways. On the first voyage, in 1990, there was a fire onboard. For any sailor, fire on a ship is right up there as a five-star crisis, along with seeing torpedo trails running towards you or discovering Leonardo Di Caprio and Kate Winslet are on board as you're sailing past icebergs.

On the second voyage they had a mechanical problem with the propeller and became stuck in the ice. They were broken out by the Japanese ice-breaker *Shirazi* and the ship managed to limp back to Fremantle for repairs.

On the third voyage, another fire broke out in the engine room.

I can only presume that bad luck comes in threes and the *Aurora Australis* did the very sensible thing in getting all its bad luck out of the way in its first three voyages.

Sitting around the table in the dining room I start a conversation with those at my table about imagining what Antarctica will be like in 20 more years. I suggest that the stations around the continent will be supplementing their income by hosting tourists. I say that the scientists will still be here, but the enormous costs of supporting them will need some type of cross-funding. After all, even Mawson envisaged whaling and mineral exploration as a means of financing the science.

I also suggest that in the future there will be such a stream of VIPs and VIP-wannabes coming in by air and that Casey Station will become a terminal not a station. Maybe the government will out-source it to a contractor to manage and then bit by bit it will all come under private hands.

Some of the others think it more likely that mining and drilling for oil will represent the biggest change to Antarctica, and someone will start it sooner or later, despite current bans. But would it be China or the USA? Or even one of the South American countries? They all have strong interests and a significant presence on the continent.

I ask what might happen if there were another Mount Erebus disaster, or a massive oil-spill from a tourist liner? Maybe that would put a freeze on tourism and scientific development both. Maybe there might be a moratorium on any new building in Antarctica and slowly the existing stations would fall into disrepair.

Some say it unlikely, but others say the disrepair of the Russian stations shows that economic fortunes can change rapidly and drastically.

'So what if the whole continent were put off-limits for a period of say 20 years and when we went back we'd find all our stations like the abandoned Wilkes Station, iced-over rubbish dumps?' I ask. And this gets me thinking about the setting for my novel. If the recreationists who are going to re-enact Mawson's trek are the first people on the continent in several decades, what has happened that has led to this? Perhaps some diplomatic row over resources? But that would hardly lead to a hands-off policy. More likely some major scientific study that found a huge detrimental effect from human presence on the continent. Let's say, for instance, that it has been discovered that the presence of human settlements is throwing out the delicate balance of the ecosystem, such as maybe even the very smallest amounts of diesel exhaust and marine pollution are leading to a breakdown of the food chain. And that makes me recall one of the Star Trek movies where earth in the future is in danger of being destroyed and can only be saved by the call of a humpback whale, but they have all been destroyed in the future. So Captain Kirk and Mr Spock and crew journey back to the past, which is our present, in an old Klingon bird-of-prey starship to bring a whale back to the future. I'm not making this up, you know, as implausible as it might seem for a movie plot.

Anyway, maybe there's been a global moratorium on whale hunting and it is discovered that human impacts in Antarctica are leading to a decimation of whale breeding or some such, and so the human presence in Antarctica is banned until whale numbers recover sufficiently.

(Note to self: think some more about this until you can get a scenario that works which doesn't involve Captain Kirk).

✳ ✳ ✳

Three days out of Casey and about two days from Davis we sight whales. I rush up to the bridge and peer into the distance with everybody else. There is always somebody who has a story about having seen a whale come right alongside the ship on one voyage, but it's like that story of something that happened to a friend's uncle's cousin's neighbour. I peer into the distance in front of the ship asking, 'Where? Where? Where?' And I'm told about 2 kilometres directly in front of the ship. I peer into the grey ocean and see a small spray burst, like a wave breaking on a rock or something. Then another right beside it. Then another. 'Three whales,' Peter the Vomit (Voyage Management in Training) says, standing beside me with a pair of strong binoculars. 'Humpbacks.'

Some of us venture out onto the side deck, but the wind is blowing moderately hard today and although the air temperature is only zero, the windchill rating is about minus 15 degrees, making it hard to stay there too long. We retreat back into the bridge and press our zoom lenses against the glass.

As the ship approaches the whales we can see more of them each time they breach, their large lumpen backs breaking the water. And I know, at that moment, what the word majestic can mean. And, like so many others, I wish it were possible for whales just to be left alone to be whales. And standing there, watching them slowly move away from us, some of the crew joke about catching one for dinner. I feel a sudden need to defend them in some way. I feel that the whaling is indefensible. I feel I'm going to rush out when I get home and buy a CD of whale songs to bring back this moment. Uh-oh, I feel another of those hippie-type Antarctic moments starting to come over me.

As we get closer to Davis Station the ice changes continually. From open sea it thickens up, like curdled milk with loose chunks of ice in it. After that it thickens some more until it looks like blocks of pavlova floating in a giant tub of champagne. After that it thins out again, more like a lily pond of white lilies on a dark pool. Then it changes to look like heavily sprinkled icing sugar floating in dark green cordial. Later we encounter open sea again, which is replaced by an ice sculpture garden floating past. Andrew, the BOM squad guy, has been busy photographing an iceberg that looks like an erect penis and he suggests we make an announcement over the ship's intercom and just see who the first people to rush up the stairs are. I tell him he's going to have a very long winter at Mawson Station, and remind him what Frederick Cook said: that we each see in icebergs what we want to see in them. Then I tell him his challenge for the rest of the voyage will be to find the matching female genitalia in ice.

   We pass one iceberg that is 55 kilometres long and while we stare at it in awe, our gaze stretching from horizon to horizon, we are told there is another one coming up soon that is about 70 kilometres long. Towards evening the sea is an enormous, tightly packed tub of vanilla ice cream, frosted where it has thawed and refroze. Then, as we get closer to the continent again, it is like pushing our way through a large sea of meringue and cream. The variations seem endless.

And finally, for the first time on our trip, we pass the Antarctic Circle at 66 degrees 30 minutes. I look around on the bridge to make sure that Andrew isn't taking his clothes off again (which he did for a photo at the Antarctic Circle, some kilometres inland from Casey Station on a trip up to the new Wilkins Runway). But we're saved from a repeat performance. It might have had something to do with our reaction to his pictures. He said at the time, 'Hey, it was very cold, all right!'

I'm poring over maps of Antarctica, sketching out where we have travelled and noting what a tiny fraction of the continent we will get to stand upon. Almost all the placenames are around the coast, mostly named after explorers and their sponsors, such as Mac-Robertson Land, named after the chocolate magnate who sponsored Mawson. There are other names though that I scratch my head at and wonder what were they thinking? Such as Whichaway Nunatuks, or Inexpressible Island.

Dumont d'Urville left a trail of French names, including Adélie Land, Glacier du Français and Cape Pepin. There are a swag of royalty lands, such as King George V Land, Queen Mary Land, Wilhelm II Land, Princess Elizabeth Land, Queen Maud Land and Edward VII

Land. The explorers tend to get much smaller landmarks named after them: Amundsen Bay, Law Promontory, the Shackleton Ice Shelf, the Scott Glacier (of which there are two—oops), the Nordenskjöld Ice Tongue and the Mawson Escarpment.

There are a few places on the map, however, where the explorers had obviously exhausted their lists of royalty, family, friends, sponsors and distant cousins once removed, which you can see in the very imaginatively named Little Glacier, Cape Goodenough, Snow Hill Island and Cape Flying Fish. But my favourite of all is the Executive Committee Range, squeezed between Marie Byrd Land and Edward VII Land in East Antarctica under the Antarctic Peninsula. I'm sure there's a bureaucratic committee somewhere that is very proud of it and each member will tell their grandchildren with great pride how a piece of Antarctica has been named after them.

Although I also imagine the little kids saying, 'What? Boring Old Fart Land?'

Davis Station

Captain Davis ran in as near the coast as he could safely venture and dropped anchor, pending the moderation of the wind.

—Douglas Mawson, *The Home of the Blizzard*

Davis Station is where things were always bound to get interesting. The station is named after the dour-faced Captain John King 'Gloomy' Davis, who captained the *Aurora*. He first met Mawson on Shackleton's 1907–09 *Nimrod* expedition and and later captained Scott's old vessel, the *Discovery*, in 1929–30 for the first of Mawson's bizarrely acronymed BANZARE voyages. An interesting thing here is that, although the two closest Australian stations are Davis and

Mawson (a mere 2000 kilometres apart), on their voyages the two men often disagreed somewhat fiercely, to the point that relations deteriorated so badly that they only communicated by written notes. And finally Mawson had a different captain appointed for the second BANZARE voyage.

You have to see photographs of Davis to believe just how dour he looked. He makes Amundsen look like a grinning hippie. If a movie were being made and the producers were trying to find somebody to play him, they'd have to resort to computer-generated imagery, like they did with Gollum in *The Lord of the Rings* movies, to get his features right.

Anyway, I digress.

We get an email from Davis Station to the ship telling us that they are just about out of water. Frozen water, water everywhere, but barely a drop to drink. Davis is known as the Riviera of Antarctica, with relative balmy temperatures and very little snow around the Vestfold Hills, where it is built. The bare rock enables much interesting science to be conducted there, but water shortages are always a problem. The station had a desalination plant brought in, but it is out of service. We are told that those of us who are going ashore should not bother taking a towel as we won't be able to take a shower there.

Vonna tells us not to worry because as soon as we land we will be taken by helicopter out in the field, and she says to make sure to pack our pee-bottles.

'Our what?' we ask.

'Didn't they give you pee-bottles?' she asks.

'No.'

She sighs. 'I'll see what we can organise.'

'As long as we're not expected to drink it,' I say.

❄ ❄ ❄

To reach Davis Station the ship has to crunch through some heavy ice, which slows our progress a little, and we are also told that those of us with planned helicopter flights might need to brace for disappointment if the weather deteriorates further and the winds increase to over 40 kilometres an hour. Up on the bridge some of the old hands are telling helicopter horror stories, which is just what you want to hear before your first helicopter ride. But I suppose it's like finding out that *Air Crash Investigation* is somehow always on television the night before you fly anywhere. Mick is saying that he was on a helicopter flight when the pilot's door popped open and they had to try and jury-rig something with hooks and straps to keep it shut. Then he tells us that he was on a chopper that had to shut down one engine as it had an oil leak and the pilot told him to prioritise the cargo in case they lost too much height and he had to start throwing some out. Then everybody seemed to have a scare story. The radio once gave out. The pilot had to put down on an ice floe instead of the ship. And of course the infamous helicopter crash on the *Polar Bird* in 2001. I've seen the footage. Spectators were all standing around the helideck watching and filming as the chopper came in to pick up cargo and it hopped a little on the deck, snared one of its landing skids and as it tried to rise it just flipped over. Bits of helicopter blades went flying left and right and every which way.

Jeeeezuz, it was something to see. But amazingly nobody was injured. Except the helicopter, of course.

I decide I'd better find something more worthwhile then listening to these stories to pass the time. So I ask Michelle from the BOM squad to explain to me the difference between a weather observer and a weather forecaster. Michelle is a Tassie girl living in Brisbane, tall with her light hair in a ponytail and seems to always have a smile. I've noticed a little competition between the observers and forecasters. Michelle tells me that weather observers believe that they deal in facts and weather forecasters deal in fiction, but she also tells me that weather forecasters use the facts that weather observers gather to help make their forecasts. Though I've seen the dartboard in the Meteorology Office at Casey Station with the different forecasts against different numbers and simply reply to her, 'Of course.'

The history of aviation in Antarctica has a very checkered history with as many disasters as successes. The first successful aviation was on Scott's 1901–04 *Discovery* expedition. Scott and Shackleton both ascended by observation balloon until it was found to have a leak and was unable to be used further. Mawson brought an airplane with him to Cape Denison, but it had previously crashed at an exhibition event in South Australia, and so was brought south without its wings to be used as an air tractor instead, at which it had some successes and some disasters—and was lost. Its remains were accidentally found under the ice in 2010.

There are many modern equivalents of adapted vehicles, such as the legendary beach buggy that was customised at Mawson Station, known as Antarctica 3. Its predecessors Antarctica 1 and Antarctica 2 were promotional vehicles for Volkswagen that went down to the ice in 1963 and 1964. Nobody has ever managed to track down the location of Antarctica 1, although it was returned to Australia in 1964 and took part in the BP Rally of that year.

The original Antarctica 3 was taken down to the ice in 1966, but the more famous replacement was a suburban Volkswagen that had the body removed, and was then cut into three for shipping to Mawson Station in 1978. At the station it was reassembled by the 'diesos' into an ice-ready dune buggy, reinforced with welded metal bars and wheeled out one day to the amazement of the then station leader. I'm told he was taken for the first joy ride, or 'jolly', in it and thereby proclaimed it a great asset to the station.

The original thin tyres had chains fitted, a perspex windscreen was built and side curtains were added to block out the wind. It was perfect for driving around on the sea ice at great speeds. Over the years, according to the story, it was rebuilt so that it was like 'Paddy's axe' (just the same as it always was though it had had six new handles and two new axe heads). At various stages it developed into a two-seater, and acquired large fat tyres for the rear wheels. It was described as 'a bloody ripper of a car for taking jollies around the ice on', with past expeditioners recounting with great fondness how they pulled it out of a skid at high speed or the ingenuity with which repairs were made to it .

But eventually it encountered the ire of Hobart head office—or the 'fun police' as they are not always affectionately known. Several attempts were made to remove Antarctica 3 from Mawson Station, but whenever re-supply ships arrived the vehicle had disappeared somewhere and nobody could seem to recall where it had last been parked. Usually it was found, buried in snow somewhere, after the last re-supply ship for the season had departed.

There is even a story that on one occasion the fun police managed to get hold of the vehicle and lock it into a metal shipping container and then bring it back to Hobart. But when the seals on the container were opened, the vehicle wasn't there!

It was finally apprehended and returned to Australia, but was later smuggled back down to Antarctica with a truck that was being shipped down. It was eventually returned to Hobart for good, and now lives in a shed at the Kingston headquarters, perhaps like Herbie the Love Bug, waiting for somebody to resurrect it back to life, or perhaps proclaim it a heritage artifact to be put on display. I'd like to think, however unlikely, that it may yet drive again, wildly and without sanctioned permission, over the ice.

Another historical vehicle of interest, a custom-built mini-trac that had the body of a Morris Minor and the snow tracks of a Nodwell snow vehicle, was tried out at Australia's stations in the 1960s.

An interesting story about one of the first motorised vehicles in Antarctica is worth telling at this point. When Captain Scott sailed south on his ill-fated *Terra Nova* expedition, he took three motor sledges. One broke through the ice and fell to the bottom of the Ross Sea when they were unloading it. After putting all the stores and men ashore, the captain of the *Terra Nova* sailed farther around the Ross Ice Shelf and came across Amundsen at the Bay of Whales, on the eastern side of the sea. The two parties dined together and Amundsen, who had publicly predicted that his dogs would prove superior to Scott's ponies or motor sledges, asked how the motor sledges were performing. Campbell told him that one of them had already reached firm land. This shocked Amundsen, who took it to mean that it had crossed the ice barrier already and reached the solid land of the continent, rather than the solid land of the seabed that Campbell was referring to.

This spirit of driving across the snow in fast vehicles continues today. For instance Kyle, our cook, has this great plan to get somebody to sponsor him to take a tracked bus or Hägglund on a road trip between Australia's stations, with him and a group of mates drinking and being yobbos along the way, and having a film company make a TV series or documentary of it. Now I don't quite know why, but nobody has yet matched his spirit of adventure with backing for his idea. Go figure.

We really know that summer is coming to an end when we reach Davis Station. The outside temperature is minus six and with the windchill factor it is minus 22. In the morning we assemble in our orange freezer suits. When we get the go, we climb down the rope ladder into the barge. The wind coming off the water cuts through a single pair of gloves and beanie like an ice bullet. Who said this was the Riviera of Antarctica?

Coming into shore I'm pleased to feel just as excited at being about to step onto the continent as I was the first time. I was a little worried that I might not. For as I'm becoming increasingly fond of saying, 'You can only take your first step onto Antarctica once.'

The Davis wharf is a jam of vehicles and cranes and people, all obviously knowing what they are doing, and we try to keep out of their way. Our bags are heaved ashore in a net and then we are hustled into a ute driven by none other than the station leader Peter. He drives us up to the helipad on the far side of the station and tells us we'll be going straight out into the field.

We crowd into the helipad terminal which, like most buildings in Antarctica, is a converted shipping container. We chat to the station staff, who are extremely friendly and they tell us they feel it is time to go home to Australia and they look forward to getting onto the ship again. Vonna introduces us and says, 'This is Nick, he's an artist. This is Lynette, she's an historian, and this is Craig, he's a writer.'

'What are you writing?' one of them asks. Of course.

'I'm writing the unauthorised biography of Vonna in which she's a six-foot-six supermodel,' I say.

The helicopters are small and sleek and red—so I know they must be able to go fast—and are just sitting there ready to go. But they've lost our bags. We congratulate them on operating just like any large commercial airport. Peter heads off in the ute to find the luggage and we walk down to a nearby shed to get our survival gear. We discover that, whereas at Casey Station all the buildings were known by their colours, here the buildings, despite being colour-coded, are known by acronyms. TAB is the Temporary Accommodation Building, SAM is the Summer Accommodation Module and SPAM is the Science Project Marshalling Area (I know, but SPMA doesn't make a word).

Earlier I had said that Casey Station looked like a remote mining camp—well, I take it back.

It is Davis Station that really, *really* looks like a remote mining camp. It is nestled on the very edge of the Vestfold Hills, which is one of the largest ice-free areas on the Antarctic continent. It is all rocky hills and fiords and the rock is dark and jumbled and it looks so much like a lunar landscape that when we're bundled up in our polar gear I keep getting the temptation to press my heavy boot print into the ground and say, 'That's one small step for man—and, ah, one giant leap for mankind.'

We collect our sleeping bags and bivy bags and pee-bottles and poo-container and our food bag and then our own bags arrive. We're ready to go now. Vonna grabs my arm and leads me to the far helicopter. There is no point in even trying to talk over the roar of the engines and rotors. We stow our bags and she pushes me into the back seat and climbs in the front. The pilot makes hand signals for us to both put on our headphones so we can hear him talking.

Then we suddenly lift off. It is the most amazing sensation. Just like dreams of flying have always felt like. I want to shout out, 'Wooooo-hooooooooooo!' but I worry it will go through the intercom and deafen Vonna and the pilot.

I feel weightless with my feet on the hard metal floor, and I sit with my face against the plexiglas windows, watching the landscape so close below us it feels like I could reach out and touch it. We soar over three lakes and the pilot tells me that the last of them, Deep Lake, is about

50 metres below sea level and he can fly down there and theoretically be flying beneath the sea.

Then we are circling around a small red-and-white hut on the edge of a large ocean inlet. The chopper touches down and we bundle out, grabbing our bags. The chopper lifts off in a storm of grit and a huge gust of wind as the second chopper puts down beside us, with Nick and Lynette.

Brookes Hut is named after the station carpenter who built it in 1972–74, and the landscape around it is lunaresque. Huge chunks of dark rock are scattered among Gondwana-grey granite. There are only occasional drifts of snow tucked in under overhangs. It doesn't seem like Antarctica, but of course it is. We settle into the hut and then go for a walk, carrying our mandatory survival packs. The wind is chilling and we step through small drifts of snow, but are mostly clambering over rock. There are strange dark lines of dolerite rock that run right through the landscape, like the creator has been practising painting straight lines here at some time.

We plan to walk to Deep Lake, but after an hour and a half we find we are back at the hut! But I suppose it is better than trying to walk to the hut and ending up at the lake. The landscape is more of a jumbled-up, tumble-down maze than those old quarries out of *Doctor Who*, which they were always running around in trying to pretend it was an alien planet, and it is just so easy to take a wrong turn and think you know where you are going.

From a distance Brookes Hut looks like a tiny backyard shed, anchored down to the solid rock with thick cables. And thinking about it, it pretty much is. Inside, it is small—only two pairs of bunks and a kitchen area—though I'm told the original hut was even smaller, so small in fact that if one person wanted to cook the other had to stay in bed. The wind picks up through the afternoon until we can hear it wailing in through the vents as it rushes past. Soon it sounds like a jet engine is throttling up just over our heads and we have to talk louder to be heard.

Vonna says that when big blows like this come in they can last a few days and we should be prepared to be stuck here. She also tells us that if there were snow around it would be blowing a blizzard and white-out, and then she tells us some horror stories of people being stuck in blizzards and how strong the winds can be and once again the many ways that people have died down here. I think of Douglas Mawson sitting out the winter blizzards in his hut and try and get my head into imagining that's where we are.

We feast on curry and rice for dinner and, while Vonna is lamenting the fact that we brought water but no beer, Nick magically produces a bottle of beer that somebody has left behind. We are at first just a little bit suspicious, of course, and presume it might be somebody's pee in a beer bottle, but when we open it, it is beer. Antarctic wonders never cease to amaze us.

After dinner I go for a walk out to the little peninsula directly in front of the hut and my attention is about a million miles away, working on having another one of those Antarctic moments, when I round a rocky knoll and walk right into the biggest goddamned Adélie penguin I've ever seen in my life. We both squawk in equal amounts of fright and I've barely got the sense to snap a picture of it so that when they find my body they'll at least know what had killed me. But fortunately the monster penguin must have fed recently on an elephant seal or a leopard seal because it lets me get away.

I get back to the hut to warn the others about the mutant monster penguin, and then I discover that there is something wrong with my camera. In the picture I show them the bird is barely waist high and doesn't have the ferocious attack look on its face at all. (Note to self: Either camera or imagination needs servicing when we get back home.)

We sit up late in the hut, writing and reading, very much as Mawson and his men would have done, listening to the wind get louder and louder. I can't resist the temptation to write in my journal: *20 February. Still Blizzarding.*

Vonna says that if the wind is still blowing like this tomorrow we won't be able to be picked up by helicopter and will be stranded here, although if worse comes to worse we could always walk back to the station as it's only about 10 kilometres away. I think of the success of our walk to Deep Lake and it doesn't bode well.

❄ ❄ ❄

It's time to tell that bit in Mawson's story that most defines him. His solo trek across King George V Land. Having spent the winter and spring preparing for their sledging operations, Mawson divided 17 of the 18 men up into several parties. There were parties heading to the south, west, east, near east and far east. Mawson was to lead the Far East Party, taking all the dogs, three sleds and the two dog-handlers, Xavier Mertz and Belgrave Ninnis.

A little bit of background on them at this point. Xavier Mertz, known affectionately by the rest of the men as X, was a Swiss ski champion and experienced mountaineer who had been recruited to teach the other members to ski. He was, by all accounts, a thoroughly likeable chap. Belgrave Ninnis, known affectionately as Cherub for his youthful good looks, was a 25-year-old lieutenant in the British army. Also a thoroughly likeable chap, who had been turned down by Scott for his expedition. They spent a lot of hours caring for the dogs during the winter, and in his journal Mawson has nothing bad to say of them, unlike some other members of the expedition.

As the *Aurora* was due to arrive at Cape Denison in early January, the men had a lot of ground to cover in a relatively short space of time and they all set out between 6 and 9 November. Mawson later wrote in *The Home of the Blizzard*: *It was a beautiful calm afternoon as the sledge mounted up the long icy slopes.*

Mawson wrote a letter to Paquita just before their departure in which he let on some of his actual concerns at the time: *The weather is fine this morning, though the wind still blows—we shall get away in an hour's time. I have two good companions Dr Mertz and Lieut Ninnis. It is unlikely that any harm will happen to us but should I not return to you in Australia please know that I truly loved you from an admiration of your spirit.*

The first days they made relatively good progress, sighting a distant peak that they named Aurora Peak. They soon worked out the best way to travel, which was to have Mertz skiing ahead and the dogs following him, with two of the lead sledges tied together. As they approached Aurora Peak they had their first nasty encounter with a crevasse, with half of Mawson's dog team falling in and having to be hauled out.

Soon they were approaching a large glacier, often the site of crevasses due to the pressure build-ups of the ice, and at one point they actually pitched their tent on a snow bridge spanning a large crevasse, and only discovered this when Ninnis fell through the snow but luckily managed to catch himself on the edge. Ninnis, in fact, seemed to be a little bit of a crevasse magnet, having several awkward falls and close encounters. On one occasion, Mawson wrote: *Ninnis's sledge fell, but fortunately jammed itself just below the surface.*

They crossed the first of two major glaciers they were to encounter and reached a height of 715 metres above sea level.

Throughout the month of December they were often hampered by bad weather and difficult terrain. Mawson recorded that ... *a dense blizzard raged, the wind reaching seventy miles per hour. There was nothing to do but lie in our bags and think out plans for the future ...*

Mawson also wrote, with a little more optimism than would prove to be the case: *The crevasses were practically past.*

The three men were, in fact, becoming increasingly done in and Mawson told them that they would press on just a little farther and would then turn about and head back to their base.

On 13 December they heard booming sounds about them. Mertz wrote in his diary that it sounded like the distant thunder of cannon, but was made by the snow masses under them collapsing their arches. He also wrote that his companions were frightened by the noise of it, having never heard the like before.

A writer of more purple prose might be tempted to describe it as a warning toll for the men, which I will certainly avoid doing, but on the next day, 14 December, disaster struck them. In his journal Mawson described how the men were travelling, with Mertz out in front again, himself on the first sledge and Ninnis on the sledge behind him. They had left one sledge behind and divided up the weight between the two sledges.

Mertz spotted the crevasse ahead of them and held up his ski pole at an angle to signal its presence. Mawson wrote in his journal: *My sledge crossed a crevasse obliquely & I called back to Ninnis, who had the rear sledge, to watch it, then went on, not thinking to look back again as it had no specially dangerous features.*

Mawson in fact sat on his sledge jotting down in his journal the details of his noon-day readings. *Latitude 68°53'53", Longitude 151°39'46".* When he looked up again he saw that Mertz had stopped and was looking back behind him. Mawson turned around and saw no sign of Ninnis there. He wrote: *I stopped & wondered, then bethought myself of the crevasse and hurried back to find a great gaping hole in the ground. I called down but could get no answer.*

He tells it slightly differently in *The Home of the Blizzard*, saying first: *As a matter of fact crevasses were not expected, since we were on a smooth surface of neve well to the southward of the broken coastal slopes.* He then tells of how Mertz indicated that there was a crevasse there and he turned his head to warn Ninnis.

Ninnis, who was walking along by the side of his sledge, close behind my own, heard the warning, for in my backward glance I noticed that he immediately swung the leading dogs so as to cross the crevasse squarely instead of diagonally as I had done …

There was no sound from behind except a faint, plaintive whine from one of the dogs which I imagined was in reply to a touch of Ninnis's whip … When I next looked back it was in response to the anxious gaze of Mertz who had turned around and halted in his tracks. Behind me, nothing met the eye but my own sledge tracks running back in the distance. Where were Ninnis and his sledge?

I hastened back along the trail thinking that a rise in the ground obscured the view. There was no such good fortune, however, for I came to a gaping hole in the surface about eleven feet wide. The lid of the crevasse had broken in; two sledge tracks led up to it on the far side but only one continued on the other side.

Mertz and Mawson peered deep into the dark crevasse but all they could see were two dogs on a shelf, about 45 metres below. One of the dogs was immobile and the other was trying to get to its feet, though obviously with a broken back. They stayed by the crevasse for a long time, calling futilely into the darkness. Mawson later wrote: *A chill draught was blowing out of the abyss. We felt that there was little hope.*

It took some time for the men to accept their situation. Ninnis was on foot, rather than on the sledge, so must have broken through the snow covering the crevasse, taking the sledge and dogs into the abyss with him. And that sledge contained most of their food, all the dogs' food and their tent. Not only had they lost a dear friend, they had lost their means of sustaining themselves against the harsh Antarctic climate.

They read a prayer service for their friend, took their bearings anew from a nearby rise and then turned around to try and get back to their base. They had to cover 480 kilometres with insufficient food.

Mawson wrote: *May God Help us.*

❄ ❄ ❄

Day two at Brookes Hut and we wake up to find the no-snow blizzard is gusting heavier than ever. The whole hut is shaking with the force of the wind. But when I look out the window the land seems still and calm. Just the rock and the hidden drifts of snow. It's quite bizarre. When I climb out of bed and look out the window in the other direction, however, I see waves on the fiord almost big enough to surf on and I watch the occasional skua in the sky being buffeted around like it is in a wind tunnel.

'How windy do you think it is?' I ask.

Vonna says the best way to estimate it is to stand outside. If the wind blows you over it is your bodyweight in kilometres per hour. She suddenly leaps out of her sleeping bag in her thermal undies and bare feet and runs outside onto the verandah and starts doing star jumps. We can hear her shrieks above the wind. She comes back in and tells us it's a beautiful balmy day and that we should go for a long walk.

I crawl back into my sleeping bag to do my best impression of the surgeon of Mawson's party, Dr Leslie Whetter, whom Mawson criticised for hopping into his sleeping bag and reading too often.

At the 2 PM radio check we're told it is too windy for the helicopters to come and get us—like we didn't know that already—and we'll have to stay out another night. Mawson was a firm believer in keeping people busy and that idle hands make for idle minds. Vonna has a slightly similar philosophy and to stave off boredom she decides that she and Nick will dress up using most of the pots and pans in the kitchen. So we tape onto them baking-tray breastplates and cheese-grater hand guards and saucepan-lid shoulder guards and upside-down cooking pots on their heads. We're very lucky to have Vonna for our guide as she's both extremely professional and also knows how to have fun with people—which from my experience is a quality greatly lacking in many guides—yet I wonder how we'd all cope if we were stuck in a hut together for nine months or more. For as the day of enforced close quarters drags on we start to discover differences among us that I suspect would just grate more than the cheese-graters on Vonna's wrists if we had to stay more than a few nights together stranded by the weather. But, who knows, maybe it would be no worse than in Mawson's Hut—though I'm thinking of his first year there, not his second, which was a time of great conflicts.

Day three we are still in the hut and Vonna's energiser batteries show no signs of running down even a little bit. She rallies us for another attempt to walk to Deep Lake. Lynette says she'd prefer to stay behind, but Nick and I agree to go. We don our clothes and boots and hats and gloves and get our survival gear together and head out into the rocky wilderness. Surprisingly, we find Deep Lake rather quickly and are there in just over 30 minutes of walking, climbing, scrambling and jumping. It is less than a kilometre across, though not too much less. I taste it and it's so salty it makes my tongue sting.

Feeling pleased with ourselves, Vonna suggests we walk back a slightly different route, which of course takes us on a long, long meandering path around endless canyons and gullies. To add to our miseries the wind is now blowing chillingly into our faces, stealing any little bit of warmth it can from any area of skin it touches. We pass the skeleton of a dead seal and a penguin carcass and don't need to state that they were walking this same route we are on when they died.

The cold and fatigue makes our muscles tense up more and soon, climbing up some rocks, I pull a muscle in my upper leg. Every step is a stabbing pain. I stumble on, but I really just want to lie down and do what the seal did. I press on, with Vonna and Nick deliberating with the map and wandering off in new directions ahead of me. It's very tempting to say, 'Slow down. I can't keep up. I hurt my leg.' But being a big boy—or a big dope—I don't. I just keep taking step after step after step, gritting my teeth and grrrring at each stab of pain.

This is what sorts out those who have the real Antarctic spirit, I tell myself. This is what those with real grit had. This is the do-or-die will that Mawson possessed that kept him going. Then I do a reality check. I'm standing there with almost no snow in sight, probably less than a kilometre from a warm hut with warm food and am making out like I'm doing Mawson's trek just because my leg hurts a bit. (Note to self: Don't be such a drama queen!)

❄ ❄ ❄

'So the stage is set once again,' says Mawson. I look up and see him sitting there in the near-darkness at the end of my bunk.

'Set for what?' I ask a little groggily. We have gone to bed early, tired out from our long day of hiking.

But Mawson doesn't answer. He is looking far away, into the distance, or the past. 'The situation was grave,' he says, nodding his head slowly.

'There are those who said that it was my fault, I know. Who have said that I was too much like Scott in that I did not learn from the masters such as Nansen, who had written on the need to spread a man's weight out over a larger area through the use of skis or snowshoes. Some have said that if I had insisted on the men wearing snowshoes, then the disaster may well have been averted and poor young Ninnis's life would not have been lost. He would not have plummeted down that dark pit of hell into an icy grave there.' He pauses again and nods his head once more. 'Perhaps. Perhaps.'

Then he says, 'But invariably those men who say that were not there. They were sitting in some warm office somewhere pondering how it must have been. They were never on the ice. They were never shivering into the force of the blizzard that plucked at your clothes and managed to force its way through to chill you to the bones. They were never sitting in a tiny tent eating dog meat.'

He stops. He closes his eyes a moment. Then he goes on. 'We knew it would be a race for our lives. Our main source of food would be the dogs that were helping to draw our loads. We ran them until they dropped dead of exhaustion. George. Johnson. Mary. Pavlova. But they were poor eating, having been fed on leather scraps and old skins and they were mostly skin and bones. The paws took the longest to boil up to become edible. Except their livers. Ah yes, those succulent large red livers. We tried to cook them, you know, but since there was no fat in them all we could do was scorch the outsides on each side and then eat them mostly raw.'

He smiles a little and shakes his head. 'If only we had known then what we know now, I many times wonder if we would have acted any differently.' He sighs and then pulls himself up erect. 'Our first priority was to fashion ourselves some form of shelter, so we made a forced march back to our abandoned sledge where we were able to cut up the runners and use the legs of a theodolite to make ourselves a tent of sorts with the remaining tent cover. It was only large enough for one man to sit upright in at a time, but it would protect us from the harsh elements at nights.

'We had to make a decision then: should we march back the way we had come, or try and get down to the ocean and hope to make our way back along the sea ice, perhaps even meeting up with the Eastern Party. In the end we decided less risk would be had by continuing back the way we had come overland.

'And how we marched. We marched through Christmas and New Year, fighting against the weather that tormented us terribly. Winds blew at us, then the temperature rose and the snow turned to slush, grabbing at our feet. And poor Mertz, often wet because he had no burberry pants to keep the water out, started to fail first. I watched his slow deterioration as he became more and more tired, not even able to write in his diary any more. The skin was coming off his legs. He was unable to get out of his sleeping bag in the mornings. I doctored him as best I could, offering him milk and other precious foods, but he was taken with despondency.

'We had only about a hundred miles to cover now and if we could manage ten miles a day we would do it in ten days. But Mertz was incapable of covering even two miles. I thought he had a fever at the time. I thought he had gone off the food. I tried to induce him to walk just a little way, but he refused, saying it was suicide for him to attempt it and that we would be better served resting the day and allowing him a chance to dry out. But I knew to wait any longer would narrow our chances of making it through.

'All depended on providence now. It was going to be an even race to the hut. We started out again on 6 January but Xavier was quite dizzy and soon caved in. We were both weak from hunger and often couldn't sleep because of the pains that caused us. I knew that I could pull through myself with the provisions at hand, but I could not leave him. His heart appeared to have gone from him. Knowing that we must march or die, I put him in the sledge in his sleeping bag and set off, but we had not gone far when he fouled his pants.

'I cleaned him as best I could, seeing that all the skin of his privates was now gone, and put him in his sleeping bag, but he was taken with fits. This fine young colleague of mine, once so strong and full of life, now reduced to this. He was the one who had skied out in front singing German songs for us to follow, now a shivering shadow of a man, as done in as the dogs had been before they died.

'I was very weak myself and knew that we had a slim chance of succeeding now. His condition had cooked both our chances. I didn't mind so much for myself, but my mind turned to Paquita and I prayed to God to help us.

'Poor Xavier ranted and raved through the night of 7 January, and he died peacefully at about 2 AM on the morning of the 8th. The life just slipped out of him and he was dead in my arms. He had been accepted into the peace that passes all understanding, and it was my fervent hope that he would be received there where a man of sterling qualities and a high mind might reap his due reward. In his life he was a man of character, generous and noble of parts.'

Mawson is quiet again for some considerable time. Then he says, 'And so now it was a race alone for me to regain the safety of our hut before I succumbed to the same terrible fate as my two companions.'

I finally understand that Mawson is giving the lecture he gave night after night after night upon his return to safety, in a vain attempt to raise money to cover some of the debts of the expedition. Reliving that fatal march over and over. I can only imagine how it must have been to dredge up the ghosts of his comrades each time he gave the talk, for now that he has seen Mertz's death one more time he falls silent. All the life seems to go out of him and his shoulders slump.

So I ask him, 'Why do you think you survived when the others did not?'

It takes a while for the question to register and then he says, 'I have thought long and hard upon that many nights. I have wondered why I survived when Mertz and Ninnis died, as I wondered why Shackleton survived when Scott died. Is there something in a man's destiny that keeps him alive—or some inner drive that helps him to evade death?'

'What was your worst moment?' I ask. 'Was it when Mertz died?'

'At the time I thought it was,' he says. 'But how often we think we are at the very lowest point possible only to find we can be brought lower. For my trials had only begun. After burying Mertz under blocks of ice I cut the sledge smaller and cooked up what food I could. My own skin was coming away continually and pooling inside my clothing. My nose and lips broke open. My fingernails were coming loose. My scrotum was raw and painful when I walked. Then the soles of my feet came away. It was terribly painful walking, but I bound them on as best I could, smearing them with lanolin and continuing on.'

He takes a deep breath now and I have to prompt him again.

'Tell us about the crevasse.'

He knows which one I mean. Of course. 'The first sign was that terrible booming sound again, somewhere beneath me. It was on the 17th. I was about halfway across the southern end of the Mertz Glacier and it was like my old friend wanted to bring me nearer to him. I suddenly plummeted through the snow and found myself dangling on the end of my tether rope. The end of my tether, see. I had time enough to say to myself, "So this is the end", but the end never came. The small sledge had overturned and was holding me there. I hung there for some time, considering my situation. My fingers were badly done in from frost, my limbs were weak and every time I tried to raise myself I fell back again.'

Then he nods his head slowly. 'I considered slipping out of my harness many times. Thinking how easy it would be to just drop into the chill darkness below. It was a moment of great temptation, to quit small things for great, to pass from petty exploration of this world to vaster worlds beyond. But I could not. I was afraid of falling and breaking my back on some ledge, like that pitiful dog we had seen fall with Ninnis. If I could not have a clean death, I would attempt to live.'

'As simple as that?' I ask him.

He turns and looks at me. 'It's never as simple as that!' Again he is silent a moment. Then he says, 'I cannot, in all honesty, say what it was that compelled me to make that climb. The desire to live. The thought of Paquita. The thought of the food bag on the sledge. All of these and more. I have little memory of how I hauled myself back to the surface. What I do have is more from what I have written afterwards. I dragged my body slowly up that thin rope to reach the surface a first time, only to have the edge of the snow there collapse and send me back down into the crevasse once more. And again I hung there, wondering if I was being tested or taunted. But I climbed again, though what was driving me on I cannot honestly say any more. But I did get back to the surface, this time emerging feet first and sliding my body across the ice to safety.'

Then he is silent as if the sheer effort of telling the story has exhausted him. I try to prompt him once more, but he won't take up the story, so I tell it. 'You trekked on for several days, falling into more crevasses, and battling the weather and your deteriorating state until you came upon a cairn, erected by your comrades that very morning, with food and a message that the *Aurora* had arrived and that Amundsen had gained the Pole. There was, as yet, no knowledge of Scott's death to report, though it was suspected.

'You made your way to the relative safety of Aladdin's Cave, a bare five miles above the Hut, but you were too weak to go on and the weather again turned against you. You sat out the blizzard in the cave until 8 February and then descended to the hut in clear weather, to find that the ship had left a few hours before. And when you related to the men left there to search for you what had happened, tears filled their eyes. You were a wreck of your former self, but you were alive.'

Death in Antarctica is a very touchy subject, despite the fact that almost all our briefings relate to ways to die or not to die. Statistically, the Antarctic actually has the world's lowest death rate of any country (if it could be thought of as a country)—but that's as an overall figure, not as a percentage. If you choose to turn your statistics that way it doesn't look so good, over 500 deaths over the last hundred years or so. The first death on the Antarctic continent was probably that of Nicolai Hanson, who died of scurvy in 1898 at Borchgrevink's hut at Cape Adare. On Scott's 1901–04 expedition, a few years later, a sailor called George Vince slid down a slippery snow slope while lost in a blizzard and disappeared into the sea.

Shackleton's famous *Endurance* expedition is often praised as having no loss of life, but his Ross Sea Party, who were laying depots for the second stage of his crossing, lost three men, including its leader, Aeneas Mackintosh.

Similar stories go on and on over the decades. Plane crashes. Falling off cliffs. Exposure to the cold. The continent can be unforgiving both to those who carefully plan and those who are foolhardy, with the line between death and survival sometimes being a minutely fine and seemingly arbitrary one.

There are too many stories to list here, yet all of them are tragic in their own way. In 1993, four Norwegians set out to copy Amundsen's trek to the South Pole in an attempt to retrieve his tent so it could be displayed at the 1994 Lillehammer Winter Olympics. But two of their snowmobiles fell into crevasses about 925 kilometres from the Pole. One of the men was injured and one killed. A four-person rescue team from New Zealand's Scott Base and the US McMurdo Station flew in, in a twin otter plane to rescue them. They landed about 3 kilometres away but the area was so heavily crevassed that it took the rescue team several hours to reach the Norwegians. The dead man was found about 45 metres down the crevasse, too deep and too tightly wedged to even recover his body.

In 1966 two members of the British Antarctic Survey were out travelling with their huskies when a blizzard blew up. After it had cleared and they had not returned the station sent a search party. They found the two men dead in the snow, one holding a shovel just outside a snow cave they had dug. The searchers had to piece together what had happened. By all appearances the two men had built the snow cave and would have survived the blizzard in it, but one of the men must have gone out to check on the dogs and got lost in the whiteout. The other man climbed outside the snow cave with the shovel, trying to guide him back in but stayed out too long and succumbed to the cold.

In fact, the British Antarctic Survey details the deaths of 31 people killed in Antarctica since 1948 working for the organisation or its predecessor, listing the causes of death and whether or not the bodies were recovered. Deaths were due to hut fire, heart attack, suicide, drowning, lost when sea ice broke up, fractured skull following a fall on rocks when out walking, crevasse fall, fall from cliff while doing ornithology work, lost on sea ice, lost in crevasse fall, exposure, lost, crevasse accident, aircraft crashed on take-off, drowned and hit by low flying aircraft! Of the 31 dead, 21 bodies were not recovered.

Antarctic historian Tim Bowden lists 20 Australians dead between 1948 and 1997 in his book *The Silence Calling* and there have been more fatalities since. We are enthralled by the wondrous nature and landscape down here, but it can be unforgiving and deadly. Each of Australia's stations has memorials to the dead, with the most deaths being recorded at the subantarctic Macquarie Island.

Many of the people who have spent a substantial time on the continent have an 'almost' story and many of them involve falling through ice or snow into water. One young woman who worked at Casey Station tells me that while crossing an ice bridge to the penguin colony on Shirley Island in the early summer, she fell through the ice up to her shoulders, with her body in the frozen water. She said she could feel the current tugging at her. Luckily her survival training kicked in and the other woman she was travelling with was able to help her out. They made their way back to the station which was fortunately close by. Had she been farther away it might have been another story.

Almost.

❄ ❄ ❄

There has been debate for many years about whether Mawson suffered from exposure to cold or to Vitamin A excess or something other, and even today it is still being debated. For many years it has been believed that he suffered from hypervitaminosis A, for Mertz and Mawson ate the livers of six dogs, which together contained many times the fatal doses of vitamin A. The word 'vitamin' wasn't even known to Mawson at the time, only being coined by Kazimeriz Funk (true name, I kid you not) that same year, although the fatal effects of eating polar dogs' livers was well known to native peoples around Greenland.

Vitamin A is needed by the body, but if taken in excessive amounts leads to the breaking down of many of body functions, with symptoms including dizziness and nausea, followed by splitting of the skin and loss of hair, and the drying out of the nasal and oral membranes. This is followed by stomach and skeletal pains from swelling in the liver and spleen. Lassitude and morbid sensitivity follow, accompanied by delirium, dementia and finally convulsions before death. The symptoms follow Xavier Mertz's last days closely.

It has been estimated that between them Mawson and Mertz consumed 60 toxic doses of vitamin A. Other contributing factors may have been the fact that Mertz was perpetually wet without his protective trousers, or that he was a smoker. In her book *An Antarctic Affair*, Mawson's great-granddaughter, Emma McEwin, relates a conversation she had with the curator of the Mawson Collection at the South Australian Museum in which he conjectured it might well have been the thyroids and brains of the dogs that caused the damage to the men.

I have my own theory that many incidents in history are caused by a multitude of circumstances, but popular interpretations prefer a single defining cause, which dominates the others in the re-telling. And when it comes to re-assembling a story out of history, people grab a preferred cause and wave it around like a banner, trying to outwave all the other single-banner wavers, when the full story is actually an amalgam of all their single causes.

I make a point to check with Brownie, the Pirate King of the Galley, that he hasn't got a box of frozen dogs' brains or thyroids that he's saving up for a special meal for us.

✳ ✳ ✳

Mid-afternoon the wind has dropped enough for the chopper to come and get us. We package our poo-bag ('Let's get our shit together!') and backpacks and assemble for the helicopters. The trip back is pretty quick and from the sky it's amazing to see just how tiny and insignificant Davis Station looks there in the distance. Just a few coloured blocks on the edge of the rock, surrounded by an enormous vastness that goes to the horizon and seeming forever onward. After we do all the compulsory cleaning and unpacking we find out that the *Aurora Australis* is not in the harbour because it dragged its anchor in the wind, having one of those 'almost' incidents, and so headed back out to sea. Also the cargo barge hit the ship while being winched aboard and has a rather inconvenient hole in it.

'What does that all mean?' I ask.

'It means you're all sleeping here the night,' says Peter, the station leader. 'And maybe the next night too. We'll see.'

They call it the 'A Factor'. The Antarctic Factor, which means whatever you plan for, expect it to go belly up and you'll have to remake your plans.

So we go for an exploration of the station, checking out all the acronym buildings, finding a place to sleep for the night and meeting new people. The Davis communal area is a little different to that at Casey. There is a library module at the end of the communal area which is very popular, with long couches and books on all sides. In fact, I'm told it was built to link two modules but the building company went broke and it was never used where it was meant to go and so it was refitted and tacked onto the end of the main building as a library. A very useful example of Antarctic recycling. I do a scan of the shelves and find, once again, that Mawson's favourite author, Robert Service, doesn't get a look in. But my two touchstones of Antarctic libraries are both there. Kim Stanley Robinson's *Antarctica* and Dan Brown's *The Da Vinci Code*.

The common area has a billiard table that can become a ping-pong table, a darts board, a wallow with lounge chairs and suitable magazines such as about pergola building and garden design, and a beautiful bar called Nina's, named after the last dog on the station in 1976. There is also a small movie theatre with 16-millimetre films in canisters. It is a very friendly station and in the evening people drink and talk and drink and laugh and drink and play loud music and drink and tell wonderful stories. It's an odd thing that we can drink as much beer as we like at Davis, but there's not enough water for a shower.

'This is a disaster,' I tell one of the blokes I'm talking to. 'We have to stay an extra night on the continent and we have to drink free home-brew beer all night!'

'Life's harsh down here,' he says.

❄ ❄ ❄

There are two things that are unique to Davis Station, which help define its character: elephant seals and physics. Perhaps we should talk about the physics first. Davis Station is considered Australia's premier base for undertaking science in Antarctica, particularly if you're a physicist, and it regularly hosts up to 80 people during the summer.

Peter, the station leader, says there have only been 55 people on station this summer, and only eight scientists—all of them physicists. (A force of physicists? A mass of physicists? A cluster of physicists?) There were meant to be another three scientists studying seals, but that will happen next summer, and the fact that this year has seen a big concentration on marine science means that a lot of work is being done from the ships out at sea. Ah, but next summer, I'm told, they expect to have 90 people on station, including a lot more scientists. During the 2008 winter there will be less than 20 people staying at Davis Station, and only two scientists—including Harriet from Western Australia, who has come down on the ship with us and will be studying microbes in sea ice. The rest of the staff will be there simply to keep the base ticking over.

Over the whole winter across the three stations on the continent, depending on how you count it, there will be three or four scientists only and support staff of almost 50. If you have a broader definition of scientist, however, and include the BOM squad staff and projects collecting data for transmission back to scientists in Australia, you can argue more science is happening than is visible.

Ah, but last year, I'm told, 40 research projects were undertaken at Davis in the summer alone, and the Division lists its programs as including population estimates of emperor penguins, the success of predators in getting food in relation to sea-ice extent in the winter, and the study of viral and microbial dynamics in water and sea ice. And of course several physics experiments, such as one involving the very impressive Light Detection and Ranging (LIDAR) device that shoots a laser beam into the sky to take an extraordinarily wide array of measurements in the upper atmosphere. Ray, the senior scientist, gives me a tour of the facilities and shows me how each of the different experiments they are running are contributing to our understanding of global climate change. He makes no secret of the fact that it is important for scientists to align what they are doing with the government's priorities.

He tells me a great story about how, in the winter of 2002, they encountered a major problem when a capacitor for the LIDAR failed. There was no chance of getting a replacement until the first ship for the summer arrived, so a solution was developed by two physicists, an electrician, a diesel mechanic, a communications technician and the station chef, who built a 'homemade' replacement using spare parts, plastic clingfilm and aluminium foil. Ray proudly showed me the famous capacitor sitting on a shelf. He also showed me how one of the plumbers had made a cooling coil, something like the back of a tiny fridge, to keep a camera system at the required temperature, saving them about $30,000. I'm impressed by the ingenuity among all the high-tech expensive equipment, and it brings to mind the many early scientists who made the most of their own equipment.

Antarctic science is divided into several categories: Antarctic marine living resources, astronomy, biology, geosciences, glaciology, human impacts research, human biology and medicine, meteorology, oceanography, space and atmospheric sciences—but almost all of it is carried out during the very short Antarctic summer. Our voyage, the last for the season, has only a handful of scientists onboard on the outward leg, researching a variety of things from tides to mosses, though we collect quite a few to take home. We have physicists and biologists and meteorologists and more. But only four people will be left ashore to conduct their science over the winter at Australian stations. Harriet examining microbacteria, and Gary with his field assistant Robyn will be studying emperor penguin chicks near Mawson Station. There will also be one scientist staying at Davis Station operating the LIDAR.

They are all great to talk to and are passionate about their science and about learning more about the unknown, and spend long periods trying to explain what they are doing and why it is important. After all, what else are we here on earth for but to discover what we are on earth for? Douglas Mawson would have been pleased to see the importance being placed on good science by good scientists, but perhaps disappointed at the way it is slowly being eroded.

The Antarctic Division's chief scientist, Dr John Gunn, later stated publicly that many science projects were being cut because of lack of funding. He said there were many important research projects that could not be undertaken and, despite once being pre-eminent in many fields of research, the Division was slipping backwards at a rate of about 5 per cent a year.

The Australian Antarctic Division acknowledges the difficulty in keeping up with the rising costs of conducting science on and around the icy continent in its *Australian Antarctic Science Strategic Plan 2011–12 to 2020–21*. It states: *… there will always be logistical and budgetary limits on the amount of science that can be supported by the Australian Government in the Southern Ocean and Antarctica, which will vary from time to time in line with government priorities …*

I'm also told that despite the wide diversity of studies underway, the majority of science is moving inevitably towards collecting climate change data. Studying the impact of increased ultraviolet light as a result of the ozone hole, and climate change, on mosses. Studying penguin poo to monitor changes in their food supply that might be related to climate change. Or studying clouds in the far upper atmosphere over the continent.

Anybody who follows science research won't be surprised to know that scientists need to follow the dollar trails to be able to do their work, and they also won't be surprised to know that climate change is a big priority with most governments at the moment. The scientists I talked to are fairly accepting of this, and say it has always been a case of framing the science they wish to do in terms of the current trends.

There are a few International Polar Year (2007–09) projects on the go as well, including the Aliens in Antarctica study, which unfortunately is not looking at UFOs, but rather the impact of introduced species into Antarctica. However, if you search the web long enough you'll find some really bizarre stories about what type of science is really going on down in Antarctica, including an extraterrestrial processing centre near the South Pole, like in the movie *Men in Black*, which is trying to cover itself as an observatory made from a cube of ice a cubic kilometre in size.

This, of course, makes me reconsider the Light Detection and Ranging (LIDAR) device at Davis Station, which projects a green laser beam 80 kilometres up into the sky. Officially, it is providing detailed information on winds, temperature, chemical composition and moisture content of each level of the atmosphere—but, just between you and me, if we wanted to signal aliens and let them know that there was a processing centre at the South Pole, it seems to me that a green laser being shot into space is the extraterrestrial equivalent of a green traffic light.

I try this theory out on Mark, a young electronics engineer at the station who will be overwintering, and he agrees that it's a very feasible theory—though I really must admit that he didn't admit this until he'd drunk at least six glasses of home-brewed beer at the bar.

Another great story I found is of the ancient city buried in the ice under the Russian Vostok Station at the Pole of Inaccessibility, which has been sending out strange magnetic readings. Oddly, most scientists I talked to had not heard of these things. What journals are they reading?

Most scientists, though, are reading the conflicting media accounts of the impact of global climate change on Antarctica. Will the ice caps melt or might they actually increase? Will animal populations be destroyed? Will sea currents change? And just about all of them are adamant that more research into all these areas is needed before any real answers can be given.

Some research will, by its nature, and because of the opportunity or a good penguin story, attract more publicity and perhaps more dollars than others. One such is the study of the impact of global warming on populations of Adélie penguins on the Antarctic Peninsula, a story that has got a lot of world press, billed a little sensationally as the slow destruction of the Adélie penguins.

Because they rely on ice to spread over the ocean to assist them in their feeding during the winter, as well as relying on the ice to recede in the summer to access their breeding grounds, changes to ice formations have a large impact upon the Adélies. The Antarctic

Peninsula in particular has been well-suited to the penguins' breeding, but that is now experiencing some of the most rapid warming and loss of ice on the planet.

Statistics from the US Polar Oceans Research Group show that midwinter temperatures there are now about six degrees higher than they were 50 years ago, which is about five times the global average, and if that rate increases the Adélie penguins there will be extinct within ten years.

Other reports state that the Adélie population on the western Antarctic Peninsula has shrunk by about 80 per cent. The cause of the rapid warming may be due to a warming of seawaters washing along the Peninsula, evidenced in the sea ice melting much earlier each year. The Adélies may adapt by travelling to more southerly parts of Antarctica, of course, and indeed some coastal populations of Adélies to the far south of the Peninsula have been reported to be increasing. Also, those penguins that don't like ice, such as the chinstrap and gentoo penguins, are moving into the areas where the Adélies once lived.

There are two researchers we are due to collect at Mawson Station who are doing studies on Adélie penguin mortality rates. They involve counting penguins and chicks over years and also comparing the extent of sea ice. Over the last five years there has been a lot of sea ice, which has prevented the adult penguins from being able to feed their chicks and mortality rates have been high. But I'm told that since an Adélie penguin can continue 'doing what they do on the Discovery Channel' up to about 20 years of age, it is not having any adverse impact upon populations yet. And one of the success factors in breeding is being an older and wiser penguin and getting a prime nest position in the colony, which is not near the edges nor too close to the centre. Location, location, location! I'm also told that older males have a preference for younger chicks. I had to ask for clarification about whether they were talking about penguins, of course.

The impact of climate change on Adélie penguins near Australian stations may be quite different to that on the Antarctic Peninsula, with problems being caused by excessive ice build-ups—due to more ice moving off the ice shelf because of warmer temperatures—rather than less ice. This of course has the climate change sceptics getting quite excited, pointing at the extra ice with great vigour and displaying the same smug self-righteousness that a man jumping from a tall building uses as he passes the sixth, fifth and fourth floors and shouts, 'See, I told you it was safe!' There is also a paradox being created by the large hole in the ozone over Antarctica, which is protecting the area from warming. But that's one of the things about climate change: its impacts can be quite different in different places. On continental Australia some places are going to get a lot drier, but some are going to get a lot wetter.

For an alternative take on the impact of climate change in Antarctica, the US Antarctic sage Fucked-Up Winterover has written: *To be honest, I haven't a clue as to what is happening with the ice caps these days. The only thing that I'm certain is increasing in size down here is my liver. Something that has definitely not increased in size is our community. Winter has begun and we are now down to about 75 souls on station. Unfortunately, not many of those souls belong to the fairer sex. Therefore enter our friend booze.*

Ah, the indefatigable spirit of human endeavour and the willingness to experiment on oneself in the name of science.

❄ ❄ ❄

I promised to mention the elephant seals—so brace yourself and get your olfactory senses ready to do some rugged imagining. For those of you who might be fortunate enough never to get up close and personal with an elephant seal, let me fill you in on a little bit of necessary background information. You need to know three important things about elephant seals. Firstly, they stink worse than probably any animal on the planet. Secondly, the only thing that stinks worse than an elephant seal is several elephant seals. And, thirdly, if anyone gives you a jar of Vicks to rub under your nose for when you are going to get close to elephant seals, remember to have it in your pocket!

Also, while they may smell terrible, at least they're ugly!

There is an elephant seal wallow lying like an outer suburb of Davis Station and the elephant seals regularly wobble their way across your path heading towards the water next to the station's pier. Watching them move, they make me think of growling and farting and burping beer-gutted old yobbos in sleeping bags who have fallen onto their stomachs and are rolling around on top of each other trying to shout something they are too pissed to say, spraying and spluttering and swearing incoherently, and then suddenly falling asleep, all lolling on top of each other and smelling like the mother of all sewer outlets. If you've ever seen yobbos behaving like this you'll know what I mean, especially if you've been partnered to one of them.

Occasionally two males in the wallow of about 60 or 70 elephant seals will rise up high and throw back their heads and make this sound like a two-stroke outboard motor with moisture in the fuel line. It is like they are seriously trying to out-gargle each other. Then they burp and fart and roll in their own shit and settle back down to sleep, thoroughly content with the world. (Is it a stench of elephant seals? A sloth of elephant seals? A stinkery of elephant seals?) Anja, a young moss researcher on the expedition, said she could still smell the whiff of elephant seal hours later, after walking up close to the wallow to take some photos. I told her that there was a scientific name for that, déjà phew.

When they move, elephant seals make a sudden lurching, wobbling forward movement, perhaps best described as lobbling, which looks like two fat people in a large hessian sack having sex. But after they've gone about 3 or 4 metres they stop for a rest for ten minutes or so before attempting a few more lunges—not unlike two fat people having sex in a sack I guess.

Up close they have really dark and sad seal eyes, but getting close enough to see that is quite a feat. It has been said that few things dead stink as much as an elephant seal alive. And the close-up smell of the elephant seal has been said to send sailors mad and lead to them casting themselves into the sea, or even leading men to attempt to trek to the South Pole, simply because it is so far distant from the smell of elephant seals.

But that's just what they say.

Peter, the station leader, however, says they have rather poor eyesight, as well as an obviously poor sense of smell, as they have been known to try and mate with the large gas cylinders that are lying around the station. And if such a mating really were possible that's a gas you just wouldn't want to ever smell.

❄ ❄ ❄

Later on Saturday Peter tells us that the *Aurora Australis* is back, the barge is repaired and we should head down to the wharf to re-board her. Peter is amazing. He seems to be everywhere at once, walking up and down roads, putting his head into offices and then heading off somewhere else, and always with the information you need to know. Those of us who have been camping out in the common area like in an airport departure lounge awaiting long-overdue flights get to our feet and look around. For most of us this will be the last view we ever have of Davis Station, so we're slow to don our heavy gear and head out the door.

Walking down the road to the wharf, the wind turns so that it blows obligingly over the top of the elephant seal wallow towards us, just so that those who have gone three or more days without a shower don't feel we're really that pongy as 20 of us crowd together onto the barge deck.

It's good to be back on the ship. It's good to have a shower. It's good to have clean clothes on. It's good to be a long, long way from the elephant seals. But I will miss Davis Station. Just describing our four days there as memorable doesn't do it justice. Memory has a way of fading or distorting some things. The memories will always be good, but it's important to know that the minutiae of details, such as the comments in the early log books I browsed through, or the way people smiled there or chatted to you, or just the feeling of standing in the light, falling snow gazing around on the last day. They might all disappear into the fog of the past, yet they are all as worth preserving as the feeling of flying in a helicopter or hiking through the Vestfold Hills.

So I'm sitting at the small desk in my cabin thinking about Mawson's motivation to keep going, which brought him through alive, and how I should use that in the book I'm planning to write. That seems to me a key thing to get right if I'm going to recreate events. Would a modern person have the same iron will and drive to make it against seemingly impossible odds? Surely, if there were a safety net there it would be easier to pull out. I'm going to have to recreate similar circumstances to make this work properly. It's going to have to all go wrong and the Mertz character will need to die rather than be picked up by the support crew. Maybe they get off course or a blizzard comes in and they get separated from the film crew and find they need to really make the return dash on their own. Or maybe they discover they've been set up and the film producers want to see if they can really do it. See if they have the same will to survive by letting them know that they are going to be left to die if they don't.

I mull on that for some time. That's the crucial point to understanding what Mawson did. Trying to find what it was that drove him on and on and on. He's written in his journals and letters that it was several different things. A desire to get as close to the hut as possible before dying so that his journal and records might be found. His desire for Paquita. All his dream and ambitions.

I know that I'm never going to be in the same situation to really put myself to the test and discover what it is that might drive me to go on rather than lie down in the snow and die. My journey of Mawson's journey is quite a different one. It is a journey of the imagination, often undertaken lying down under my doona with my eyes closed.

I don't think he'd be impressed to know that. If I open my eyes and find him sitting there beside me, asking me what I'm doing I'll say, 'Nothing. Just daydreaming.'

And if he doesn't believe me, I'll change the subject and ask him, 'Why did the penguin cross the road?' I'm sure he won't know the answer. To go with the floe.

All at Sea Again

The dense pack had come, and hardly a square foot of space showed amongst the blocks; smaller ones packing in between the larger, until the sea was covered with a continuous armour of ice.

—Douglas Mawson, *The Home of the Blizzard*

With an extra 39 people on board from Davis Station, we suddenly find the ship very small and there are small factions of discontent and grumbling building among some of the round-trippers. There are quite a few younger people among the Davis stationers, who have just come out of what one of them described to me as a very long uni residence party. As soon as they got on the ship they ran around locking cabin doors and putting clingfilm over the toilet seats in some cabins.

A few of the round-trippers were less than impressed and started saying that the A Factor didn't stand for the Antarctic Factor, it stood for the Arsehole Factor. I'd be fairly critical too, except for the fact that I know I used to behave quite a bit like that in my youth.

It's easy to spot those from Davis at mealtimes, as they pile endless fresh vegetables and fruits onto their plates and go back time and time again for more. Although it's fair to say that the food on the stations is pretty good, the food on the ship is spectacular. Brownie, the Pirate King of the Galley, working with Kym and Kyle, spoils us with treats that include mushroom pies, eye-fillet steaks wrapped in bacon, a huge variety of soups and chicken cooked a dozen different and succulent ways, all accompanied by an enormous array of vegetables that he magically manages to keep fresh. Yeah, okay, maybe I should concede and call it a restaurant.

We have two new cabin-mates who are physicists. One is from the Ukraine and one is from Switzerland. I'm considering calling them Ninnisdenko and Mertz. They moved into our cabin with all their gear and there was so little room left that I found I had to go for a long walk around the ship, to give them space to pack some of it away before bedtime.

I'm warned that Ninnisdenko can be a bit odd, but since he only seems to wake up for meals and otherwise sleeps all through the day and then sits up until the very early hours in the cabin playing zombie and maze games on his laptop, with all the lights out, I have no way of finding out.

❄ ❄ ❄

There has also been a lot of talk on board about how close we came to spending the winter at Davis Station. Those who were on the ship at the time say that when the ship dragged its anchor it drifted perilously close to two rocks, just squeezing between them by nothing but good fortune. I, and most everybody else who heard the story, or its embellishments, immediately thought of the *Nella Dan*, the Antarctic Division's re-supply vessel that ran aground at Macquarie Harbour in 1987 and was so badly damaged that it had to be sunk out at sea.

'It would have been a very interesting time,' one of the old hands tells me. 'We might have had a barge that was holed, a ship run aground or holed, and we'd all be hunkering down for the winter at Davis Station and looking for a way to get the expeditioners out of Mawson Station, maybe overland, to join us. It would be a very cozy winter, sleeping in hallways and wherever they could cram us all.'

'Nah, they'd get us a ship,' said one of the other old hands. 'They'd come and get us out before the winter.'

'Only if a ship were available. And if it came too late in the season it couldn't get past the ice and we'd have to fly everybody out to it in a helicopter. It could take days.'

'Better than us all having to stay for the winter.'

And so it goes. But the ship didn't get stuck and the barge was fixed and we are able to go on our happy way—except for those still pissing into clingfilm on their toilet seats.

❄ ❄ ❄

Mawson was safely back at his hut in February 1913, but the ship *Aurora* had steamed out of Commonwealth Bay only hours previously. Fortunately, the men had repaired the wireless mast and they were able to signal that Mawson was safe and request the ship return and collect him. He packed his gear in anticipation of leaving, but the *Aurora* was unable to pick them up due to bad weather and the pressing need to collect Frank Wild and his team from the ice of the Shackleton Ice Shelf before they were stranded there, unprovisioned, for another year.

Mawson and the six men left as a rescue party would have to spend another winter on the ice. It was a great disappointment to him, but all he wrote in his journal was: *12 February. Calm weather—remarkable that we have such calm and only when the ship away.*

In *The Home of the Blizzard* he later wrote: *We still fostered the hope that the vessel's coal-supply would be sufficient for her to return to Adélie land and make an attempt to pick us up. But it was not to be.*

It was to prove a long and difficult year for Mawson, but he was heartened by the fact that they would have wireless contact with the mainland, but it proved frustratingly difficult to send and receive messages, particularly to Paquita. The first telegraphic message he sent to her said: *deeply regret delay only just managed reach hut effects now gone but lost my hair you are free to consider your contract but trust you will not abandon your second hand douglas.*

To which she replied: *deeply thankful you are safe warmest welcome awaiting your hunters return regarding contract same as ever only more so thought always with you all well here months soon pass take things easier this winter speak as often as possible.*

Mawson wrote often in his journal about the frustration of only getting partial messages through the wireless and Paquita became frustrated that she did not receive more messages from him either and that he seemed to put first priority on official telegrams.

❄ ❄ ❄

After reading Douglas and Paquita's letters I always find I'm thinking longingly of Sharon. I know Dougelly might appear and claim that I just say that for the narrative structure, and that I've no real idea what it is like to be in Antarctica missing somebody—but I will defend myself by telling him that if Sharon were here she'd stick large icicles into his suitably shaped body orifices if she heard him say that. Anyway, at times I find I don't want to be with people, I just want to go to the rear rail of the ship and reach out over the ocean towards her. After four weeks I'm passed the novelty of separation, and have become more than over-familiar with sleeping alone in a thin bunk, crowded in a small cabin with three other guys.

So I ring her on the ship's phone inside the small cleaning cupboard, smelling the Sunlight—soap that is. I wait for the satellite link to make a connection and to hear the phone ringing. It will be about 10.30 PM at home I estimate, not too late, and it will be nice to give her a surprise call. She picks up and I say loudly down the line, 'Hey Sweetums!' Her startled shriek is distant and broken by the poor connection and I try and talk to her for some minutes before we are cut off. I try again but the line is no better. It is like she is down a deep tunnel, shouting up to me and the echo and the distance are distorting and stealing her words from me. I try ringing back four times, but each time can only hear a few of her words, and the final time I can't hear her at all. I say, 'I hope you can hear me, but I can't hear you, but just in case you can I want to tell you how much I miss you and how much I love you.' I talk on into that dark distant tunnel for some time, calling endearments into the darkness of silence, and then I say goodbye and hang up.

A frustrating dissatisfied feeling hangs around me for hours afterwards. Douglas might nod and say now I was starting to get the feeling right.

❄ ❄ ❄

The Antarctic Division people tell me that the difficulty in recruiting staff to go down to Antarctica has become so severe that they have gotten email from their personnel area asking if anyone can suggest any good ideas to help recruit suitable people. Over the years the appeal of the place seems to have dropped. Several say that in the old days, maybe 20 years or so ago, people went for the adventure. Then there was a period in the 1990s when people went because the money was good. But now it was getting harder to appeal to qualified people on either of those points. Lloyd, the ship's doctor, said he was rung up and asked if he'd come down again as station doctor as they needed somebody with some experience and he has done eight winters over the years. There are quite a few old greybeards on the ship who among them must represent over a hundred years of experience on the ice. But many of them will be retiring before too long and there is a particular shortage of younger skilled tradespeople, it seems, with complaints that some are too specialised in narrow fields and others lack experience—hence the old-timers are called on time and time again.

For young tradespeople Antarctica is not as distant and exotic as it once used to be and most can get better money at the mines in Western Australia. Doctors, in particular, are hard to recruit. The Division prefers to employ doctors who have experience in remote area medicine, as they are used to handling all manner of diverse medical situations. There is little incentive for doctors to come to Antarctica though, especially for the winter, because it takes them out of their businesses for a year and adds little to career development. It has been suggested that if doctors were able to gain some professional development points or remote medicine qualifications from serving in Antarctica they might find it more attractive.

The overwintering doctor at Casey this year is Heleen, a Dutch doctor who has studied tropical medicines and worked in developing countries. She says she is expecting a quiet year on the station and will complete some studies as a distance student—with the emphasis on distance. She is going to be the only woman there over winter but says she has the men under control. I don't doubt it. She is pretty, yet pretty terse if she needs to be.

Mick, the all-Australian larrikin, has been down to the ice nine times in 12 years. He is one of the 'repeat offenders' who has a special attachment to Antarctica, particularly as he met his wife there. She was one of the scientists at Casey Station one year.

Andrew from the BOM squad, by comparison, has been down to the ice four times. He will be overwintering at Mawson Station this year, and he says that he has a twofold motivation. The extra money he earns as a part of his Antarctic allowance will make a significant difference to his superannuation when he retires in two years, but you can just see that the adventure of it all is as big a drawcard for him. After all, not only is he an avid outdoorsman but, as I previously mentioned, when he drove over the Antarctic Circle on his way up the Wilkins Runway inland from Casey, he jumped out of the Hägglund vehicle and took off all his clothes for a photo by the sign there. You sure as hell don't do that if you're only there for the money.

Perhaps the Division should consider re-running Ernest Shackleton's famous advertisement that supposedly attracted hundreds of applicants: *Men wanted for hazardous journey. Small wages, bitter cold, long months of complete darkness, constant danger, safe return doubtful. Honour and recognition in case of success.*

Unfortunately no one has ever located a copy of this ad, so perhaps it is one of Shackleton's myths that he was occasionally fond of creating.

But when it comes to getting recruits, some people come knocking on the Division's door asking to be given a job in Antarctica. Tom, who has been down at Davis Station for the summer working as a carpenter, told me that he left Darwin and went to Hobart because he wanted to work in Antarctica, and he went to the Antarctic Division's headquarters, sat in their tearoom playing guitar with a sign on his head that said, 'I want to go to Antarctica'. Oddly enough, they didn't give him a job. But the security guard there gave him some good advice, telling him to go and get a tradesman's ticket and then they'd probably employ him.

So he did and they did.

I was talking to one of the two Debbies, Deb the environment officer, and when I told her what Tom had told me she got very excited, telling me the story was legendary in the Division and everybody knew it, and that I had to point him out to her. So I did.

We are very lucky to have so many living legends on the ship with us.

❄ ❄ ❄

'So what's your take on the secret Nazi bases,' I ask Mawson when I look up and see him looming over me in my bunk. He gives me that million mile stare and asks, 'Which secret Nazi bases in particular would that be?'

'You must have heard of them,' I say.

'Of course,' he says. 'I've heard of them. And I've heard of the abominable snowman.'

'But there are all these reports about them.'

'There are reports of abominable snowmen too.'

'No, there are these stories from British soldiers who went to Antarctica just after the war and they found all these tunnels in the ice, and they sent in commando teams to see who was hiding in there, and they could hear all this fighting and only one man got out alive and he was wounded or something and he told how they'd found all these Nazis in there, living in underground bunkers. But they hushed it all up, of course. They say that's the real reason why the Americans went down to the ice in force in the 1950s, in Operation Highjump, to find and wipe out the Nazi bases. They said that they found lots of them and bombed them. They said that Martin Bormann, Hitler's personal secretary, was alive down there.'

Mawson nods his head, urging me to go on.

'And, well, the Americans hushed it all up too and they say that if there are any more Nazis still down there, they'll be in deep freeze by now.'

Mawson sits there a moment and then says, 'Don't you think that the story sounds just a little fanciful?'

And now I start to bristle a little. 'Fanciful?' I ask him. 'What about Bathybia?' I've been saving this one up for the right time. He reddens a little.

'What about it?' he asks, and I can see the defensiveness creeping into his voice.

'Well, you can't tell me that it wasn't just a little fanciful?'

'No more fanciful than Lovecraft's "The Mountains of Madness",' he says.

'But Benicio del Toro is trying to make a movie about that.'

'And are you saying that nobody would make a movie out of Bathybia?'

'I know I wouldn't.'

Now let me digress just a little and explain something. In 1907–08, when Mawson accompanied Shackleton's *Nimrod* expedition, the expeditioners printed the first book in Antarctica. It was titled the *Aurora Australis*—the same name as our ship. And Mawson wrote a story for it called 'Bathybia'. It tells how a group of expeditioners penetrate deep into the interior of Antarctica and find this huge valley with a near-tropical climate, filled with giant insects, like on that island in *King Kong*. And they make a raft and travel along the river through this land, which they call Bathybia, and they fight off all manner of monsters that he describes as giant mites and water bears, until the river takes them right into the very deep centre of this strange land. They live off the local vegetation and right near the end they climb a huge snow-bound mountain and find a strange cylindrical beast buried in the snow. They dig it out and then go to bed pondering how the hell they are going to return to their base, but the beast thaws out and attacks them, and then, in Mawson's own words … *Our comrade was frantically struggling with his specimen, and into the melee we threw ourselves. The din grew louder and slowly but surely, out of the confusion rose a voice, which smote clear upon me. 'Rise and shine you sleepers, 8-45, time for down table!' There in the passage was the horrid figure of the night-watchman replacing our washing-up bowl, which had just served him as a breakfast gong.*

Yes, you guessed it, he suddenly wakes up and discovers it was all a dream.

H P Lovecraft's story 'The Mountains of Madness' has some similarities in that is a story of an Antarctic expedition that discovers the remains of winged creatures and a large abandoned city at the top of a mountain range, and slowly works out that the strange slave creatures that were engineered by the advanced winged creatures have survived their creators and are still alive in the dark recesses below the city. Like many of Lovecraft's stories, it's about something nasty and frightening down a deep dark hole. I'm not sure what Freud might have made of this obsession, or whether he had any vagina fears, but I digress within my digression.

'Do you know what I tell writing students when I'm instructing them about the basic do and don'ts?' I ask him.

He shakes his head. Of course he shakes his head. How would he be expected to know? But I've been saving this up too.

'I tell them that if they ever end a story with "and then I woke up and found it was all a dream", I'm going to fail them.'

He just stands there for some time, looming over me and I ask him, 'Did you see that in the movie *The Thing*, how the alien can assume the shape of people and mimic them?'

And Mawson says, 'That might go a long way to explaining Jeffryes' abominable behaviour.'

'I thought you didn't believe in the abominable snowman?' I ask him.

'I didn't say I didn't believe in it,' he says. 'I said it was fanciful.'

'Like giant mites and water bears living in a tropical jungle in a valley in Antarctica?'

He deems not to answer.

Mawson Station

Never was landing so hampered by adverse conditions, and yet, thanks to the assiduous application of all, a great assortment of materials was safely embarked.

—Douglas Mawson, *The Home of the Blizzard*

We are lucky to be reaching Mawson Station last on our trip as it is particularly scenic, often being described as the station that most feels like Antarctica, with the ice and mountains literally starting at the back door, as well as having a lot of heritage. For many people it is clearly their emotional favourite. But it is going to prove memorable to us for other reasons.

Nicki sits us all down for a pre-Mawson Station briefing and lays it on the line. 'This is where things are going to get interesting,' she tells us. If I said Davis Station was where things got interesting, then Mawson is going to be really, *really* interesting, and this is where everyone's professional skills are going to be put the test. A large iceberg is wedged across part of the mouth of Mawson's Horseshoe Harbour, strong winds—those ferocious Antarctic gales known as 'katabatic winds'—are forecast and the station has not had a re-supply in two years, so getting the job done is going to be both necessary and difficult.

'Otherwise,' as she tells us, 'worst case is we could have 15 extra people on board coming back with us.'

It is really that serious. If we are unable to re-supply Mawson Station it will not have enough fuel to stay operational this winter. Mawson has one of the best natural harbours in Antarctica, and normally the ship could anchor within 100 metres of the shore, but because of that iceberg blocking the harbour mouth we're going to anchor over a kilometre away and try and get the fuel hoses and barges operating though the gap between the iceberg and the west arm of the harbour. If the winds pick up over 30 knots though, which is highly likely at this time of year, the barges can't operate and the ship will move out to sea so as not to risk damage on the nearby rocks.

We can see the offending iceberg on the webcam that the station has set up. The most pessimistic reckon we won't be able to complete the re-supply and will have to consider closing Mawson for the winter. The optimists reckon that the iceberg will drift off to block some other harbour before we get there. If we aren't able to manage the re-supply it will be a big disappointment for many, not just those like Gary and Robyn who hope to be studying the emperor penguins over winter, but it will break Mawson Station's record of being the longest continually staffed station in Antarctica—and that's a record that many feel particularly proud of and would like to retain.

I asked one of the ship's crew if that would put any extra pressure on them to get through the ice or to take extra risks to get in, and he said, 'No. If it's not safe, it's not safe.'

Nicki has said, 'Wild theories on how to move the iceberg lodged in Horseshoe Harbour at Mawson are still being passed around the ship. Rest assured that there will be no use of explosives, no secret missions to attach tow lines and drag it away and the ship will not ram it to pieces—just to mention a few of the rumours. The most likely solution is as simple as parking the ship farther out and running a longer fuel hose to the station.'

Added to that there is a thick build up of ice around the coast, and the ice is layered, which means it is the result of several years build up and is very strong. If we don't find an easy way in we will have a conundrum. We can get through it by really pouring on the power and crunching our way through it, but we might use up all the fuel intended for Mawson Station in doing it, so we'd arrive there with not enough fuel to re-supply them for the winter.

Nicki is as cheerful and confident as ever in telling us all this, but you can tell that it's a worrying combination of problems to manage. That A Factor again.

✳ ✳ ✳

I'm thinking that the vocabulary of Antarctica is an odd one that is probably quite confusing to people who are not used to it. Many of the words sound like they might be something else. For instance, neve, which is compacted snow on top of ice, sounds more like it is a naive upper-class twit. A nunatak—a mountain peak that sticks up through the ice—sounds like a growth on a dog's leg. Moraine—an accumulation of rocks dumped by a glacier—sounds more like a bad headache from eating ice-cream too fast. Katabatic—fierce Antarctic winds—sounds to me like a type of Balinese cloth design. Scree—loose rocks covering a slope—is the sound of fingernails scraping across a blackboard. Mukluks—reindeer-skin boots—is a horrible mess in the kitchen caused by teenagers who have come into money easily. And a megaberg is a large suburb. Melon hut is a hat for an unusually large head. Slushy is an elderly alcoholic woman. Hägglund is a province in Sweden. Skua is a seafood kebab. Blue ice is a yuppie drug. And crampons is a form of mild toxic shock syndrome. And sastrugi is Russian for what the fuck was that bump that caused me to bang my head on the roof of the Hägglund and get mild concussion (trust me on this one—it happened to me and everyone cried, 'Sastrugi!').

❉ ❉ ❉

After dinner we are at the edge of the ice that is surrounding Mawson. A sheer long shelf of ice stretches east-west as far as we can see, stark against the dark ocean water. And in the distance behind it we can see the dark, ice-free peaks of the mountains behind Mawson Station, sticking out of the clouds like floating islands. It is truly awesome.

The ship tries the ice in several places and cruises up and down looking for a lead in through it, but by nightfall we still haven't found a way in. The wind has picked up now and the snow blowing off the edge of the ice sheet across the dark water makes me shiver just to watch it. 'Now this is Antarctica,' we keep saying on the bridge, where a crowd has gathered, looking longingly at the continent in the distance. 'Really, *really* Antarctica.'

Standing at the ship's rail, trying to capture the howl of the wind and the rush of the snow blowing across the ice as a moving image is enticing. But no matter how good a video camera each of those who venture out into the wind has, they look disappointed when they replay it. Nothing looks as spectacular as the ice in real life. For some things down here you just need to concentrate on experiencing them. Stand there in the chill wind and feel it on your skin and in your watering eyes and try and hold it in your memory.

❄ ❄ ❄

Getting through the ice is proving difficult. After 24 hours we've gone less than four nautical miles and still have 12 nautical miles of solid ice to break. The ship, doing what it does best, rams the ice, rides up on it and then settles slowly down with its weight cracking it apart, then we slowly reverse and run at the ice again. Each thrust takes ten minutes or so and we advance maybe 30 metres. Do the sums. That's less than 200 metres an hour—about the speed of an elephant seal lobbling along.

Nicki tells us that overnight we only covered one nautical mile and it will take about 60 hours to reach Mawson Station at that rate. Trying to sleep is difficult and it feels like we're in a freight train crashing into an ice-block factory repeatedly.

Through the next day our progress slowly increases but by sunset, and a very spectacular sunset that has most everyone with a camera crowding onto the side decks to see if it is possible to take too many photos of a sunset, we still have about eight nautical miles of ice to break our way through. We can see the lights of Mawson Station now and are taking bets on whether we will be there in the morning or the next afternoon.

In the twilight I go up to the bow of the ship and lean over. Up close the ice is a huge expanse of low shadows and light snow drifts against a icy-white metal surface. Pushing on top of a length of ice and coming to a standstill, the ship reverses about 200 metres and then pours on the power. Advancing up the channel it has just opened, it seems to launch onto the new ice and slide across it with a crunching and cracking. It is stupendous to feel the lift in the ship as it mounts the metre-thick ice and see the way huge cracks form as the weight of the ship breaks it. The dim twilight and the sound of the cracking across the vast expanse of soft-lit ice are also something no camera could ever catch. This portable high technology that we invest so much trust in to capture images and memories just seems so inadequate now.

Gordon, our new doctor who has joined the ship at Davis Station in exchange for Lloyd, joins me and we watch the ship break its way forwards, 100 metres or so at a time.

'There are times when you just need to put your camera down and watch,' I say, feeling another one of those Antarctic moments coming upon me. Gordon, whose probably had his fair share of Antarctic moments, just nods his head in agreement.

❋ ❋ ❋

And then suddenly, there we are. We wake up in the morning and we are sitting outside Horseshoe Harbour, looking at that pesky iceberg and taking in the wonder of the continent yet again. Waking up to see a station outside the window is like waking up on Christmas Day. Small coloured buildings look like toys or presents, sitting there among the rock and the snow.

We are fitted out with immersion survival suits and taken up to the helideck and flown the few hundred metres to the station. Soon we are standing on the continent again. It feels just as exciting. This rock. This ice. This land. This Antarctica. The first thing we notice is that Mawson is cold. Really cold. About minus 10 degrees, but with a minus 25 windchill factor.

We are not on the station long, but long enough to do a little bit of poking around, getting the layout of the living quarters, seeing the husky museum and bar and library, and then we're squeezing into a Hägglund and are driving up the icy plateau outside the back door of the station. The caterpillar tracks slip and slide a little on the ice as we climb, but we continue up, up, up, and are soon on the blue ice of the continent, bumping and shaking over the continual uneven surface. Dark jagged mountains lift up out of the ice around us, looking like rock icebergs that are floating in the ice.

It takes about an hour to reach Hendo's Hut at the foot of Mount

Henderson, which is another shipping-container hut, but very tiny and icebound. It is a bargain-basement hut, but it has a multimillion-dollar view that stretches back down the mountainside, across a glacier and crevasse and frozen lake, and then right across the broad white icy plateau down to the ocean and Mawson Station.

I thought I had been in Antarctica proper when we'd driven over the ice and snow at Casey Station and I thought I had been in the Antarctic proper when we saw the sun set over the Vestfold Hills near Davis Station, or walked around the penguin rookery on Shirley Island, or crunched our way through thick sea ice on the good ship *Aurora Australis*. But when we got up on the plateau inland from Mawson Station it felt like everything we'd experienced to date was Antarctica with L-plates. It is more awesome than awesome and really makes me think I'm starting to run low on suitable adjectives.

Even if we get stuck here by the weather, just sitting by the window for a few days would be more than fine.

Hendo's Hut is a strange design. It is only about 2.5 metres by 4.5 metres and the air vents are such that they seem to let all the cold air gush in and let the hot air from the heater gush straight out. As a result the hut never seems to get above zero degrees, but it is a lot warmer in than out. The wind is picking up and up and up and we watch the fog come in and obscure our view. Sitting in the hut, I have cold toes even inside two pairs of thick socks and my felt bootliners.

Being quietly hut-bound with Vonna is, of course, impossible, so we start inventing games and things to pass the time. First we create the real estate ad for Hendo's Hut: Rustic living. Sleeps four. Great ocean views. No noisy neighbours. Frosted glass fitted throughout.

All-weather verandah. Close to nature. Environmentally friendly airconditioning. External ensuite toilet.

Going to the toilet is quite a challenge, not just the 'crap and wrap' logistics, but the sheer effort of battling the wind and cold to go and expose your privates over a frozen toilet bucket. We start debating what the temperature might be outside, as there is no thermometer here. I reckon it is at least minus ten, but Nick goes to the toilet and comes back and says he feels it is only minus seven. I ask, 'What did you measure that with? Shrinkage?'

He says, 'I don't have a scale to compare it with. Perhaps they should put something like that in the Field Manual.'

❄ ❄ ❄

Mawson Station was established in February 1954 by the legendary Phil Law in an area charted and claimed by Mawson on his 1931 voyage. The exact site was chosen from photographs the Americans had taken during Operation Highjump in 1946–47. That first winter ten men stayed and built the first quarters there. By 1966 there were more than 50 buildings and the current station retains a mix of the new and old.

Interestingly, that 1954 voyage was also confounded by ice. The ship had to stop many kilometres out at sea and the expeditioners drove across the sea ice in the old tracked vehicles known as weasels to reach the shore and start building the station.

The logs of the station record the event well: *5 February 1954. Offloading at the ship commenced at 0600 … When the two weasels were unloaded I ran one back to the edge of open water and found the ice solid enough … All proceeded well until 9.5 miles where a large open lead (4 yards wide) was encountered. Unfortunately, just prior to this, we lost the aircraft co-operation whilst it was refueling. As we were unable to bridge this lead we had to follow it until it narrowed. We chose to turn left as there was a large grounded berg about half a mile away and we hoped to be able to cross on the drift in its lee … The floe used as a pontoon took the passage of the first weasel but due to lack of experience, the driver of the second weasel dropped off the end of the bridge too hard and broke the floe. It was doubtful whether the floe would stand a second passage by the weasels.*

Dave, one of the old-timers on the ship, gave a presentation just before reaching Mawson on the weasels, demonstrating his devotion to them in spite of all the evidence—reinforced by Bill's memories of the early 1960s—that they were cantankerous vehicles and broke down repeatedly. Dave showed us pictures of the original three weasels going over the sea ice into the area soon to become Mawson Station in 1954. I notice that many of the expeditioners on the ship have a greater affinity with the early ANARE days than they do with the heroic era of Mawson and can't get enough of these types of talks— they love the sentiment of how things were done in the old days, when you didn't ring up Central Office and ask what to do, you just went ahead and did it.

Dave showed us the evolution of the weasel from a World War II vehicle, how Australia acquired them, and the difficulty he had in obtaining parts for the weasel he has restored at the Division's Central Office. He has even spent two years unsuccessfully trying to locate a lost weasel in Antarctica, and is now pretty sure he knows where it might be, and is also pretty sure that he won't get any more funding to search for it.

He laments the fact that people don't get as excited about the weasels as he does. 'It's a pity that people don't recognise the heritage value of them,' he says. 'They should, but they just don't.'

Many of the talks given demonstrate what I've observed on the ship: that if you want to get an easy laugh, make a joke about Central Office. It is a tradition that dates back to the very earliest days when the toilets at Mawson Station were known as the Law Hut. It's not unique to the Antarctic Division, of course, but I suspect that Central Office is greatly misunderstood and actually has a very commendable sense of humour and flair for double entendres unexpected in a modern bureaucracy. A copy of the Division's recent change management workshop was stuck up on the whiteboard in the mess—sorry restaurant—for anyone to read and the opening sessions were entitled 'Opening the space and introducing the tools'.

Intentional or not, old-fashioned schoolboy-humour comedians like Benny Hill would have been proud of them.

❆ ❆ ❆

Walking around outside in the wind up on the plateau I really get to feel what it must have been like living in the home of the blizzard. The katabatic winds are so strong that they make it hard to balance as I walk. And they are so cold that any bit of exposed flesh stings. I have my goggles carefully pressed tight over my balaclava and beanie, but they fog up after every second step. 'They can put a man on the moon, but they can't make goggles that don't fog up,' I moan. But when I take them off to wipe away the condensation it has already frozen to ice. And the wind makes my eyes water which freezes and sticks my eyelashes together.

Back in the hut it takes hours before we warm up. And the bottles of water that we have left on the floor freeze while we're eating dinner. It is a two pairs of gloves and three pairs of socks cold. It is colder than those walk-in freezers that some butchers have. It is colder than the worst winter night in Canberra. It is colder than chopping ice out of your freezer with bare hands. It is colder than carrying a bag of party ice a long distance. It is colder than a debt collector's smile. It is colder than Ivan Milat's heart. But it is warm inside our down sleeping bags with flannel liners and the chill on my exposed face freezes a smile there.

As it slowly gets dark outside, at about 10.30 PM, the darkness of the mountains and the lightness of the snow slowly merge together into one.

The next morning is 1 March, which is the first day of autumn in Antarctica, and it feels the temperature has dropped even lower as a result. But it is a very special day for me. We dress up in our double socks and lots and lots of thermals and pants and fleecy tops and freezer suits and balaclavas and beanies and step out into the bright sunshine. We are going to be picked up by helicopter today and taken to a new hut and we need to check the wind strength.

We walk around the corner of the ridge that shields us from the worst of the wind and the force of it nearly knocks us over and it cuts through everything we are wearing. We turn around and walk down the mountain instead, sheltered a little from the wind. But coming back up is incredibly difficult with the wind blowing at us. And as the path gets steeper and steeper, I'm huffing and puffing like those guys in the Mount Everest documentary that the dickheaded guy had been screening on the ship. I count each step and try to get to 100 before I stop for a rest. One—uh—uh—uh, two—uh—uh—uh, three—uh—uh—uh. The wind blows flurries of ice at us. Thousands of tiny ice bullets that sting and sneak into my goggles. I stumble a little. Goggles up. Zing-ping-kating go the tiny ice bullets on my face. Goggles down. Eleven—uh—uh—uh. Twelve—uh—uh—uh. Thirteen—uh—uh—uh.

When we finally reach the hut and pile inside there is steam coming off our heads and out of our clothes.

'Goddamn,' I say, 'If Mawson had to struggle through this every day I have a new admiration for him. Or perhaps sympathy.'

And, of course, looking back down the slope we have just climbed up, below the hut, it now seems such a little way. 'Everybody knows that distances in Antarctica can be deceptive,' I say.

The choppers come and get us at 3 PM and they say we have to go out to the plateau to meet them. It's just over 100 metres away, but it means we have to cross the ridge between the mountains to get there and the wind is funnelled into that gap like an industrial wind tunnel. Walking out, with the weight of my pack and water container, I can just make headway against it, but then I have to go back and get our poo- and piss-buckets and our rubbish. I stick the rubbish bag inside my freezer suit, making me look like the Michelin Man on his way to Jenny Craig's, and then try and walk back through the wind tunnel.

Without the extra weight of my pack I have trouble putting one foot in front of the other. I am starting to get tired and have to really fight not to lose the buckets. If they blow out of my hands they will certainly bust open on the rocks and hard ice and not only will I be an environmental vandal, but there will be a long line of frozen piss stretching all the way back to Mawson Station many kilometres away. And the frozen turds would be collected by geologists for years to come, wondering what rare rock they'd found until they took it back to their base and it thawed out.

If it gusts as I'm taking a step forward, I can't get my foot down and am blown backwards. I have to think to myself that I'm Mawson and I can do this. I bend into the wind further, hanging on tighter to the buckets, which by the force of the wind are back behind my body, my arms stretched back like I'm towing something. I shout at the raging wind. Aaaaaarrrrggghh! And slowly I make my way past the worst of it.

Then the choppers are there and we are climbing aboard. Leigh, the pilot of the helicopter I'm in, says they are recording gusts of 75 kilometres per hour. God knows what they were in that gap in the ridge then.

Then we're up in the air, feeling the buffeting a little, but climbing up, up, up. Then we are effortlessly gliding over the sudden vastness of the plateau below us. It is almost too much for my brain and eyes to take it all in at once. We are as high as the tall dark mountains. We can see crevasses and contour lines running across the ice field. We can see wind scours around the base of mountains where the ice has been worn back into smooth curved walls. We can see what is just below us and we can see what is far away. We can see the ocean and we can see the ice horizon of the interior. We can see smooth ice and we can see crazy random patterns in it. We can see frozen lakes and we can see snow drifts. We can see dark nunataks and ruptures in the ice. We can see sudden blue ice lines that run in parallel across the plateau. We can see pressure ridges and we can see strange shapes that we can't even name. We can see it all but I have to keep staring and staring and staring to comprehend what I'm seeing.

It truly puts the awe into awesome.

We fly over the top of a crashed Russian plane that looks for all the world like a small Airfix plastic model plane that has been stepped on. Then we are circling around a huge natural amphitheatre in the rock that is Fang Peak. What a great name for a mountain.

Fang Hut is a huge improvement on Hendo's Hut. It is also small, but is built like it was designed by Ikea, with a table that folds up and down and nicely fitting bunks and the heater not directly under the vent. We settle in and melt ice for water and make a cup of tea and walk around and around the hut, admiring the mountains that surround it closely on three sides.

In the afternoon I climb one of the smaller mountains around the hut, even though Vonna says it is a hill, between Fang Peak and Mount Parsons. It is a slow climb up loose brown rocks that slip under my boots, but it is not too hard going. I climb up onto the saddle alongside Fang Peak and the weather is so calm and clear now that I decide to keep going and do a dash to the summit of this smaller mountain. With no sherpas or camera crew to carry my gear or ego, in fact with no gear at all to carry, I trudge slowly upwards.

Of course the peak is always just over the next rise, but finally I'm standing up on this pile of loose shale rocks at the summit. I can see all the way back to the ocean, and all the way back to the mountains where Hendo's Hut was. I can see the iceberg-filled ocean in the distance and mountain-filled plateaux all around me. What a feeling! It puts the marvel into marvellous and puts the spectacle in spectacular.

I sit there, feeling on top of the very world, ignoring the two taller peaks about me, and then finally start the slow walk back down, sliding the last bit of the descent on my stomach on the ice, which puts the fun into funtastic.

I check on our map and discover that the mountain I just climbed has no name. So, considering this is my birthday, which is the reason this is a very special day for me, I decide to name it. It is now Mount Craig in Antarctica, next to Fang Peak. And in case you're ever in Antarctica, Mount Craig can be found at 67°47'8"S and 62°34'0"E. Yeah, I know that surveyors aren't allowed to name mountains after themselves and I know that there's some committee somewhere that has to officiate on and approve the names of Antarctic landmarks, but just in case they were the ones who named the Executive Committee Ranges, I'm not going to risk it. This will just be between me and you and the rest of the world.

I look on the map and estimate that it is 932 metres high. Then I start to wonder if it needs to be above 1000 metres to be a mountain?

I'm sure there's some rule about that somewhere. Maybe it should be Craig's Peak? Or Craig's Knob?

(Note to self. Do not ask anybody on the station if they'd like a jolly to Mount Craig, nor if they like to climb Craig's Knob.)

We are amazed at how heavy our piss-bucket is becoming. It is nearly half full after only two days. So I decide, in the interests of science, to do some rough sums. I estimate that if we stayed in the field for a year we would fill a piss container of about 3650 litres. And a station of about 20 people would accumulate about 18,250 litres a year, which is just over one shipping container full of piss. And as there are about a thousand people living in Antarctica each winter, they must accumulate about a million litres of piss, or about 50 shipping containers full. Yet when I announce my findings to everyone in the hut they only ask me why I've spent half an hour figuring that out—of course, I don't have a really good answer. But it makes me wonder again just how those early explorers must have driven each other crazy being in close confines for so long. Ranulph Fiennes writes in his books on trekking across Antarctica how small traits in a good friend can nag at you until you hate it, or them. How did Mawson cope in his close confines for so long? I find that after a few days in cabins together we are all finding traits in the others that drive each of us crazy. One of us tells too many lame jokes. One of us says, 'Let's get going!' and then spends half an hour sitting around while everybody else gets packed. One of us seems never to hear things that are said and always has to be told two or three times. One of us has rather average map-reading skills but thinks they are very good. One of us just can't understand why the others don't think of things just the way he or she does. One of us thinks that sitting and contemplating the ice, rather than running around and jumping on it and climbing on it, is wasting opportunity and time. One of us lets one in the party get away with saying things that the other two can't get away with saying. One of us—each of us—has some trait that clearly annoys at least one other person in the group. Over a few days it is very clear how maddening it must be over a whole year.

During Mawson's second winter in Antarctica he was tormented by madness as much as he had been tormented by the blizzards in his first year, although the madness was not just his. In his journal of the first year he repeatedly comments on the weather and how it affected everyone. In his second year he repeatedly comments on the wireless operator, Sidney Jeffryes, and how he affected everyone.

Mawson had already rejected an application from Jeffryes to join the expedition, and that decision proved to a better one than was made by Captain Davis and others who later accepted him. Jeffryes started out the year fine, but began to deteriorate mentally as the darkness set in, causing all the men in the hut deep concerns. In his journal Mawson chronicles in great detail Jeffryes' erratic behaviours, including repeatedly neglecting his wireless monitoring work and believing he had been insulted by others and wishing to fight them.

Mawson started off with mild comments, such as on 7 July 1913: *I think that his touchy temperament is being very hard tested with the bad weather and indoor life. A case of polar depression. I trust it will go away now.*

But by 11 August he was writing: *No sane man could surely act like he does.*

Jeffryes was by now claiming that he knew the others were plotting to murder him and that the doctor was analysing his urine in secret and he began taking the crystal out of the wireless set when he wasn't using it. The key problem for Mawson was that Jeffryes was their only skilled morse operator.

Things came to a head in early September when Jeffryes was caught sending a message to the relay station on Macquarie Island, stating that the other five men had gone insane. Jeffryes stated that Mawson had him under a hypnotic spell and the other four were plotting to murder him.

By the end of the year, with the return of spring and the wildlife as well, Jeffryes showed considerable signs of improvement but it did not save him from being committed to an asylum for life upon his return to Australia.

I can't help but wonder if Mawson recalled the account of the madness that stalked the *Belgica* that he had read in Frederick Cook's account during the previous winter. If so, he makes no mention of what he thought of it in his notes. But he does talk about his own state of mind, and there is a very interesting quote of Mawson's that I have read a few times: that he felt he was going mad from too much writing. For some time I considered beginning my book with the quote, but then found it was actually a misquote. It has been recorded in books such as Lennard Bickel's *Mawson's Will* as: *I find my nerves in a serious state. From the feeling I have in the base of my skull I am suspicious I may be off my rocker soon! My nerves have evidently had a great shock—maybe too much writing has brought this on. I must rest more.*

But what he wrote in his journal, as edited by Fred and Eleanor Jacka, was: *I find my nerves in a very serious state, and from the feeling I have in the base of my head I [have] suspicion that I may go off my rocker very soon. My nerves have evidently had a very great shock. Too much writing today brought this on. I shall take more exercise and less study, hoping for a beneficial turn.*

It is interesting to know that many famous historical quotes don't always stand up to scrutiny, but that's how history and the recording of history often goes. My interpretation of events and stories on this voyage will undoubtedly disagree with the interpretations of others who were on the ship with me. This shouldn't be a surprise though. History has always been such. When Ned Kelly was hanged, for instance, one newspaper reporter in attendance recorded his last words as, 'Ah well, it has come to this.' Another reporter, however, recorded them as, 'Such is life.'

Ah well, such is the life of the writing of history or recording of events.

❄ ❄ ❄

The Subversive Antarctic Historical Society had a meeting at which they talked about the psych test that overwinterers have to do. They all seem to have a story about it. It is described to me as the same questions asked ten different ways. But, I'm told, the very last ten questions are different again, and have been known to include such questions as, 'When you walk past dark places do you hear voices telling you to do evil things?'

'You've got to be kidding!' I said.

'Nope,' I was told, and what's more people are said to have ticked that box in the past.

'What happened to them?'

'We are told they were referred to specialist advice.'

Two of the expeditioners on the ship told me that they had failed their last psych tests and were only permitted to go down for summer stays. I wonder if that means they ticked the box about the voices from the dark places and it has been decided not to let them be there when it gets dark in the winter. Another guy, one of the electricians, told me that when he did his first psych test, many years back, he was asked what he thought of having women in Antarctica. He told the psychologist that he thought it was a good idea. He watched the man write something in his notes and smile like he'd given him the right answer, and then he added, 'But they should issue one to everyone.'

Usually if a ship is bringing back overwinterers there will be an army psychologist on board to work with those coming back, but our voyage is classed as a re-supply voyage only, so there is no psychologist, regardless of the fact that we actually will be picking up several overwinterers. I asked for an explanation of the logic of it and was told not to look for logic in it.

Now that's a little crazy.

❄ ❄ ❄

We wake up to an amazingly sunny Sunday under Fang Peak and we hop into the Hägglund that the last party we had swapped over with at the hut had left us when they flew out in the helicopter. We drive across the plateau to Rumdoodle Hut, nestled under Rumdoodle Peak, about 8 kilometres away, following the cane line across the ice. The cane line is, as the name suggests, a line marked out by tall bamboo cane markers with tins on them. Usually beer tins. In clear light you can follow the cane markers and if the weather is crap and the GPS isn't working you can use a radar in the Hägglund to find the beer tins on the cane sticks.

Out on the plateau the surface is rock-hard ice, but not flat. It is rough and uneven, and looks like the surface of a wind-rippled pond that suddenly froze. The weather today is absolutely magical and we all need to don our sunglasses to block out the glare. We reach Rumdoodle Hut quickly enough and are gobsmacked. It is gorgeous. It is wonderful. It puts the other huts to shame. We unpack and Nick and Vonna go off to jump on rocks and climb up and down mountains, but Lynette and I sit on the verandah of the small hut looking over the ice, contemplating that frozen landscape before us. There is absolutely no wind. It is the first day in Antarctica that has ever been so still and so silent. The sky is the most blue blue a sky could ever be. It could easily be a beach scene there before us with the white, white sands at our feet and the clear sparkling blue ocean running out over the horizon, with dark islands lifting up in places.

It is such a beautiful sight and as soothing as any tropical beach I've ever sat on. But it is so silent. So still. So perfect. The only movement is the slow glide of the sun and the even slower drift of the ice. But we are reminded it is Antarctica when Lynette picks up her cup of tea, which she had put down a few moments before, and tugs at the tea bag, pulling out the contents in a frozen cup-shaped block.

It is not always so idyllic here, of course. On the cliff face behind us we find the remains of an earlier cabin that winds had dashed against the rocks. We find wood scraps, a hinged block of wood and an old saucepan. Huge boulders have rolled down off the cliffs above us and the ice is slowly carrying them away to the sea as it moves off the plateau at rate of a few centimetres each year. The boulders stand out on the ice like the Twelve Apostles off the coast of southern Victoria.

And Lynette starts telling me about Syd Kirkby, whose biography she is writing. She has an enormous admiration for him. For his achievements as an Antarctic surveyor, exploring and surveying more of Australia's Antarctic Territory than anybody else. His larrikin spirit. His will to overcome adversities. It's a different Lynette than I've encountered before, this willingness to open up and share thoughts from her work with me. We're all conscious, I think, that our time on the continent is coming to an end soon and we are starting to be more reflective about what we've seen and thought.

She also tells me the most amazing story about Mount Rumdoodle. Syd named it as a sort of joke. There was this book from 1956 entitled *The Ascent of Rum Doodle*, by W E Bowman, which tells the farcical account of a group of Englishman who attempt to scale the mighty Mount Rum Doodle, 40,000½ feet (over 12,000 metres) high in the country of Yogistan, accompanied by 3000 porters. The book was a favourite of early Antarcticans and mountain climbers and I have even heard it suggested that each station leader should have a copy so as not to emulate the behaviours in the book, which ends up with the hapless mountaineers climbing the wrong mountain.

'It was one of his favourite books,' she tells me.

And then I share with her what I think. Sitting there, on this most perfect of perfect days, I say that the view out of the large glass window at Rumdoodle Hut is only equalled by the view out of the window at Dylan Thomas's cottage in southern Wales, looking over the inlet to the sea, the hills and rock paths all around. And I say that it's a pity that Dylan Thomas never spent any time in Antarctica. I'd love to see how he wrote about it. But he didn't, so I decide to try and channel his spirit and rewrite his marvellous opening line from *Under Milkwood*: *To begin at the beginning: It is spring, moonless night in the small town, starless and bible-black, the cobble streets silent and the hunched, courters'-and-rabbits' wood limping invisible down to the sloe black, slow black, crow black fishing boat bobbing sea …*

That's how he did it. This is how I did it: *To begin at the beginning: it is an autumn cloudy night on the vast Antarctic continent, starless but bright, moonless white, the wind moaning and searching across the slow moving, floe white, slow white, so white glacial ice …*

(Note to self: not bad, but don't give up day job.)

Later we go for a walk across the ice and discover that the most fun you can have in Antarctica with your pants on is to climb to the top of a hard-packed snow ridge, walk along the ridge, and then pull out a plastic garbage bag each, sit on them, kick off and go weeeeeeeeeee down the ice slope. Powdered snow and ice flies up from where your boots touch the ground as the ice under the snow bumps like a million-finger massage using fists, as you shoot down the slope at Olympic speeds, only stopping when you hit the really hard ruts of the blue ice lake, where you lie on your back, looking up at that blue, blue sky, feeling the snow and ice chips melting on your face and where they have gone down inside your clothes, and you're laughing and laughing like you are ten years old.

Then you jump to your feet and cry, 'Again! Again!'

And then to top it all off, while lying there at the bottom of the slope after the second even faster descent you see the sun setting slowly behind the mountain or hill I named after myself. Nick takes photos and I tell him he can say that he now has the evidence that the sun shines out of Craig's Knob.

That evening we talk about Sidney Nolan's Antarctic paintings and how well he captured the chaos and the feeling and emotions of Antarctica that the clean-line white-and-blue photos can't capture. A single shot is one thing, a single slice of what Antarctica can be, but it is rarely what it feels like. Capturing the feeling of the weather and the days taken to get to a place and the wind and the feeling of struggling against the cold and snow and then looking at a spectacular formation. A more abstract eye is needed to really, *really* capture the feeling of it.

The obsession of the camera is humbled later that evening, the night of the most perfect day in Antarctica ever, and what will be our last in the ice kingdom of the interior. We will be back on station tomorrow, and then back on the ship, in central heating and electric lights. I wake up at three in the morning. Wide awake. And I wonder why I'm awake. So I crawl across Nick's sleeping bag and look out the window to see what it looks like out there.

'Wake up! Wake up!' I say. 'There's the most amazing aurora out there!' The others shake themselves awake and look through the window. There is huge bright green question mark in the sky, rising up from the north. I press my face closer to the glass. What I see makes me jump off the bunk and grab my freezer suit and gloves.

Outside the aurora stretches from horizon to horizon, this huge spectral cloud that glows and dances, forming and reforming. There was too much of it to see it all at once, and I had to keep turning my head back and forward, watching the white and soft green glow fade away and then form up somewhere else. One moment to the north. Then the south. Gliding away behind Mount Rumdoodle and shining over the peak like a spotlight and then dancing out again, rolling around in circles and then turning back the other way. It was a ballet of light, swimming and gliding and floating and totally entrancing. We stood there until our toes and cheeks froze to the point we couldn't even properly mumble, 'Fan-fucking-tastic!'

And of course even the best camera has no chance of capturing it. We climbed back into our sleeping bags after the spirits of the south had danced away into the darkness, glowing ourselves. 'It was magical.' 'It was spectacular.' 'That was the most amazing aurora I've ever seen.'

And as I fall back to sleep I remember how Mawson had described auroras at a similar time: *13 March. Great display of aurora in evening.*

He was clearly quite a poet himself, but knew not to give up his day job either.

✿ ✿ ✿

And so it was time to return to Mawson Station and get to sit in its Red Shed and walk around the many coloured blocks that make up the different buildings there, and discover why so many people have a soft spot for Mawson (the station, not the man). The first notable thing are the huge twin wind turbines that generate up to 80 per cent of the station's power, depending on the available wind. They cost hundreds of millions of dollars to transport and construct, but the turbines are proving a useful way to help defeat the cost and tyranny of shipping in oil.

One of the largest expenses for the Antarctic Division is the fuel costs, for fuelling a re-supply ship as well as the station. We have needed to provide Mawson with at least 300,000 litres of fuel—you can do the sums yourself to see how much that will cost. In the end, working through half the night, and laying the fuel lines across one arm of the harbour and battling ice on the water, the crew has been able to supply almost 380,000 litres in quite an heroic effort. Those who worked all through the night can be found sleeping all over the station in odd corners, in the library under fiction and non-fiction, in the little museum and on assorted couches. And at lunch they have the red bleary eyes that you'd normally mistake for a drunkard, but it is from the long hours, harsh weather and dedication to get the job done. And thanks to that dedication Mawson Station will continue to keep its record as the longest continually operating station on the continent.

I was told a story about the Italian-French Concordia Station, which is located a long, long way inland from Casey Station, near the

75th parallel. I'm told it is an amazing example of high-technology and conservation. The station recycles almost everything. Waste water is processed to the point it can be drunk and parts of the station close down when they are not in use to minimise energy costs. It is enviable to see just how little energy the station uses and how effectively they can reduce their impact.

Other stations don't have such a good reputation. The Russian stations in particular have become poorly funded, not just to the point where broken machinery is left lying around, but to the point that expeditioners are left lying around too and can't be guaranteed that they will be collected by ship each year. At the Chinese stations, I'm told, the temperature inside their former buildings was kept at about zero degrees, which was considered acceptable, and staff were expected to wear suitable clothing inside as well as outside. That has changed somewhat with their new buildings, but on the Australian stations acceptable inside temperatures allow staff to wear thongs and T-shirts, with a room temperature of about 18 degrees Celsius. Yet for all the costs of running the Australian stations, they still rate fairly well in terms of minimising impacts upon the environment.

Mawson, the man not the station, was by today's standards an environmental vandal, killing the wildlife, leaving rubbish and junk around, crapping in the snow. But that is measuring the past by today's standards and it is as unfair as measuring us by the standards of the future, whatever they may be.

❄ ❄ ❄

Any history of Mawson Station would not be complete without a story about the dogs. Each station has a unique accompanying story that helps define the station's individuality: Casey Station has Wilkes Station, Davis has the pong of elephant seals and Mawson has had the dogs. There are some old-timers who were around when the huskies were still at the stations and they talk of the dog-days like they were another time that we will never understand.

All three Australian mainland stations had dogs, but the last dogs were at Mawson. The dogs were originally from either Greenland or Labrador, well used to the snow, cold and ice. The first dogs were taken to Mawson Station in February 1954 and were put to work pulling sledges as they had for Mawson and other early explorers. People talk and wrote of the early dogs, such as Mukluk and Oscar, as if they were legends from the heroic age.

Mawson devotes considerable space in his journals to the dogs, how they are behaving, who has borne pups and so on, and it is apparent the men fussed over them as if they were personal pets or substitute children. In March of his first year he wrote: *Several families were born at this time, but although we did everything possible for them they all perished, except one; the offspring of Gadget. This puppy was called 'Blizzard'. It was housed for a while in the veranda and, later on, in the Hangar. Needless to say, Blizzard was a great favourite and much in demand as a pet.*

Blizzard became Mawson's favourite dog.

Frank Hurley wrote in great detail in his memoirs of the *Endurance* expedition about the individual personalities of each dog and how traumatic it was for dog-team leaders when the dogs had to be killed and eaten. Nobody wanted to eat from a dog that had been his own to care for.

There are many reports and memoirs written though the 1960s, '70s and '80s that have similar close and affectionate references to the dogs that Australian expeditioners worked with. Those who handled dogs swore by them, saying they were so much more efficient than the primitive weasel tracked vehicles, and if you really got into a fix you could do what Mawson did and eat them.

But with increased technology and the growing need to protect Antarctica's environment, the days of the dogs were numbered. In 1987, the first warning came with a report written by Lyn Goldsworthy of the Antarctic and Southern Ocean Coalition, who visited Antarctica as an observer and submitted a report that stated that the huskie dogs at Mawson Station mauled penguins, polluted the environment, failed to contribute to the morale of people at the station and were an alien species, the presence of which could not be justified.

This triggered a groundswell of support among people who wanted Australia to keep the huskies. Letters were written to politicians and the media and petitions were circulated, and the Australian government did not accept the recommendation of the report to have the dogs removed. But the signing of the Madrid Protocol in 1991 was the end of the fight as it included a clause that specifically prohibited dogs from being in Antarctica. Politically, it was seen as a trade-off by Australia, sacrificing the dogs to obtain agreement on stricter environmental protection overall. At the time only three nations still had dogs: Australia, Argentina and Britain. A lot of effort was made to find a suitable home for the dogs and most went to the Voyageur Outward Bound School in Minnesota, USA, near the Canadian border.

However, a few that were deemed too old to continue as working dogs were left in Antarctica until 1993. Letters from expeditioners and accounts from the time are strikingly moving, with some expeditioners writing farewell letters to their favourite dogs and telling in very emotive words how it felt to lose their faithful animals. The last five dogs were Morrie, Bonza, Welf, Elwood and Ursa, and after arriving back in Australia four of them were featured at an open day at the Antarctic Division, with a thousand people coming to see them.

In fact, depending on your morbidity and anal-retentiveness for definitions, there are several dogs, or remains of them, still on Australian Antarctic Territory. For instance, the frozen remains of one dog, nicknamed Rex, is still on the ice near Mawson's Hut. The head is said to be well preserved as is the neck, but much of the body is bones poking out of frozen mummified skin.

And there is another dog that gets around on Australian stations— the legendary Stay, who features in many group photographs and accounts of modern Antarctic life. Stay is not your average huskie though; he is actually a fibreglass guide dog for the blind donation box that has taken on a new life. He was originally taken to Davis Station in 1991 for publicity and fundraising purposes, and also as a symbolic gesture of protest at the imminent removal from Antarctica of the huskies, but has since become a well-loved mascot for Australian Antarctic staff.

It is a great Antarctic honour to have Stay stay on your station and there is a long-running guerilla war among stations, kidnapping Stay or hiding him to prevent him being kidnapped. The first kidnapping occurred in the 1992–93 summer when Mawson Station expeditioners decided Stay would be better off at their base. But the next year Stay was stolen by Davis staff. In the years since Stay has been to all the Australian stations, including Macquarie Island, and has been hidden in ceiling cavities and in traverse vans on the ice plateau to evade kidnappers. Stay's adventures also include losing a leg in a brawl, taking part in several traverses, and even reportedly one trip to the Arctic. In 2006 some adventuresome Davis Station expeditioners, led by Chris who is on our voyage and looks like Angry Anderson's younger brother, took Stay with them to visit the Russian Progress Station and the Chinese Zhongshan Station, about 360 kilometres away. Being the Chinese Year of the Dog, Stay proved a big hit.

I had great expectations of meeting Stay and perhaps doing an interview with him (or her as some contend) but unfortunately Stay is currently staying at Macquarie Island. Nevertheless, looking through the many station group portraits that feature Stay at each of the bases we visited, it was heartening to know that at least one dog remains standing in Antarctica—as much a symbol of heroic irreverence as a symbol of the days of heroic dog sledging.

❄ ❄ ❄

I've a certain soft spot for dogs and for anyone who loves their dog. I love reading the stories of those who have worked with huskies in Antarctica and I stare in wonder at the two stuffed dogs at Mawson Station, Noogis and Vida, wondering what they were like to run, feed and play with. Those people on the ship who have dogs talk about them fondly and affectionately as if they were describing family members. Vonna, Nicki and Lynette are all convinced they have the cleverist and most individualistic dogs in the world. That's silly, of course, because I have the cleverist and most individualistic dogs.

In her emails, Sharon often tells me that our four dogs are proving very good at keeping her company and she has been busy cooking for them and taking them for walks in the evening. I'm glad she has them there—at nights particularly. It's good to know that dogs have this way of almost knowing if you are feeling down and then coming and sitting with you, or bringing you a wet-chewn toy, or rodent carcass, as if surely playing chasings or fetch will be as much fun for you as it is for them. I have a picture of them above my bunk on the good ship *Aurora Australis*, alongside a picture of my three grown-up kids and one of Sharon.

For there is a certain type of dog happiness that only owners of happy dogs can know. It's the happiness of ruffling them around the head and behind the ears, avoiding their happy searching tongue, and it is the look in their dark eyes when they sit close to you. It's a bond of mutual trust and affection and dog-human bonding that farmers know and some beach fisherman and many bushmen know, and Antarctic expeditioners who have had huskies know.

But, conversely, there's a terrible, terrible sadness and grieving when any person, man, woman or child, loses their dog. I dread the day that any of our four joyful, loveable, exuberant, mischievous dogs dies—and when I read the words of the men who had the huskies taken away from them I can feel the grief in their words, as I can feel the grace in the words of the prayer for the dogs, penned by an expeditioner at Davis Station in 1961. *Look kindly, O Lord, on these thy creatures, for we are utterly dependent on them, and they, like us, are utterly dependent on thee.*

❄ ❄ ❄

Douglas Mawson and Paquita continued to write each other letters that they could not post during the second year apart, counting down the days until they would be together again. Mawson wrote to his fiancée on 15 April 1913: *Time has largely healed my scars and now perhaps I would be more selfish in consideration of yourself. It may have appeared to you in your love, a very sordid matter—the theme of my bald statement—nevertheless I would not have you marry me for consideration of aught but true love and not then if gnarled by any seeming imperfection.*

And she wrote to him on 21 April: *Oh Douglas how I long for you! All these eighteen months have you been constantly in my thoughts as you are for ever in my heart. And now more than ever. I have heard all I could about the hut & your life there & picture myself with you helping—loving you. Oh how I hope my love helped you on that journey that it upheld & supported you as I should have had I been there.*

On 10 June, in the darkness of midwinter, he wrote: *What would I not give now to slip in to you—asleep—and steal the honey from your lips, sweeter than all else—and then perchance dame nature, doing her work well, would have you dream that I was well and happy to the seventh heaven of delight.*

But the time apart was starting to show as well. On 17 August Paquita wrote: *Can a person remain in such cold and lonely regions however beautiful and still love warmly?*

And then on 21 September she wrote: *But this everlasting silence is almost unbearable. I don't want to doubt you dear but I'm afraid of the fascination of the South. All the members say they would go again & here is Shackleton off again. Will a calm life ever satisfy you?*

When her letters were finally delivered to him with the *Aurora's* return to Cape Denison in December 1913, the day after Christmas, their third Christmas apart, he wrote a letter to her answering all her questions, including repeating her question and this response to it: '*You won't go away again will you?*' *No dearest, nothing like this will happen again—rest assured.*

It proved, however, to be a promise that he couldn't keep.

❄ ❄ ❄

After four days up on the plateau out of contact I'm busting to ring Sharon and my kids and to hear their voices again. It's odd that four days feels such a long time. It's a joy of modern Antarctic life that it's possible to get a message to your loved ones from almost anywhere. We got a very crackly message passed on to us via radio wishing me a happy birthday from Sharon while in one of the mountain huts. I'm also busting to check my emails for any messages from her. Four days! Mawson would think me a wuss. But then again I check my email five or six times a day when I'm on the ship on the off-chance that she's sent me something. I also wonder if I'm being as falsely optimistic as Mawson was when I tell her that I'm never going to go away like this again.

Back at Mawson Station after our days up on the plateau it feels like we're at Club Med Antarctica. Showers. Toilets. Central heating. Wonderful food. It is strange to think that just two hours earlier we had been standing in the most amazing wind scour, which is the Antarctic equivalent of Wave Rock in Western Australia. Tourists would drive hundreds of miles to see this if they could. The ice wall has these enormous dark bands in it from rock and dirt that have been picked up in years and decades past. In some places chunks of rock are stuck up in the ice above our heads, getting ready to fall when the wind scours the ice back just a little more. And on the ice all around us are these strange dark blue circles that you can peer through down deep into the ice, like blue glass windows into a subterranean cellar. On the drive back it feels like my head is full and can't fit any more wonder into it.

But there is a further surprise for me at the station. There is a huge cake with a chocolate plaque on it that reads: *Happy Birthday Craig, love Sharon*. Frank, one of our cooks, and one of the nicest guys you're likely to meet in Antarctica, has baked it based on a special recipe that Sharon has sent through. I'm gobsmacked yet again. More so when I'm told they had plans to fly it out to me by helicopter but were too busy with refuelling logistics.

I'm so awed that I don't want to cut the cake and destroy it. To my mind it's Antarctic heritage!

And Mawson Station is the station for heritage, as lots of the earliest buildings are still there, but it is also the location of a controversy over what constitutes heritage. In the early decades of Australian Antarctic settlement, being a very blokey place, it was not uncommon to find pin-ups and soft-core porno-pictures decorating the walls and workshops. However, as more and more women started coming down to Antarctica and challenging the blokey culture there was more pressure to remove these. In the late 1980s and early 1990s in particular there was pressure from those who have been described as 'anti-pornography feminists' armed with sexual harassment legislation.

Initially, public areas were cleared of pin-ups and porno prints, but private areas were considered private for the showing of privates, but one female station leader even banned pin-ups in private quarters. This got a bit of media coverage in Australia at the time, generally being treated as an overreaction. But those who were on ice at the time tell me that a few blokes had insisted on sticking pin-ups in places where they could easily be seen when their doors were opened, to be deliberately provocative.

Porno pin-ups have generally been a part of a culture that modern sensibilities wanted removed, except in one case—the Mawson Station Sistine ceiling—and its desecration in 2005 caused quite a bit of grief and anger among many of the men and women I talked to who had been to the station at some time.

But let me give a little bit of background. At Mawson Station, dating back from the early 1970s, in the old carpenter's hut, the tradesmen had stuck up *Playboy* centrefolds, or girlie pictures to use the language of the time, all over the ceiling of the old carpenters' hut. Over the years a large part of ceiling was covered with neatly taped-up girlie pictures, and it became known as the Sistine ceiling, surviving the 1980s and '90s, when sexual harassment issues were strongest. But in February 2005, the night before the last crew of the year were due to fly out, the Sistine ceiling was destroyed, with all the pictures being torn down and ripped into pieces. The incident both shocked and surprised many, including women I talked to who had found it an historical fascination more than demeaning.

'These were all 1960s and 1970s type pinups,' I was told by one of the women on our ship. 'If you could see a nipple in there anywhere it was a pretty rare thing.'

In fact, when one expeditioner showed me her photos of the ceiling in all its glory there were more than a few nipples on display and even some rare Antarctic beaver, but the tone was fairly subdued, so the tenor of what I was told was true, even if the nipple-count of memory had altered. And I should say, looking at the photos of the pin-ups, I had a memory moment of my own, pretty certain that I recognised a few of them from my teenage years—though I'd be willing to be proven wrong by some archivist.

Of course, there were also pin-ups at other stations. The team dismantling the old British base on Danco Island in 2004 described a 'toilet complete with original *Playboy* pin-ups from the '50s'. And Phil Law once recalled that the Australians were always astonished at the number of nude photos on the walls of the American stations. The Japanese, however, according to Antarctic legends, went one step further, having a lifelike sex doll known as Antarctica, which scientists at the Showa station used 'to keep warm during the long Antarctic winter'.

Two immediate assumptions that had been made too quickly regarding the destruction of the Sistine ceiling, according to people who were there at the time, were that it was a woman who did it and that it was one of those who had just left the station. The argument goes that it could just as easily have been one of the men, and it could also have been one of the people on station, timing the vandalism to the night before the expeditioners flew out to Davis to meet the ship there to make it look like one of those leaving was responsible.

We might never know who had assumed the right to play heritage vandal or moral police for everyone, but the winterers later decided to do their bit for conservation and heritage and spent a considerable time sticking the pictures back together. They are now preserved in this absolutely amazing handcrafted wooden book on station. It is a box made out of different types of wood, with metal-worked letters on the cover that state 'The Heritage Girls of Mawson'. The box is bound with brass clasps and a craftsman has spent a lot of time on it to make something so beautiful

Inside are almost a hundred *Playboy* centrefolds, ranging from the early 1970s through the 1980s, each carefully restored, stuck down on tissue paper or paper, some sealed with contact. If they were laid out, if you know what I mean, you could probably get a full chronology of *Playboy* Pets of the Month for near two decades. And I can imagine everyone on the station sitting around a large table with all the pieces spread out before them, like a giant jigsaw puzzle, holding up nipples and lips and thighs and trying them out on different pictures, trying to get the right part on the right body.

And then I'm thinking we should form a foundation to raise money to restore the ceiling to its full glory, like the Mawson's Huts Foundation, and we could call this one the Mawson's Muffs Foundation, and they could employ an arts fellow to come down and do all the hard work on it. And we could attract support at one of those Sexpo events, and at sex shops. And we could get well-known pin-up gals to do publicity and fundraising. And we could get corporate sponsorship from the 'adult' industry.

(Note to self: I think I've been away from home too long.)

❄ ❄ ❄

An interesting turn of events for young Dave, the electrical engineer who has just joined the Antarctic Division a few weeks before this trip. It was to be a familiarisation voyage for him, but he has now been asked if he will stay on at Mawson Station for the winter to replace one of the tradesmen who is not able to stay now. Dave has to think about it a bit and is divided on whether to stay or not, but in the end decides he will stay.

'In my job I might never be offered a chance to overwinter again,' he says. But of course Dave is drastically short of the types of things that a wintering expeditioner would have packed to last the winter. Like the rest of us round-trippers, he has only packed 30 kilograms of stuff. So a Save Dave committee is formed and people donate clothes and camera film and all kinds of things to help him through the winter. Others give money to buy him a large jumper from the ship's shop.

It's nice to be helping him out—but then again Dave is a nice guy, and I can't help but wonder that if the person in need was a bit of a dick would they get as much support? Of course I'm thinking of that dickhead with the Everest documentary here, if you can recall him. Although I'm sure I'd actually soften my attitude a little and find a pair of dirty underpants to pass onto him.

※ ※ ※

There have been two more deaths in Antarctica this week. A helicopter at the German Antarctic station of Neumayer II crashed, killing its pilot and a researcher and injuring three other passengers. Our helicopter safety procedures have always seemed overly stringent, but after news like this nobody complains when we are told over the ship's intercom that helicopter operations will be commencing and the helideck and the bridge are completely out of bounds.

And in October 2010 a helicopter crashed while ferrying staff from the French re-supply vessel *L'Astrolabe* to the French Dumont d'Urville station, killing all four on board.

One of the old-timers sums up the attitude to helicopters in Antarctica well when he tells me, 'We can't really do without them, but by God they can be dangerous bastards and good at killing people.'

Antarctica seems to have more than its fair share of plane and helicopter mishaps, and in the 2010–11 season one of Australia's small CASA 212-400s, which are used to fly between the stations, was damaged on landing at the Bunger Hills research camp, about 430 kilometres west of Casey Station. The plane hit a sastrugi, which caused serious damage, leaving it unable to fly. But fortunately none of the four people on board was injured.

✳ ✳ ✳

The weather has turned bad and most of us are sent back to the ship. It moves out into the sea ice to sit in comfort while the winds howl and blow at Mawson. After two days of moping and staring out at Mawson Station through binoculars the winds drop enough for us to return and resume cargo operations. Also many of us are allowed to go back to the station for the day. We board a little orange boat that is officially called *AA2 (Aurora Australis 2)*, but I prefer to call it Mini-Me, and we get to step onto the continent one more time before our final departure.

Coming back to Mawson has a nice feeling to it. It is no longer unfamiliar. The people there wave to us and say hello. One of the first people we bump into is Narelle, the station chief. We ask her where to find a few things we're after and she shows us where to go. Like Jeremy at Casey and Peter at Davis, she has things running well and it looks like it's going to be a good winter for everyone at Mawson.

I go to the library to continue some research into Dougelly and other things. I work my way along the shelves and I note that there are two copies of *The Da Vinci Code,* and a very nice hardback edition of Kim Stanley Robinson's *Antarctica.* They have a lot of books on Mawson, of course, but I can't find a copy of anything by Robert Service. Dougelly would be disappointed. There are, however, many of the same books as the other stations have: Wilbur Smith, Mathew Riley, Tim Winton, Tom Clancy and Robert Ludlum. But there are some books I hadn't seen at other stations. A lot of Virginia Andrews and also a swag of Dostoyevsky. (A concentration of Dostoyevksy? A Karamazov of Dostoyevsky?)

I also find a large book produced by the US National Science Foundation that lists all the names of all the places in Antarctica. I look up Craig and find that there is a Craig Ridge. It is a small ridge located in the Ellsworth Mountains, located at 77°31'S, 86°04'W. It was named in 1963–64 after the helicopter crew chief who assisted the US scientific party there.

That gets me thinking again about that committee which has to approve all the names for Antarctica, and I wonder just how on the ball they are. After a few minutes searching I find the following impressive list of landmarks, and their locations in case you ever consider visiting them:

Dick Peaks (67°40'S, 49°36'E)

Mount Bumstead (85°39'S, 174°10'E)

Beaver Glacier (83°24'S, 169°30'E)

Fuchs Dome (80°36'S, 27°50'W)

The Pricker (54°01'S, 37°19'W)

Shagnasty Island (60°44'S, 45°38'W)

Mount Dick (80°49'S, 159°32'E)

Roots Heights (72°37'S, 0°27'E)

Shag Rock (66°00'S, 65°38'W)

And Cape Circumcision (54°25"S, 3°21'E)—of which there is surely a good joke about taking a 'short cut' to reach.

There is also the very famous Una's Tits, which you can even check out on Wikipedia. They are two very impressive ice-capped basalt towers that guard the entrance to the Lemaire Channel on the Antarctic Peninsula. They are said to have been named in honour of a buxom lass who lived on the Falkland Islands and who clearly captured the attention of the overwintering expeditioners upon their return to relative civilisation in the 1940s.

Looking around further I'm shown into the back of the movie screening room nearby where there is a collection of old films, including a 1940 copy of *Pride and Prejudice*, which is the subject of an anecdote that Tim Bowden tells in *The Silence Calling*. According to the story, one year in the 1950s the expeditioners on Macquarie Island watched the movie many times over, even turning the sound down and doing the voices. As a result they all developed very polite Jane Austen mannerisms to their speech, which was probably also useful as a way to maintain civility among the group. But when Phil Law arrived with the re-supply ship in the spring he was amazed to discover everyone conversing in this archaic genteel and well-mannered style.

Later I talk to a few of that station staff over dinner and find that those who are preparing to spend a winter here are getting all psyched up, and those who are preparing to return home are also getting psyched up for that. I've heard that expeditioners from the New Zealand station who fly in and out find the speed of return a bit dislocating, which more expeditioners might experience when the airlink is used more. On the ship people have a bit of time to prepare themselves mentally and go through a transition period before returning, though many have already said that five or six days would be sufficient, not the 12 days we expect to take to get back to Australia.

I wander down to the old station buildings after dinner, before the barge is due to take us back to the ship, and I go inside the old accommodation quarters. They are small metal-clad buildings with between four and six bedrooms in them. They have a design not unlike many modern Ikea children's rooms, with a bunk bed situated on top of a desk. They have no doors, only old curtains, and there is a very cold-looking common-use shower at the end of the corridor. I look around and find some old graffiti on the walls: '32 fucking days left', '26 fucking days left after Sunday', '19 fucking days to go!' 'Five to go!' 'Two to go. Yippee!'

It's just a feeling I have, but I guess that winterer was already all psyched up to go.

I go into two more of the old accommodation buildings. They are also chill and desolate. The wooden furnishings are still there, but personal effects and posters and carpets and so on are all gone. Compared with the luxury of the Red Shed, it has a faded feel of the past about it. Before I step out the door I notice coloured light bulbs strung up on a wire hanging from the ceiling. Christmas lights perhaps? The colours are red and green and blue, not unlike the modern sheds of the station.

Then I go down to the old Chippy's Hut. This is where the Sistine ceiling had been. On the ceiling the outline marks are still there where the pin-ups had been taped. I can walk down the centre of the hut and count the places where each woman had been. Interestingly, some of the women told me last night on the ship that I should have a closer look at the Heritage Girls of Mawson because there were two photos in there that a female expeditioner had taken of herself to include in the collection. Sure enough, I went and looked and there were two photos, the same size as the pin-ups, that were not taken from a magazine, showing a rather sexy looking woman in ski boots and black knickers and bra, bending forward on the snow, so you could not see her face.

It was a nice shot and one of the Mawson Station guys walked past while I was looking at it and I asked him if he knew who it was. 'Yes,' he said. 'I'd recognise that arse anywhere.'

After leaving the Chippy's Hut I go across to the dog huts where the huskies used to be kept. The ground around the huts is covered in bones, the last remains of some treat for them. There are three very small huts there that contained the dogs' food, medicines for treating them and a kennel for bitches to have pups. In the second hut there are still frozen dog food boxes and on the wall is a long line of pegs with the names of the dogs above where their lead or harness would have been. Bonza. Morrie. Ursa. Luvan. Io. Arne. Thunder. Plato. Groo. Zipper. Bundy. Bear. Merlin. Cocoa. Choofer. Oscar. Goohaw. Jedda. Lowbo. Tom. Sprocket. Cardiff. Blackie. Welf. Elwood. Brendan. Kirsty.

I wished I had seen those dogs and had been able to match the names to each one. And then I go into the next hut, the smallest, where the pups were born. When I open the door the smell of dog rushes out to me. I stick my head in and breathe it in. For a land that is generally without smells, the faint lingering trace of dog is very strong and if I close my eyes I can almost imagine they are still there.

Almost.

But these old buildings are a thing of the past, or so I thought, until walking back in quiet contemplation, one of the station workers asks me if I'd seen his room in the old accommodation building.

'Which one?' I ask him.

'The red one,' he says.

'When was that?' I ask him.

He strokes his chin a little and looks to the past and tells me it was in the mid-1990s. I'm also told that Dave, the weasel-loving Antarctican, had stayed in bunks in the old huts many, many times. I love that about Mawson (the station, not the man), that the past and the present still exist like that. And the expeditioners who stay there seem to have a strong understanding of the past because it is present all about them.

And proving there is always another surprise in store, I see some of the young scientists from our ship trudging across the station and they invite me to join them to visit a distant building and see some science in action. The long, white aeronomy building contains a vast array of sensitive equipment measuring all kinds of things in the upper atmosphere, but the real interesting bit is being taken down to the old cosmic ray observatory, which is accessed through a trapdoor and down a long, deep spiralling staircase that has all been carved out of solid rock. The machines down there are in this vault, also carved out of the rock, sealed behind a door, over 20 metres deep. If ever there were a secret base in Antarctica, then it would look something like this.

And then—finally—it is time to return to the ship. The little orange boat Mini-Me runs us out to the *Aurora Australis* four passengers at a time. Standing there, down by the wharf, I look around at the station and around at the snow and ice and up at the plateau and think, well, this is it. This is the last time I'll stand upon Antarctica. The little orange boat is at the wharf, waiting for us to climb aboard, but I find my feet are suddenly heavy. There should be at least 40 words to describe the feeling of leaving Antarctica, as there are those 40 words for snow. But not one of them seems to my mind to be adequate as I step upon the boat, find a place to stand and watch as we pull slowly away from the shore. Away from the dark rock. Away from the ice. Away from everything.

The dark line of water between us and the icebound continent gets larger and larger as we chug out to the ship.

There is a quiet melancholy upon all of us in the little boat as we let the chill of this place bite one last time. We're going to be anchored here by the station for another full day, allowing the departing Mawson Station staff to have their farewells, and I reckon that if I had chucked a tantrum, like some previous arts fellows had done, I might have been allowed to go back to the station to continue some research or other. But to tell the truth I don't like reliving the sadness of leaving again and again. And also I'm finally starting to feel that the big Antarctic adventure-shaped hole within me is adequately filled up and now it is that Sharon-shaped hole that I most want and need to fill.

❄ ❄ ❄

That night I'm back on the ship with all my notes of the past few days spread out about me, dozing a little, and I look up and see two people looming over me. It takes me a moment to recognise them.

'It's about this book of yours,' says Scott. 'We're awfully concerned about it.'

'Yes,' says Shackleton. 'Very concerned.'

'Why's that?' I ask them after a moment.

'Well, I can see that your heart's in the right place, but there're a lot of things about Mawson that are not generally well known,' Scott says.

'Is that right?' I ask him.

'You'll have to trust us on this, but we know him quite well. Did you know that we both knew him personally and wanted him to be on our expeditions?'

'I think I read that somewhere,' I say.

'It's tragic really,' says Scott. 'If he had come on my expedition, perhaps things would have worked out quite differently.'

'Yes,' says Shackleton. 'Perhaps he'd have died too.'

Scott ignores the snide comment.

'Let me tell you something about Mawson,' Scott says. 'He considers himself so much better than anybody else, because he never let his science be tainted by a race to the Pole.'

'Always the science,' says Shackleton. 'Like only a scientist can truly appreciate Antarctica.'

'And the fact that he lived!' says Scott. 'Aren't you getting sick of hearing that he lived? If he had died in a tent with Mertz it would be different of course. Then he'd be just like me. Then he wouldn't be so holier than thou.'

'You're implying that I should have died too then?' asks Shackleton. 'That's what you're saying, isn't it.'

'Of course I'm not.'

'You're saying that if Mawson and I had died too then we'd all be on level footing, and you say that because you think if we had all died then you'd come out looking the best of the three of us, isn't that right?'

'That's absurd.'

'It just eats you up that we got back alive and you didn't!'

'We are here to talk about Mawson, not me.'

'Of course we are, but why does it always have to come back to you?'

'I think it always comes back to you!'

'Whose a little cry-baby missing his pedestal? Has somebody knocked you off it?'

Scott scowls deeply. He gives an airy upper-class sniff of his nose and turns to me. 'Anyway, Mawson is being hypocritical. He says he's only interested in science and is always going on about how the only good expeditioners are those with scientific backgrounds, but his 1929 to 1931 voyages were a little thin on science and were nothing but masquerades for land grabs.'

'Do you know,' says Shackleton, 'that many of the places he claimed he didn't even set foot upon. He just stuck an oar out of the boat and touched a bit of rock near the shore and said, I proclaim this British territory. At places he wasn't much closer to the continent than I was on the *Endurance* expedition.'

'Ah yes,' says Scott. 'That's an important point that's been lost in the mists. He did not claim it for Australia, he claimed it for the British Empire!'

But I cut in. 'There's a question I've always wondered about. Why do they call your expeditions after the ships you sailed in if the expeditions are actually on the land?'

The two men look at each other a moment, puzzled and then say. 'It's just how it's done.'

'Why do you need a reason for everything?' Shackleton asks. 'Can't you just accept some things are what they are?'

'Like finding Scott and Shackleton in my cabin telling me how I should rewrite my book.'

'Precisely.'

'Yes. Precisely.'

I lie back and sigh. 'So what do you think I should be doing?'

'Well,' says Scott, assuming a very diplomatic air. 'We think, actually, that you're backing the wrong horse here.'

'What horse?' I ask.

'Well, when I say horse I mean it as a metaphor, of course.'

'So I'm backing the wrong explorer, am I?'

'Well, that's a rather blunt way of expressing it, but in a word, yes.'

'Let me guess then,' I say. 'I suppose what you are here to tell me is that I shouldn't be writing about Mawson, and that I should be concentrating instead on an explorer who better summed up the heroic age through his perseverance and determination and achievements.'

'Yes,' says Scott.

'Something like that,' says Shackleton.

'So I should write about Amundsen?' I say.

The two men's jaws drop noticeably. 'Amundsen!' hisses Scott, like he suddenly has asthma.

Shackleton pats him on the back as if he is clearing some obstruction from his airways.

'Amundsen!' hisses Scott again.

'No?' I ask

'No,' says Shackleton. 'You should be writing about us. You should be expounding our greatness, talking about how we shaped people's understanding of the icy continent and how we shaped people's understanding of the human spirit.'

'Did Mawson bring all his team out alive, against impossible odds?' asks Shackleton. 'No, he did not.'

'Did Mawson choose to die with his men rather than save himself?' asks Scott. 'No, he did not.'

'Did Mawson have a telemovie made about himself staring Kenneth Branagh?' asks Shackleton. 'No, he did not.'

'Do we need to go on?' Scott asks.

I sit there for some moments and then ask, 'Tell me, do you do this a lot? I mean drop in on authors uninvited and try and convince them to write about you instead of any other Antarctic explorer.'

'Oh yes,' says Scott.

'Frequently,' says Shackleton.

'It's a harsh world out there,' says Scott, 'and if you don't get out there and sell your story, what's going to be left of you?'

'Yes,' says Shackleton. 'Ask Wilkes and Nordenskjöld and all those others that nobody has ever heard of. Ask them what it's like to slip out of the public's imagination.'

'They'll tell you what it's like,' says Scott. 'It's like being, well, it's like being...'

'Dead?' I ask.

'Worse than dead!' says Scott. 'It's like being forgotten!'

'So why aren't you writing a mini-series or a movie rather than a book?' Nick asks me, after I prompt him to ask it.

'Well, it's been done,' I tell him.

'When?'

'Twice actually. The first time was back in the early 1980s when David Parer and his wife Elizabeth Parer-Cook went down to Mawson Station and filmed *Mawson the Survivor*. They used the station staff even, with the station leader playing Mawson as he was a big strong wiry bloke and he had to do the re-enactment of pulling himself up out of the crevasse. He reckoned afterwards that it was one of the hardest things he'd ever done. That from a fit bloke who hadn't just trekked hundreds of miles with not enough food. The latest was done in the 2006–07 summer and was called *Life and Death in Antarctica*. Tim Jarvis wanted to do a sort of re-enactment of Mawson's lone trek, and wanted to do it on Mawson's original trail, but the area was too heavily crevassed for safety, so he had to do it out of Davis Station where there are less crevasses. The purpose of the film was to find if he could manage on the calorific intake that Mawson was restricted to. As far as I know though he didn't eat dog's liver and suffer a similar vitamin A poisoning, but on a reduced diet he wasn't able to pull himself out of the crevasse twice. Only the first time.'

But Nick doesn't seem that interested in all the details.

'Also of interest,' I add quickly, 'the film uses a fairly large amount of *Mawson the Survivor* footage, so if you only have the chance to see one, see *Life and Death in Antarctica* and it will be like you've seen both.'

In fact, we had a special screening on the ship and I was intrigued to see how they did the recreation of Mawson's epic march. They took it up from the point where Ninnis had died, so Tim Jarvis and his Russian companion John were to undertake the return trip playing Mawson and Mertz. They used kangaroo jerky instead of dog meat and they had pemmican and the same type of biscuits that Mawson had. Oddly though, the program actually concentrated very little on the day-to-day tribulations of the pair. Every ten days a doctor checked their weight and general health and so on, and they had an occasional grumble about how difficult the sledge was to pull over the snow and how hard it was to walk into the wind, but there was not as much detail on what it was like to be doing the re-creation as I would have liked. The crevasse scene was good though, watching Tim Jarvis as Mawson trying vainly to pull himself to the top. I couldn't help but wonder if his life had really been on the line, without a film crew and all up there to help him if he was stuck, might he have made it? That's going to be something for me to think about in my story.

Later I hunt down some of the film fans I know and we get into this game of who would play Mawson in the movie. Nicholas Cage?—too dopy looking. Tom Cruise?—too short. William Hurt?—maybe, but is he getting a bit old these days?

Gary Cooper is suggested—if he were alive. The same for Charlton Heston.

Lynette suggests Eric Bana. Not tall enough we decide. But then Bill suggests William McInnes. He's obviously thought about this a bit already. We all look at each other and nod. Yes, he'd be great. He has a longer nose, but he'd carry the height and authority of Mawson well, we agree.

So it's finally settled. If my book gets made into a film I want William McInnes to play Mawson. And me—well, Eric Bana can play me. I'd be happy enough with that, even if Sharon might tell me I'm dreaming.

Coming Home

*We immediately set to work getting all the records, instruments and
personal gear ready to be taken down to the boat harbour in anticipation
of calm weather during the day.*

—Douglas Mawson, *The Home of the Blizzard*

O ur thoughts have all now turned to home and the ship finally
turns for home too. We steam out into the ice surrounding
Mawson and nature gives us the most spectacular send-off we could
ever imagine. The sun drops through the clouds into a thin strip of
blue sky above the horizon and lights up the clouds above and the
water below and the icebergs in between in a surprising array of golds

and oranges, reds and purples that leave us almost in tears to watch the slow-changing splendour of the display. It is glorious. It is magnificent. It is beyond any adjectives I might have at my command, even if I hadn't used them all up. We line the rails and the bridge and feel blessed that our last sight of the continent is such a magical one. It will stay with us for many, *many* years.

Several people squash into small corners on the deck with their hoods up tight, keeping to themselves, having a private moment with their feelings and the continent. Others photograph madly, almost desperately, one last chance to capture the uncapturable.

I stand up on the monkey island deck until the sun has fully set and until my fingers are numb in the minus eight-degree temperatures, even inside my gloves, and my toes are shivering, even inside two thick pairs of socks. The cold stings, but I'm going to let it sting as much as I can bear. This is my farewell embrace from the continent.

❆ ❆ ❆

The next morning we wake to the sound of crunching ice. Up on the bridge it is surprising to see how broken up the large pack ice is. This same ice that slowed us down for four days is now presenting no problem for the good ship *Aurora Australis*. I'm told that there have been very large swells on the ocean that broke up the pack. A reminder of the power of the elements. We can feel the rise and fall of the swell already, even though we're in the ice still. Once again we line the windows to photograph seals and penguins.

By mid-afternoon the ice thins out and is suddenly gone. We have, in one 24-hour period, seen our surroundings go from pack ice with icebergs, to smaller bergs, to bergy bits, to growlers to brash ice and now to greasy ice—or silken ice, as I prefer to call it. The slow rise and fall of the swell looks like the ocean is moving in slow motion. Then we sail into open water. We have left Antarctica. In his book *The Ice*, Stephen J Pyne says, *Ice is the beginning of Antarctica and ice is its end.*

Soon we move into a snowstorm and flurries dance and whirl around the deck, as if giving us yet one last farewell from that great icy continent. I stand outside on the deck in it and surprisingly it does not feel so cold, even without gloves and a beanie. Perhaps there is some ice in my blood now after several weeks in Antarctica.

The weather-forecasters say that nasty weather is looming ahead of us and we can see dark clouds out there on the horizon. We are due to have a barbecue on the trawl deck this evening—which means that we won't be a dry ship for the party, with the regulation three beers being broken out of high security. And if the seas ahead are as rough as we're told to expect, then it certainly won't be a dry ship as we've seen waves wash across the trawl deck in the past.

But as it turns out the weather is not too bad and several whales even put on a performance on either side of the ship, and some very spectacular-looking icebergs drift past. It's a beautiful backdrop. So we stand around as if we're in somebody's backyard, moving from group to group, telling stories and drinking and, of course, with a few drinks in us we soon start talking about sex. Most of us are missing it I guess (I guess? I know!) and a few of the slightly grogged-up guys are circling the fewer women there like skuas circling a penguin colony.

Ah, the eternal optimism of the alcohol-fuelled male!

One of the inevitable questions that people ask of expeditioners, particularly those who have overwintered, is about sex in Antarctica. I know this from experience (I mean, since I asked so many of them about it myself). Women have been involved in Australia's Antarctic program as expeditioners since 1975, and have wintered since 1981, though the ratio of men to women is still very disproportionate, and it is difficult for a woman to avoid male attention. Some expeditioners tell me that it is a good case study of man/woman reverting to their animal roots (not that kind of roots!). Typically, a single woman will find she is the centre of attention of a circle of men, who will vie for her attention, and after she has chosen a mate (who might just be a best buddy) things will quieten down. However, I'm also told that for a woman to have a best buddy, people will usually presume that they are sleeping together. (Well, to be frank, it's not actually sleeping that they presume.)

There has been a lot of focus on women in Antarctica over the last 20 years and some interesting books have been written on the slow acceptance of them into the Antarctic blokey culture. Talking to expeditioners, it seemed to me much less of an issue than I had expected it to be, and perhaps we are finally getting close to the point when we no longer need to think of it as exceptional and also realise that the issues between the sexes in Antarctica are not that very different from the issues between the sexes we have everywhere.

One young single woman told me that before she went to Antarctica she was told that it would be like *Big Brother* on ice—which she said wasn't true all of the time—but was more true than not after a drinking party. There is another legendary story that I've been told by many people, about one former female expeditioner who made up a roster, taking turns with the men on the station before she eventually settled on one for her partner. Sort of like 'try before you buy', which, naturally enough, pissed off most of the other men and caused quite a bit of friction.

Another of the women told me that having a choice of male expeditioners was best described as 'the odds are good—but the goods are odd'.

Another expeditioner told me that there was a general attitude that while down on the ice all marriage statuses were cancelled. Also that although some tried to keep their relationships secret, it was very difficult in such small communities.

No matter how you look at it, sex in Antarctica is a sticky business. Expeditioners are often warned that if they wish to have a relationship, or even a fling, with a fellow worker they should remember that it might not last and yet they will have to sit across the breakfast table from that person for the rest of their time down south—which can get very awk-awk-awkward, as the penguins might put it. One of the results of this is that masturbation is perhaps a little more prevalent and also a little more openly discussed than it might be at most social dinner parties in the better suburbs. There is a saying that Wednesday night is wanking night—followed by the adage that every night is a Wednesday!

It is, of course, a rare station that hasn't had a romance of some kind and there are numerous stories of longterm relationships and marriages that have resulted, one even of a couple who got along so well on the voyage home that he proposed to her just after the ship berthed in Hobart.

Not all stories end so happily though. One that was often repeated to me is the background story to Nikki Gemmell's book *Shiver*. Nikki (yes, there seem to be a lot of Nicks and Nickis and Nikkis who travel to Antarctica) went down to Antarctica as an arts fellow in the mid-1990s and had an affair with one of the station workers. She wrote and published *Shiver* in 1997 (referred to widely in Australian Antarctic circles as THAT book), which recounts the story of a young woman who goes to Antarctica and falls in love with an expeditioner and has a fairly graphic affair with him.

The problem was that, as Nikki herself has pointed out, the novel was autobiographical and people were very easily able to identify the characters in the book, with the result that friends and family back in Australia were exposed to indiscretions that might best have been left on the frozen continent. On her website Nikki Gemmell has written: *I 'crossed the line' as a journalist—fell in love with someone I was interviewing … *Shiver* is my most autobiographical novel. After I completed it I felt stripped. I'll never write in such a raw way again. All writers are cannibals in a way, but with this book I cannibalised my own life more than anyone else's.*

Another reason that the book made such a deep impact on the Antarctic community was that the man she had the affair with later died in an accident in Antarctica in 1996, having a fall while walking alone off station, giving the story a very tragic ending. I'm told that *Shiver* is currently being made into a film, which some believe will resurrect the ill feelings all over again.

An earlier THAT book, also written by a woman who travelled to Antarctica and told all, was *My Antarctic Honeymoon*, written by Jennie Darlington, who accompanied her husband, Chief Pilot Harry Darlington, on the US expedition in 1947 under the autocratic Finn Ronne. Finn's own wife, Edith, decided at the last minute to go with her husband and convinced Jennie to come along too, and they overwintered with 21 other men in a small station they established on Stonington Island in Marguerite Bay, on the western side of the Antarctic Peninsula.

Jennie got pregnant in Antarctica, although the child was born in the USA, and is perhaps the first child conceived down on the ice. But in her book she was fairly blunt in outlining Finn Ronne's faults, describing him as the 'Ahab of Antarctica'. Naturally enough, her book was very popular with the men under his later command, as he was by all accounts a psycho-boss, censoring his scientists' personal telegrams and regularly cheating at games. He attempted to ban the book on his bases and would fly into a rage if he found anybody reading it. Which of course only added to the desire of many men under his command to have a copy.

As to our ship, there is one existing couple on board, and some couples who are very close, but we appear to be a long way from the earlier days when the *Aurora Australis* was known as the 'Love Boat', largely fuelled by the boozy parties on board. But I suspect that comparisons with the good ship *Venus* might be like the mythical sightings of killer whales from the bridge—more talked about than ever confirmed. Our ship seems dry in more ways than one. Lloyd, the doctor as far as Davis Station, had condoms outside his surgery in help-yourself bags, alongside the seasickness pills and Panadols. He told me that he hadn't noticed any diminution in the condom supply, and I considered messing with his head by taking one out every day and then suddenly putting them all back.

On a topic related to sex, Lloyd had been asked by one of the expeditioners if it was true, as he had been told by a friend of his who works on census databases, that 37 Australians have been born in Antarctica. Lloyd told him that it was probably a statistical glitch, or people filling in the forms wrongly on purpose, like the people who list Jedi Knight for religion on the census form. However, he did say that the Argentinean government flew a pregnant woman down to their Base Esperanza in 1978 so that Emilioo Marcos Palma became the first person born on the Antarctic continent, to cement their claim to the territory by dint of birth and citizenship. Not to be outdone, the Chileans, who are claiming overlapping territory, flew down a pregnant Chilean citizen and in 1984 Juan Pablo Camacho was born on Frei Montalva Station. Several stations on the Antarctic Peninsula now have families with children attending schools on them, but not the Australian stations.

Lloyd won't say who it was, but he told me that one Australian expeditioner had got pregnant deliberately several years ago so that she could overwinter and have a baby in Antarctica. He said she had tried to keep it secret but it had been discovered, and then the powers that be 'invited' her to return to Australia, which she obediently did.

And while many expeditioners might find a stay in Antarctica a long and celibate one, they should perhaps discover the 7–7 Challenge, which is undertaken by uninhibited young women, normally from North America, who try to 'hook up' with a man from each of the seven continents—and it is Antarcticans who always present the biggest challenge to them. So while their odds might not be so good while down on the ice, they may improve notably above average upon their return.

❄ ❄ ❄

So I'm sitting there in my cabin with Mawson again and we're not talking about the past this time, we're talking about the future.

'So what do you think is most likely?' I ask him. 'Will it be possible to keep Antarctica a preserve of scientists?'

'I should think so,' he says. 'Do you know what we had inscribed on Ninnis and Mertz's graves?'

'Tell me,' I say.

'Erected to commemorate the supreme sacrifice made by Lieutenant B. Ninnis and Dr X. Mertz—in the cause of science.'

'But people have been dying for commercial return for a lot longer than they have been dying for science. What if one of the non-treaty countries starts drilling for oil?'

'It's too difficult.'

'It's getting easier every year.'

'It's too expensive.'

'It's getting cheaper every year and the price of oil keeps climbing.'

'There's too much hazard from ice.'

'Like in the North Sea where they currently drill?'

He mulls on that a moment.

'Or will the continent be covered in hotels?' I ask. 'Or maybe they'll just create tourist zones on the Antarctic Peninsula. Or maybe they will have people moving down there to live, starting a new country with Antarctic citizenship? Or maybe they will find a way to make money, processing penguin poo or something and big companies, with no national affiliation, will move in, or maybe there will be a territory war or maybe another large disaster and it will be declared off-limits to everybody or maybe …'

'Stop,' says Mawson, 'This is all together too much. And all too fantastical.'

'Not so fantastical really,' I say. 'Just not preferable.'

He sighs. 'It used to be so much easier,' he says. 'The continent was largely uncharted, we knew so little about it but we had something clearer to aim for. A better understanding of it.'

'But you wanted it kept for the scientists.'

'And rightly so. Antarctica should be primarily the domain of scientists being left to carry out important science—it should not be about chasing short-term economic outcomes, or treaty requirements. If you seriously want to understand our planet in crisis then you need to better understand the processes at the Poles. And only scientists can best do that.'

'But now it seems almost everybody wants a slice of it.'

'But they won't if nobody owns it.'

'So therefore shouldn't anybody be able to visit it?'

He scowls. I'm seeing a lot of scowls from him lately. 'I think it's time you declared your position,' he tells me. 'Are you pro-science or anti-science?'

'Can I be both and be neither?' I ask him.

'I don't see how you can,' he says.

'Can you imagine a day when important decisions about science are taken by society rather than by politicians and by scientists?'

'More fantasy,' he says.

'No. Just a possibility. The future is never there until you reach it.'

'What does that mean exactly?'

But instead of answering him, I ask him something I've been saving up. 'If it's zero degrees today, and it's going to be twice as cold tomorrow … how cold will it be?'

Now, that's what I call a scowl!

Gary, our penguin expert, who we have left at Mawson Station, has worked as a guide for several Antarctic tourist voyages and said that he noticed a major change in the industry about the year 2000. Up until then the majority of operators were there because they had some relationship with Antarctica, through having been an expeditioner or some strong love of the continent, but the gradual creep of operators who saw it purely as a business opportunity began increasing.

He said that most operators do a very good job still, and comply with the Antarctic Treaty requirements and are very conscious of their impact on the environment.

I asked him how long it might be until there were a hotel on Antarctica and he said that in effect there is one there already. A Chilean station on King George Island, which is the largest island closest to South America off the Antarctic Peninsula, has accommodation which they make available to people who fly in or visit by ship. King George

Island is crowded with stations, and he said there is one bay that has five stations on it, almost touching each other.

He said the biggest threat from tourism to Antarctica will be if one of the larger ships gets into some trouble. The big ships, which carry over a thousand passengers, currently don't land, they just cruise around the area. But he said that each season there is generally one incident with a ship hitting ice or running aground or having mechanical problems. No real surprise, statistically, if there are about 40 ships going back and forwards over the length of the summer season.

Concerns were increased with the sinking of MS *Explorer* in November 2007 when it hit ice and the hundred or so passengers aboard had to be rescued. Footage of the large ship sinking was played around the world, with the orange lifeboats full of people drifting about in the sea for five hours. Having done our lifeboat drills I was sure it was not a comfortable time for the passengers.

The *Explorer* was, in fact, an historic vessel, the first ship built specifically to take tourists to Antarctica. It was launched in 1969 under the name *Lindblad Explorer*. To some, the accident had only been a matter of time and at a conference of Antarctic Treaty nations in May 2007 there were reports of concerns about tourism and the need to address safety issues. About 46,000 tourists visit Antarctica each summer, at the latest count, which is almost an eightfold rise on 1992–93 figures of 6750. Although a rescue of the hundred or so people aboard the *Explorer* was possible because of the proximity of other ships and aircraft, if one of the larger ships, such as the *Golden Princess*, struck similar troubles, rescuing the 2500 passengers and 1200 crew could well be a logistical impossibility.

And the *Explorer,* which was only one of half a dozen ships to either run aground or run into trouble in recent years, had been specifically ice-strengthened, unlike some of the large cruise ships. Gary said the possibility of fuel leaking from a big vessel that got into trouble would be very serious and would be quite disastrous on Antarctic ecology.

But whatever you might think about it, Antarctic tourism is a growing business as more and more people are lured to the icy oceans of the south. The first Antarctic tourist, if we define a tourist as somebody who paid for their fare to the southern continent, may have been the Norwegian-born Australian, Carsten Borchgrevink, who sailed on the whaling ship *Antarctica* in 1895. Also, the 19-year-old Phillip Brocklehurst reputedly paid to go on Shackleton's 1907–09 *Nimrod* expedition, and Apsley Cherry-Garrard, who accompanied Captain Scott's fateful *Terra Nova* expedition and wrote one of the finest accounts of the heroic age ever, *The Worst Journey in the World,* paid one thousand pounds to be a part of the expedition.

Bernard Stonehouse of the esteemed Scott Polar Research Institute in England, who has been a polar researcher since 1946, has been studying the impacts of tourism in Antarctica since the 1990s. He has said that many scientists are against tourism as they believe it will get in the way of doing science. However, he said that he began to change his own views as early as the 1960s when he met tourists who knew an enormous amount about his research and realised they were strong advocates for polar conservation.

His study has also found that there is no strong evidence that tourism is having a major impact on the plants, wildlife or landscape of the Antarctic. In fact, tourists have done less damage than scientists who have had the run of the continent since the 1950s and have only recently begun seriously cleaning up their impacts. Within one generation, tourism has become the largest human activity on the Antarctic continent and it is largely self-regulated. However, Stonehouse also said that because of the size of the tourist ships now starting to come to Antarctica, the potential for an accident is high and the impact of such an accident would be very severe. He advocates a safety network to limit any risk to human life and the environment.

Which brings us to tourist disasters. And any discussion of tourism in Antarctica sooner or later comes to the Mount Erebus disaster of 1979 in which 257 people died. Air New Zealand began running tourist flights over Antarctica in February 1977. The flights were promoted as a unique opportunity to view Antarctica, and experienced Antarctic guides were able to point out landmarks and historic places over the plane's public address system. To ensure all passengers had an opportunity to view the scenery, they usually took a maximum booking of 85 per cent capacity, leaving the aisle seats empty, and having passengers take turns sitting by the windows.

Flight TE901 on 28 November 1979 was the 14th such flight. Sir Edmund Hillary had been scheduled to be the guide that day, but had to cancel due to other commitments. The pilots for the flight were Captain Jim Collins and co-pilot Greg Cassin, neither of whom had ever flown over Antarctica before, but they were experienced pilots nonetheless. The flight was made simpler by the fact they would be flying on a pre-programed flight path around McMurdo Sound. Or so they thought.

The flight left Auckland just before 8.30 AM, and as they approached the Antarctic continent, about noon, they descended to 3050 metres, a safe operating height, well above the 1830-metre limit. They then flew over what they believed to be the smooth flat ice of the Ross Ice Shelf, and the pilot advised that he was dropping to the very low altitude of 610 metres to enable passengers to view the ice. There was, however, a layer of cloud that blended into the white of Mount Erebus in front of them, obscuring it from sight. The first the pilots knew that the 4020-metre high volcano lay directly in their path was at 12.49 PM when the altitude device sounded, warning them that they were too low. Six short seconds later the aircraft collided directly into the mountain. Erebus, incidentally, although named after one of Sir James Clark Ross's ships (the *Terror* and *Erebus* expedition of 1839–43), was the son of the Greek god of chaos and was known as the embodiment of primordial darkness.

Having lost contact with the flight, rescue teams were dispatched from the nearby McMurdo Station. They searched along the assumed flight path, but found nothing because the plane had not been on the route it should have been on. Later that night debris was seen on Mount Erebus, but it took 24 hours before search-and-rescue parties were able to land there and confirm that it was the remains of Flight 901. All 237 passengers and 20 crew were dead. A huge recovery effort was made to retrieve the corpses, which comprised 200 New Zealanders, 24 Japanese, 22 Americans, six Britons, two Canadians, one Australian, one Swiss and one French. Tragically, the remains of 44 of the victims were unable to be identified.

The years following the disaster were marked by enquiries and accusations and counter-accusations as to who was to blame, with the finger being pointed at the pilot for descending too low and the company for changing the flight coordinates at the last minute and not informing the pilots. A Royal Commission cleared the pilots of blame and accused the company of trying to cover up the truth. However, this was taken to the Privy Council in London, which overturned some of the findings. The result, as often happens when legal battles are fought tooth and nail, is that the victims, those who died in the crash, and their families and loved ones, had the ordeal dragged on and on, rubbing the emotional wounds deep. So the Erebus disaster has cemented itself into the New Zealand psyche in a way that is hard to compare with other national traumas.

Air New Zealand is unlikely to resume sightseeing flights over Antarctica, but Qantas, by comparison, began its tourism flights again in 1994 and in 2010 started sightseeing flights aboard an Airbus A380, carrying 450 passengers.

For a final word on the Mount Erebus tragedy it is worth hunting down Kiwi poet Bill Manhire's magnificent 'Erebus Voices', which he presents as a dialogue between the mountain and the dead, starting with the voice of the mountain, which ends with the lines: *I am the one with truly broken heart. / I watched them fall, and freeze, and break apart.*

And as you read it, recall that almost all the wreckage of the aircraft is still on Mount Erebus and can be clearly seen in warm weather.

❊ ❊ ❊

The final 12 days at sea pass slowly. The temperature finally climbs above zero, but fog sets in and the swells increase. More and more of us resort to the seasickness tablets and once again I find that song going around in my head, 'Did you boogie with your baby in the back row of the movie show?' I also find I've started dreaming of sun-baking, stretching out in the sun's luxuriant warmth. I also had a peculiar dream about driving back home from Antarctica and getting lost on the way and finding that the maps I had didn't have all the rights roads on them.

Mawson doesn't tell us what strange dreams he had on his return voyage to Australia in 1914.

Now the days start to drag. The early seafarers used the term 'the doldrums' to refer to when the wind disappeared and their ships sat for days and days in the heat of the mid-Atlantic waiting expectantly for the breezes to blow again. The Antarctic equivalent is being stuck in the ice, waiting for the winds and waves to come and break up the floes. But for us, the doldrums is the slow, almost two week-long voyage home, waiting, day-by-day, to get closer to Hobart, where the journey ends and so many of our loved ones will be waiting for us.

We are all talking about Groundhog Day Syndrome (GDS), trying to remember what day it is and trying to come up with ideas for what we might do to break up the sameness of the daily routine. But there is a strange lassitude that has overtaken most of us. We sleep in. Check our emails. Eat lunch. Go to a lecture. Check emails again, just in case there's been something new. Read or watch a DVD. Eat dinner. Check emails. Watch a DVD or read. Sleep. And then it all starts all over again the next day.

Those things we used to do, like going up on the bridge to watch the ice, have also been overtaken by a certain boring sameness. Endless ocean in front and behind, just like it was the day before. It's strange to think how exciting that same ocean had looked on our voyage down to Antarctica. The limbo-like feeling is exacerbated by the rolling of the seas, as many of the people on board are taking those dreaded seasickness tablets which bring on a state of near-zombieness, making it a little harder to think or do things. Sleeping at nights is awkward with the strong roll of the ship. One moment your head is higher than your body, which is fine, but then your feet and stomach are above your head, which isn't really fine at all.

Looking around the restaurant in the evenings you'd swear you were sitting in a bus station with people who have just climbed off a 12-hour bus ride and are sitting up through the night to catch their next bus. The most animated conversations at meals go something like this:

'Planning anything big this weekend?'

'Thought I might go out and see a movie, you know.'

'Anything special?'

'Not sure. Maybe I'll just stay in and watch a DVD though.'

'Yeah, that'd make a nice change from going out.'

Or we make jokes about going to the casino or the bar, or having the ship's steward bring us a cocktail while we lounge by the ship's pool.

A few lucky souls have reports and things they need to work on and those wandering the ship like they are stuck in limbo look at them with a little envy. In between checking his emails for about the 50th time in a day, one repeat-offender expeditioner tells me, 'You can never really get home again quickly enough.'

It all makes me think of the opening lines of Kenneth Slessor's wonderful poem, 'Five Bells': *Time that is moved by little fidget wheels, is not my time ...*

I'm sure there was an episode of *Star Trek* that was something like this, where they were trapped in a timeless zone that just went on and on and on, and I'm sure if I could remember the plot I could find some message in it for us. But my brain just isn't working properly today. Just like yesterday. And just like tomorrow.

Mawson's later life was a mixed one. After being knighted in 1914, he found the public lost interest in his achievements as both the impact of the deaths of Scott and his party and the beginning of World War I had filled the collective imagination. Mawson organised the BANZARE follow-up expedition to Antarctica in 1929–31, which led to the creation of the Australian Antarctic Territory in 1936, and then he turned his energies to writing up the many scientific reports based on their research. And he was still involved in the planning of Australia's Antarctic program. His Antarctic past forever defined him in many people's minds and his past continued to follow him, even with Sidney Jeffryes writing to him several times over the years, quoting scripture and saying that the asylums he had been interred in were nests of Freemasons who were his enemies.

Mawson had his own enemies, both within the bureaucracies of academia and government. In later years he could well have written to Jeffryes in sympathy, about the gradual control of science and Antarctic issues by his enemies. He disliked the fact that the Australian National Antarctic Research Expedition (ANARE) was controlled by the government and felt privately run expeditions had many advantages over state-run ones, even though he had to work hard for several years afterwards to clear the debts he had incurred for his own.

Mawson also believed that Antarctic exploration should find a way to pay for itself, through possible exploitation of minerals, but also through whaling in the southern oceans. Mawson also backed controlled culling of local populations of animals, such as the seals on Macquarie Island. He was always a strong-willed man but in his last years was a man from another era. He retired from teaching in 1952 and died from a cerebral haemorrhage in 1958.

❄ ❄ ❄

Later that night I wake up and find Mawson sitting on the end of my bed. Actually he's sitting on my legs. Thankfully, Ninnisdenko is not there playing zombie-vampire games in the darkness.

Mawson looks a little unhappy.

'Is there something wrong?' I ask him.

'I'm not particularly happy about the way you are describing me,' he says.

'But you were a conservative, pernickety old git in your later years,' I tell him.

'No, I wasn't,' he says. 'I was very progressive. I insisted that my two daughters study science and I was strong about the conservation of Antarctic sea life.

'Let me quote you something,' I say, digging around for my notes. '*It so happens that man is a combination of certain qualities—woman of others. There is a fundamental dissimilarity just as surely as there is similarity. In the biologists' classification the female represents the passive vegetative state—the male is the active animal state. The generalisation is true of woman and man no matter how much the new woman may think to the contrary.*'

He scowls at me. As ever.

'Or this: *Is it not likely that the hordes of Asia, unaffected by these changes may override roughshod the dwindling population of future Europe—and our proud Empires of today be a thing forgotten as the regencies of Egypt and Babylon which also did fall to the insidious germ of social change.*'

'That was a different era,' he says defensively.

'That was sexism and racism and a conservative, pernickety old-gitishness.'

He closes his mouth tightly. Then he says suddenly, 'You've been talking to Scott and Shackleton, haven't you?'

I tell him I can neither confirm nor deny that.

He reddens. 'Those scurrilous reprobates! They are so stricken by petty jealousies of each other that they are fuelled by bile. They are so obsessed with outdoing each other that they can't bear the thought of a book being written about any explorer other than themselves.'

'That's pretty strong,' I say.

'But it's true,' he says. 'Did they promise you fame and fortune if you wrote about them? Did they tell you that the only way to get a bestseller was to write about them? They'll promise you anything.

They are bitter and twisted old men who have had far too many books written about them already.'

'Ah,' I say. 'I see. Bitter and twisted.'

'Yes.'

'And far too many books already.'

'Yes.'

'And there's no jealousy happening here?'

'Preposterous!'

'And let me guess,' I say. 'They don't just hassle authors, they hassle publishers and editors and the bookbuying public too?'

'I wouldn't put it past them,' he says.

'Yes. Scurrilous really,' I say.

'Absolutely.'

'The egos and insecurities of the men!'

'That's right.'

'Well, if they come past again I'll tell them you asked after their health,' I say. 'And I don't want to make you paranoid, but they could be down in Lynette's cabin this evening talking to her about her book. She's in D20.' I watch him disappear quickly and then go back to sleep.

❄ ❄ ❄

And suddenly it's only a few more such sleeps and we'll be back in Hobart. Since we crossed the line of convergence between Antarctic and warmer waters, every day has got a little warmer. The ship is filled with a sense of rising excitement and anticipation, particularly among those who will have loved ones waiting on the dockside for them.

The ship is abuzz with activity again. Packing and washing and repacking and cleaning out cabins and throwing away rubbish and swapping email addresses and photographs. People talk about what they are going to do the first night in Hobart. There is going to be the customary piss-up at the Custom's House Hotel by the docks for many, but others will choose to go home to children and spouses, and some will travel on farther to homes interstate or overseas.

The excitement of seeing family again is apparent on people's faces. Even demure middle-aged women say how nice it will be to get their hands upon their husbands and how they expect to see them stomping at the dockside in the warm Hobart sunshine, like love-sick beasts, impatient to get their hands on them too. Another younger woman tells me that she can't wait to be back in Hobart so that she can 'moor to her boy'! The blokes tend to be a little bit more direct, but let's just say their comments are underpinned by similar loving sentiments.

Yet there is paperwork and customs preparation still to get through and we are told to expect two hours or more to clear customs once we are tied up at the docks. It's odd, but after seven weeks, that two hours seems unreasonably long.

Out on the helideck the hacky-sack players stand in a ring that grows larger each day. Others wait on monkey island for that first fabled scent of the eucalypts that it is said can be smelled by our aroma-deprived noses about two days out of Hobart. And the sunshine outside on the decks is glorious. The ship's meteorological computer tells us that it's only about 12 degrees, but it feels like an Australian summer day to us. People turn their faces skyward to be kissed by the sun's warmth, peeling off layers of clothing and letting the sun caress their limbs. A home-shaped smile spreads on our lips.

Soon, soon, soon, we chant silently. Soon there will be green trees and the smell of tarred roads and the fumes of cars and buses and the sounds of a city and people and brick buildings and the luxurious grass of parks and the oily fish-and-chip smell of Hobart's wharves and the cries of seagulls and the sounds of traffic and the advertising signs and then there will be shops and television and newspapers and magazines and people, people, people!

Some of us, who have been away a winter or longer, grow a little apprehensive at the thought of re-entering that other world and having to relearn social norms and deal with strangers and changes and chaos at every turn. But still, they say, it will be good to be home. Yes, it will be wonderful to be home. It will be glorious. It will be heartwarming. And Antarctica will seem, for a prolonged moment, more than that several thousand kilometres of broad ocean away.

But it will always be there. As it will always be in our memories. In our thoughts. In our dreams. We will be home, or in transit to home, carrying a part of Antarctica with us that nobody from customs and none of the heritage purists can ever demand that we leave behind.

They say that Antarctica changes you. They say that after Antarctica nothing is the same. They say so many things that I'm starting to wonder not just what that really means, but who the hell *they* are? But I do wonder in what way I might have changed, and whether I will know it before I find I just fit a little differently into things than I did in the past.

I will trust in Sharon to slap me back into an acceptable shape though.

I imagine that times will come when I will long for that clear chill air of the Antarctic plateau again and the feel of gazing on icebergs at sunset, and the sound of massed loony penguins and the special buzz of Antarctic moments. But I have it all tucked away into a special memory cupboard that I will be able to delve into whenever I feel the need to escape into those past and wondrous moments. And I will be keeping the key to that really, *really* safe.

We are very fortunate to have so many living legends on the ship with us, and as the voyage nears its end more and more of them are discovered over casual conversations. In addition to Bill, who wintered at Wilkes Station in 1961, and Tom, who had the most novel job application idea, there is Sharon, who coordinates the aircraft ground support for Davis Station. She received the prestigious Polar Medal, which is included in the Australian honours system, for her work. There is also Leigh, the helicopter pilot, who has been coming down to Antarctica for 40 years and Dave, the weasel-lover, who is probably the longest serving multiple-winterer on the ship and Ray, who has been going south for about as long as either of them, and whose passion for Antarctica is only equalled by his passion for science.

They are heroes, all of them. And there are more.

Brownie, who runs the gallery, deserves a medal for the thousands of dollars he raises for Camp Quality. Young Dave deserves one for staying on for the winter at such short notice. Mick for being the sort of person you'd trust your life with—if Scott had taken him with him he'd probably have survived (and then gotten really drunk). Leslie for running the barge through all kinds of shitty weather. Nicki and Rob and Peter for maintaining calm in a sea of turmoil. The two Debbies for their professionalism. Almost everyone I sit down with on the ship and talk to is a hero in some way (except the Mount Everest documentary dickhead, of course).

I've gotta tell you, as we get closer and closer to home I feel lucky to have known people such as these.

❄ ❄ ❄

Douglas and Paquita were so impatient to be together at last that much of their final correspondence dealt with where exactly they would meet and what privacy they might have. Paquita was keen to meet Douglas on the ship and get him into her arms as soon as she could but, having seen the *Aurora* before it left to collect her man, she decided that wouldn't be the best. Heaven knows what she had in mind really, but she did frequently remind Douglas how 'warm' she was going to be and that she was now 'a woman!' I have very much the same adjectives in mind when I'm thinking about being reunited with Sharon again, but I suspect that I might be falling prey to a common fault of historians in reading the meanings of the present into the words of the past.

After all, what can we really know of what was in a person's mind and heart only from her written words? Surely it is only a facet of a very multifaceted life that we all live and surely we would all hate to think that a biographer might be poking around with our lives in the future, based only on our emails, correspondence and written records. They are instructive, certainly, and sometimes they are all that we have to go on in reconstructing figures from the past, but all biographers necessarily puts something of themselves in there as well, evidenced by the many different interpretations of a figure from the past that different authors create.

I imagine Douglas Mawson is looking sternly over my shoulder and reading over what I'm writing. He's going to go off his nut, giving me a lecture about how dare I presume to know what he might think or might say or might anything at all. But he'll be polite in his use of language and will tell me that I need to be more scientific in my approach.

I'll listen quietly and then I'll ask him, 'So is a haemorrhoid in Antarctica a Polaroid?'

Then he might leave me alone for a bit to get on with finishing the book.

Paquita and Douglas had their longed-for reunion at the South Australian Hotel on North Terrace in Adelaide. She had travelled from Melbourne and the *Aurora* moored on 26 February 1914. They were married soon after, at Holy Trinity Church, Balaclava, in Melbourne on 31 March, and left the day after on a cruise to Europe, where Douglas was knighted in England in June. Their first of two daughters, Patricia, was born in Melbourne in April 1915.

According to my estimates of the time between being knighted and having a child, officially making him *her* knight, perhaps more out of than in shining armour, did them both a world of good.

❄ ❄ ❄

The Subversive Antarctic Historical Society are talking about the things that nobody is meant to talk about—but that's what they do. They are not policy specialists, but they know what they know and they see things how they see things. The conversation, boiled down, goes like this: Australia states it is in Antarctica to conduct science, but in reality is doing less and less science and more and more logistical support. At Casey Station this summer, as has been mentioned earlier, there were only 16 days of science and there are no scientists there at all over the winter. The cost of supporting the stations is increasing to the point that over 80 per cent or so of costs are just to keep the infrastructure going and as costs are cut, or drop relative to the increasing operational costs, it is the science that falls off the end. But Australia wants to keep a foot in Antarctica. As does Japan and Korea and India and Russia and France and China and Argentina and South Africa and Chile and Brazil and the Ukraine and the USA, and so on. Are they all doing good science down there? Well, most are, but not all, and much of Australia's science is still very good. But on balance, should your science define your logistics or should your logistics define your science? There is no majority rules decision on that one. The discussion then turns to the premise that most of the countries down south are there mainly because they know that one day the cost and scarcity of oil will mean that it is economically viable to drill for it around Antarctica. At that point those nations who have a presence in Antarctica will be the ones making the claims on mineral rights and so on. The Antarctic Treaty, although it is quite a diplomatic piece of work in finding a balance between territory claims that some nations want recognised and the desire of others not to have any territorial claims recognised, is still basically a voluntary treaty. Politically, it is described using ephemeral words like 'resilient' or 'evolving'. However, once one or two members (or non-members) start finding dollars in the ice, there may be an equally voluntary 'resilient' and 'evolved' mad rush to join them, with perhaps one or two dissenting high-moral voices, who probably get their energy from some other source.

Australia is going to find it increasingly difficult to support the cost of three Antarctic stations as well as the station on subantarctic Macquarie Island, and has already held discussions about leasing Mawson Station to the South Koreans, who decided in the end to build themselves a second station elsewhere. As landlord of a leased station, to whoever might wish to lease it, we would still probably have to provide some maintenance and some support, but we would suddenly be earning some money from our presence. And that's the real magic word when talking about the future of Antarctica that everyone agrees on—presence. And money. Everybody wants to be there when the investments start paying off. For some it is scientific outcomes. For some it is territorial outcomes. For some it is being ready to score a piece of the big pavlova when it's time to start cutting it up—and digging and mining and extracting.

Almost everyone in the Society is very sentimental about Mawson Station, being the longest continually staffed station in Antarctica, but Casey has the airlink and Davis is in a great ice-free location for science and for drilling and mining—so it is most likely Mawson that would be the first to go, they say, or be closed for a winter—although others feel the station on Macquarie Island would be more likely to be closed first. When stacked up against the other two stations all Mawson really has is heritage and science—neither of which are likely to be the big Antarctic currency of the future.

Like Stephen Barnwell's Antarctic dream dollars, the currency of the future for Antarctica is something we can only conjure up at the moment, but given the state of the world and our history of dropping high principles for energy and revenue, it is something we can more easily imagine than the fictitious colony of Nadira.

❄ ❄ ❄

I'm in our small cabin alone, packing my bags. We'll be in port in a few hours and I'm looking forward to seeing Sharon down there in that detention centre that they reserve for family and friends. I'll take a photo of her from the ship so I can compare her happy expectant face with that sad teary one I photographed as I left her.

We have to try and clean our cabin so that it doesn't look like four bachelors have been sleeping here for a month, and then we have to have our bags ready for customs to inspect. We're told they will x-ray our baggage and do the normal customs searches on us. 'For what?' I ask. 'What can you possibly be bringing back from Antarctica? Snow?'

In fact, there is a prohibited list, and I'm told every year some people get busted for trying to bring things into Australia that are prohibited. Firstly, any fruit and vegetables from the ship. Yeah, I know they were all acquired in Tasmania to start with, but that's a blanket rule. And then there is any Antarctic Division property that people might be trying to make off with. I heard a story about an expeditioner trying to bring in an engine. And let's not forget stones. It is completely forbidden to bring any stones from Antarctica back into Australia.

If you think about it, it makes some sense. Only about 3 per cent of Antarctica is ice free, and if every expeditioner or tourist who visited picked up a small stone, like an Adélie penguin does, why then in maybe 500,000 years or so there might be no ice-free areas left. (But don't add global warming to that equation.) It doesn't stop there. Just imagine what might happen if every one of those expeditioners who visited Antarctica took a stone and then visited the Grand Canyon in the USA, and dropped that stone in to see how deep the canyon was, well in maybe 500,000 years there might be no more Grand Canyon, just a giant pile of stones.

It's important not to lose your perspective on these things.

Then I look up and there's Mawson. 'About your book,' he says gravely.

'What about it?'

'Aren't you running out of time to start it?'

'Why do you say that?'

'The trip is nearly over.'

'Well, this book is nearly finished.'

'But what about that other book? The one you've been talking about.'

I shrug. 'I'm thinking I'll write it some other time.'

'If I wanted to write a book I'd just sit down and write it,' he says gruffly.

'No, you wouldn't.'

'Yes, I would. Like a sledging expedition. I wouldn't mess around with paperwork and things, I'd do all my own preparations and just set out and do it.'

'But you never sat down and wrote *The Home of the Blizzard* like that. You had all that second winter to work on it and you didn't get it finished.'

'I had most of it finished.'

'And I seem to recall that it wasn't even you who did the hard work on it. It was Archibald McLean, your chief medical officer.'

'I wrote it. He just edited it. Worked it over into a better shape, you know.'

'Notwithstanding the fact that it is the rewriting that is a lot harder than the writing?'

He glares at me.

'So are you going to write a book about me or not?' he demands.

'Haven't I just done that?'

'I don't think so. No. I think you've gone and written a book that's all about yourself.'

'You say that like it's a bad thing.'

'You told me that you were going to write a book about me.'

'Well—based on you. It was going to be a recreation, remember.'

'But you haven't written anything at all of that yet. You've just talked about it.'

'But I've written this book.'

'But it's just about you.'

'Not just about me. It's about all the people I met on my voyage. It's about their stories as much as anybody's.'

'But it's your interpretations of their stories. Like I'm only an interpretation of your idea of me!'

'Let's call it a re-creation of you,' I say.

He is quiet for some time then, and has that look on his face of a man pondering how to get out of check in a chess tournament.

And then I add, 'And I'm looking at the modern heroic era.'

'What modern heroic era?' he asks. 'There's no such thing. The heroic era died out with me. I was the last of the heroic explorers.'

'Almost everybody I have met on this trip has been a modern hero,' I tell him. 'Heroic tradespeople. Heroic sailors. Heroic cooks. Heroic scientists. Heroic bureaucrats even. They don't always agree on how things should be done, but they all have that heroic drive to live and work with Antarctica, and to understand the continent better in some way. Or through that to understand themselves better.'

'You call that heroic?'

'I certainly do. And do you know what it most reminds me of?'

'What?'

'You. It is your spirit that drives them, that is alive in them.'

He is quiet for a long time and gives me the closest thing I've yet seen to a smile.

'So you sort of have written a book about me?' he asks. 'A re-creation, as you call it, of me?'

'Well, I'd thought that initially, but now I'm thinking there's an ever better book I can write, having been down to the ice and experienced so much.'

'And that will be more directly about me?' he asks eagerly, walking right into it.

I can barely keep a straight face as I tell him, 'Notwithstanding the fact that it has been repeatedly stated that it would be based on you,' I say, 'I'm thinking there would be more interest if I wrote about Scott or Shackleton.'

(Note to self: Don't forget to mention the surprising shades of reds and purples one sees.)

Books on Antarctica

For those who do not have the good fortune to travel to Antarctica, there are many good books that will help you to travel there. Likewise many Antarctic expeditioners use books to remind them of home. Mawson took a small but quite diverse library, named the MacKellar Library after its donor, and it included titles from polar exploration, but also books such as: *Lady Betty Across the Water, Lorna Doone, The War of the Carolinas, The Trail of '98, Virginibus Puerisque, Marcus Aurelius* and *The Unveiling of Lhassa.*

In *The Home of the Blizzard* Mawson wrote of the important place books played in their lives: *The Hut is dark, and a shaded burner hangs by a canvas chair in the kitchen. The wind is booming in gusts, the dogs howl occasionally in the veranda, but the night-watchman and his pipe are at peace with all men. He has discarded a heavy folio for a light romance, while the hours scud by, broken only by the observations.*

These are the books that I found helpful, or are referred to in the text, and I also read them mostly at peace with all men.

Philip Ayres, *Mawson A Life*, The Miegunyah Press, Melbourne, 1999.

Louis Bernacchi, *To the South Polar Regions: Expedition of 1898–1900*, Hurst & Blackett Ltd, London, 1901.

Lennard Bickel, *Mawson's Will* (aka *This Accursed Land*), Macmillan, Melbourne, 1977.

Tim Bowden, *Antarctica and Back in Sixty Days*, ABC Books, Sydney, 1991.

Tim Bowden, *The Silence Calling: Australians in Antarctica 1947–1997*, Allen & Unwin, Sydney, 1997.

W.E. Bowman, *The Ascent of Rum Doodle*, Max Parish, London, 1956.

Apsley Cherry-Garrard, *The Worst Journey in the World*, Picador, London, 1965.

Janet Crawford, *That First Antarctic Winter: The Story of the Southern Cross Expedition of 1898–1900 as Told in the Diaries of Louis Charles Bernacchi*, South Latitude Research Limited, Christchurch, 1998.

Nancy Robinson Flannery, *This Everlasting Silence: The Love Letters of Paquita Delprat and Douglas Mawson 1911–1914*, Melbourne University Press, Melbourne, 2000.

Harold Fletcher, *Antarctic Days with Mawson*, Angus & Robertson, Sydney, 1984.

Nikki Gemmell, *Shiver*, Vintage, Sydney, 1997.

Tom Griffiths, *Slicing the Silence,* University of New South Wales Press, Sydney, 2007.

Michael Hall and Margaret E. Johnston, *Polar Tourism: Tourism in the Arctic and Antarctic Regions*, John Wiley & Sons, Chichester, 1995.

Roland Huntford, *Scott and Amundsen*, Hodder & Stoughton, London, 1979.

Roland Huntford, *Shackleton,* Hodder & Stoughton, London, 1985.

Frank Hurley, *Shackleton's Argonauts,* Angus & Robertson, Sydney, 1948.

Fred Jacka and Eleanor Jacka (eds), *Mawson's Antarctic Diaries,* Allen & Unwin, Sydney, 1988.

C. Laseron, *South with Mawson,* Harrap, London, 1947.

Phillip Law, *The Antarctic Voyage of the* HMAS *Wyatt Earp*, Allen & Unwin, Sydney, 1995.

Alasdair McGregor, *Mawson's Huts*, Hale & Iremonger, Sydney, 1998.

Emma McEwin, *An Antarctic Affair,* East Street Publications, Adelaide, 2008.

Don McIntyre with Peter Meredith, *Two Below Zero*, Australian Geographic, Sydney, 1996.

Bill Manhire (ed), *The Wide White Page,* Victoria University Press, Wellington, 2004.

Harvey J. Marchant, Desmond J. Lugg and Patrick G. Quilty (eds), *Australian Antarctic Science: The First 50 Years of ANARE,* Australian Antarctic Division, Hobart, 2002.

Douglas Mawson, *The Home of the Blizzard*, William Heinemann, London, 1915.

John May, *The Greenpeace Book of Antarctica*, Greenpeace Books/ Dorling Kindersley, London, 1988.

Robyn Mundy, *The Nature of Ice*, Allen & Unwin, Sydney, 2009.

Stephen Murray-Smith, *Sitting on Penguins: People and Politics in Australian Antarctica*, Hutchinson Australia, Sydney, 1988.

David Parer and Elizabeth Parer-Cook, *Douglas Mawson the Survivor*, Alella Books/ABC Books, Sydney, 1983.

Stephen J. Pyne, *The Ice: A Journey to Antarctica*, University of Iowa Press, Iowa City, 1986.

Kathleen Ralston, *Philip Law: The Antarctic Exploration Years 1954–66*, Ausinfo, Canberra, 1998.

Kim Stanley Robinson, *Antarctica*, Random House, New York, 1997.

Shelagh Robinson (ed), *Huskies in Harness*, Kangaroo Press, Kenthurst, 1995.

Sara Wheeler, *Terra Incognite: Travels in Antarctica*, Jonathan Cape, London, 1996.

Edward Wilson, *Diary of the Terra Nova Expedition to the Antarctic 1910–1912*, Blandford Press, London, 1972.

Useful Names to Know

Roald Amundsen The Norwegian member of the big four heroic age explorers. First man to reach the South Pole, to cross the North-West Passage and most likely first to sight the North Pole (in an airship). He had initially planned to attempt to reach the North Pole, but when Frederick Cook and Robert Peary both claimed to have reached it in 1909, he headed to Antarctica and the South Pole. Criticised at the time for his professionalism in an era of ardent amateurism, he relied on dogs as transport and food, his years of research in the Arctic and thorough planning to be the first to reach the South Pole on 14 December 1911. Robert Falcon Scott, by comparison, who insisted on man-hauling sledges most of the way, reached the Pole on 17 January 1912 and died in his tent with no food or fuel just 18 kilometres from a food depot on the return journey. Clearly a moral victory for Scott though.

ANARE One of many Antarctic acronyms, it stands for the Australian National Antarctic Research Expeditions, which encompasses government and non-government expeditions to Antarctica. It was established in 1947, one year before the Australian Antarctic Division, which was set up to administer ANARE.

Antarctic Treaty The defining international treaty that governs all activity on the continent. It was signed by 12 nations on 1 December 1959 and came into force on 23 June 1961. There are now 47 signatories to the treaty, which is due to expire in 2041. The treaty and its related agreements (known as the Antarctic Treaty System) ban mining, military and environmentally damaging activities in Antarctica.

BANZARE Acronym for the British, Australian [and] New Zealand Antarctic Research Expedition. Led by Mawson, the expedition involved two voyages to Antarctica between 1929 and 1931. A British Empire initiative, it was driven more by geopolitics than science and was the expedition on which Mawson claimed Australia's large Antarctic territories—although he actually claimed them for Britain.

Fabian Gottlieb von Bellingshausen Led a Russian expedition to Antarctica, and in 1820 became the first person to lead a ship over the Antarctic Circle since Captain Cook in 1774. He circumnavigated Antarctica and sighted land inside the Antarctic Circle. Upon his return to Russia there was no interest in his discoveries. Nowadays, however, the Russians claim him as a hero.

Louis Bernacchi Tasmanian physicist on Borchgrevink's 1898–90 expedition, who wrote a very graphic account of the overwintering, describing Borchgrevink as a 'numbskull' and insane. Bernacchi also accompanied Scott on his *Discovery* expedition of 1901–04.

Carsten Borchgrevink Anglo-Norwegian who led the Southern Cross Expedition of 1898–1900. He had sailed to Cape Adare on board the whaler *Antarctic* in 1894, when several of the party, including Borchgrevink, all claimed to be the first to have stepped ashore on the Antarctic continent proper. He returned to Cape Adare in 1899, established a hut there for overwintering and later led an expedition onto the Ross Ice Shelf. Despite his achievements, his self-promoting and criticisms of his leadership led to him being dismissed as more of a showman than a scientist.

Edward Bransfield British explorer who sighted the northernmost tip of the Antarctic Peninsula in January 1820, two days after Bellingshausen had reported seeing something that perhaps looked like land. The British claim Bransfield as the first to definitely sight the Antarctic continent.

Frederick Cook Either an heroic explorer or a fraud, or a bit of both. Spent a winter trapped in the ice aboard the *Belgica* in 1898–99 as the ship's doctor, with a young Roald Amundsen, who praised him highly, stating that the Belgian Antarctic Expedition owes a great debt to Cook. Cook's book, *Through the First Antarctic Night*, detailed the scurvy and madness suffered by the crew. But two of Cook's later great achievements appear to have been faked. The first was climbing to the peak of Mount McKinley in Alaska in 1906 and the other was being the first person to reach the North Pole in 1908.

Captain James Cook On his second round-the-world voyage, aboard the *Resolution*, he and his crew became the first men to cross the Antarctic Circle in 1773 and 1774, although he failed to sight the Antarctic continent. He wrote: *I can be bold enough to say, that no man will ever venture farther than I have done and that the lands which may lie to the South will never be explored.*

Dumont d'Urville French explorer, crossed the Antarctic Circle in January 1840 aboard *L'Astrolabe*, and landed on an island just off the continent, at what is now Adélie Land (near Mawson's Hut at Commonwealth Bay), where the French Dumont d'Urville Station is located. He also encountered Wilkes and Ross on their Antarctic voyages. If he had not become an Antarctic explorer, he would be best known for finding and obtaining the Venus de Milo statue 20 years earlier.

Adrien de Gerlache Belgian explorer in command of the *Belgica*, the first ship to overwinter in the Antarctic ice (in 1898–99), as well as the first party to undertake an inland excursion on the continent. He came close to having the first mutiny in Antarctica too when he announced his plan to overwinter. His first mate was Roald Amundsen and ship's doctor was Frederick Cook, who largely kept the expedition together.

Heroic age The era of concentrated exploration of Antarctica from about 1895 to about 1922. It encompassed the achievements of 'the big four': Scott, Shackleton, Amundsen and Mawson. Including the lesser known explorers, there were about 16 major expeditions from eight different countries. Not to be confused with the contemporary age of heroic bureaucracy.

International Geophysical Year, 1957–58, an international year of science. In Antarctica, it triggered much of the modern research bases and programs, including the building of the USA's Amundsen-Scott Base at the South Pole and the McMurdo Sound base, the largest on the continent, which is sited in the region claimed by New Zealand.

Sidney Jeffryes Radio operator during the second winter of Mawson's 1911–14 expedition. He suffered mental illness during the depths of winter and accused the other men of trying to murder him; he was relieved of his duties. On return to Australia he was placed in an asylum.

Xavier Mertz A Swiss ski champion who was one of Mawson's two companions on the sledging trip across King George V Land in 1912–13. He died on 7 January 1913, from exposure, dysentery, a toxic dose of Vitamin A poisoning from eating their dogs' livers, or a bit of all of these.

Belgrave Ninnis One of Mawson's two companions on his fatal sledge trip across King George V Land in 1912–13. Ninnis fell down a crevasse with most of the expedition's food and their tent on 14 December 1912. He was only 23 years old.

Otto Nordenskjöld Swedish explorer who led the *Antarctic* Expedition of 1901–04, losing his ship but finding its crew before being rescued. He was put ashore at Snow Hill Island off the Antarctic Peninsula to overwinter in 1902, but the ship was caught and crushed in the ice on its return journey in 1903, forcing the crew to make their way to Paulet Island to survive the winter. A three-man party had earlier set out to reach Nordenskjöld, followed by a six-man party from Paulet Island. Miraculously, all the parties met up, and in late 1903 were rescued by an Argentinean ship. Nordenskjöld brought back many fossils that indicated that Antarctica had once been warmer and may have been joined to a larger continent, as Mawson sought to prove.

Nathaniel Palmer A US seal hunter, who at the age of 22 captained the ship *Hero* and sighted the Antarctic Peninsula. He also claimed to have set foot ashore in late 1820, supporting the American claim that if they could not prove to have the first person to sight the continent they had the first person to have stepped onto it.

James Clark Ross British explorer who chanced upon the Ross Sea in Antarctica in 1841, crossing the Antarctic Circle as far as the 'Barrier' of the ice shelf, establishing a farthest south record of 78°11'S, that stood until the 20th century. He named the two volcanoes on Ross

Island in the Ross Sea, near the Ross Ice Shelf, after his two ships, the *Terror* and *Erebus* (the ships were named after his two dogs, perhaps having exhausted possibilities of using Ross in their names). His ships were later used by Sir John Franklin to attempt to chart the North-West Passage across the American continent and were lost with Franklin and his crew. Ross's last expedition was a fruitless search for them.

Robert Falcon Scott *See* Roald Amundsen.

Ernest Shackleton One of the big four explorers of the heroic age. He took part in Scott's *Discovery* expedition from 1901–02, where they were both members of the three-man party attempting to reach the South Pole. They turned back 770 kilometres short and he and Scott both blamed the other. Shackleton returned to the Antarctic aboard the *Nimrod* in 1907–08 (with Mawson on board), and came within 150 kilometres of the South Pole. On his 1911–14 expedition, the ship *Endurance* became stuck in pack ice within sight of the continent; after the ship was crushed he led his entire party to safety, first trekking across the ice and then undertaking a perilous boat journey to South Georgia Island to obtain help, surviving against all odds. He died on a fourth expedition to Antarctica before reaching the continent, at the age of 47, and is buried on South Georgia Island.

Charles Wilkes Commanded the United States Exploring Expedition of the Atlantic and Pacific Oceans, from 1838–42, and ventured into Antarctic waters in 1839 and 1840, sighting land. He sailed along the edge of the pack ice south of Australia for over 2000 kilometres, which was taken as evidence for there being an Antarctic continent. Wilkes encountered d'Urville's *L'Astrolabe*, but both accused the other of snubbing them and sailing away. There is also an ongoing dispute over whether Wilkes or d'Urville was the first to sight the continent.

Hubert Wilkins One of Australia's most accomplished, yet least known, Antarctic explorers, who pioneered Antarctic aviation. He first went to Antarctica with John Cope's ill-provisioned 1920–22 British Imperial Expedition, which achieved very little, and served as an ornithologist on Shackleton's fourth and last expedition on the *Quest*, which also achieved very little. He returned to Antarctica in 1928, after an unsuccessful attempt to sail under the North Pole in a submarine (declaring sabotage), and was the first person to fly a plane over Antarctica. Wilkins made three subsequent expeditions to Antarctica with the American millionaire Lincoln Ellsworth (who had flown over the North Pole with Amundsen). Had he been born a generation earlier Wilkins would probably have been one of the big names of the heroic era. Fittingly, the ice runway near Australia's Casey Station is named after him.